Teaching Mathematics
in the
Visible Learning Classroom
Grades K–2

Teaching Mathematics in the Visible Learning Classroom

Grades K–2

John Almarode, Douglas Fisher,
Kateri Thunder, John Hattie,
and Nancy Frey

CORWIN Mathematics

FOR INFORMATION:

Corwin

A SAGE Company

2455 Teller Road

Thousand Oaks, California 91320

(800) 233-9936

www.corwin.com

SAGE Publications Ltd.

1 Oliver's Yard

55 City Road

London EC1Y 1SP

United Kingdom

SAGE Publications India Pvt. Ltd.

B 1/I 1 Mohan Cooperative Industrial Area

Mathura Road, New Delhi 110 044

India

SAGE Publications Asia-Pacific Pte. Ltd.

18 Cross Street #10-10/11/12

China Square Central

Singapore 048423

Library of Congress Cataloging-in-Publication Data

Names: Almarode, John, author. | Fisher, Douglas, 1965- author. | Thunder, Kateri, author. | Hattie, John, author. | Frey, Nancy, 1959- author.

Title: Teaching mathematics in the visible learning classroom, grades K-2 / John Almarode, Douglas Fisher, Kateri Thunder, John Hattie, and Nancy Frey.

Description: Thousand Oaks, California : Corwin, a SAGE Company, [2019] | Includes bibliographical references and index.

Identifiers: LCCN 2018040267 | ISBN 9781544333298 (paperback : alk. paper)

Subjects: LCSH: Mathematics—Study and teaching (Early childhood) | Mathematics teachers—In-service training.

Classification: LCC QA135.6 .A46 2019 | DDC 372.7/044—dc23

LC record available at https://lccn.loc.gov/2018040267

This book is printed on acid-free paper.

Executive Editor, Mathematics: Erin Null

Editorial Development Manager: Julie Nemer

Senior Editorial Assistant: Jessica Vidal

Production Editor: Tori Mirsadjadi

Copy Editor: Christina West

Typesetter: C&M Digitals (P) Ltd.

Proofreader: Tricia Currie-Knight

Indexer: Sheila Bodell

Cover Designer: Rose Storey

Marketing Manager: Margaret O'Connor

Certified Chain of Custody

SUSTAINABLE FORESTRY INITIATIVE

Promoting Sustainable Forestry

www.sfiprogram.org

SFI-01268

SFI label applies to text stock

19 20 21 22 23 10 9 8 7 6 5 4 3

Contents

List of Videos

Note From the Publisher: The authors have provided video and web content throughout the book that is available to you through QR (quick response) codes. To read a QR code, you must have a smartphone or tablet with a camera. We recommend that you download a QR code reader app that is made specifically for your phone or tablet brand.

Videos may also be accessed at resources.corwin.com/vlmathematics-k-2

Acknowledgments

We are forever grateful for the teachers and instructional leaders who strive each and every day to make an impact in the lives of learners. Their dedication to teaching and learning is evident in the video clips linked to the QR codes in this book. The teachers in Charlottesville, Virginia, have graciously opened their classrooms and conversations to us, allowing us to make mathematics in the Visible Learning classroom visible to readers. The learners they work with in the Charlottesville City Public Schools are better simply because they spent time with the following people:

Dr. Kateri Thunder, PreKindergarten Teacher, Burnley-Moran Elementary School

Mrs. Alisha Demchak, Kindergarten Teacher, Burnley-Moran Elementary School

Ms. Jessica Pedersen, First Grade Teacher, Burnley-Moran Elementary School

Mrs. Rachel Caldwell, Fourth Grade Teacher, Burnley-Moran Elementary School

Mrs. Calder McLellan, Mathematics Specialist, Burnley-Moran Elementary School

Mr. James Henderson, Assistant Superintendent, Charlottesville City Schools

We are extremely grateful to Superintendent Dr. Rosa Atkins for allowing us into the schools and classrooms of Charlottesville, helping to make our work come alive.

Ms. Adrien Paulson is an excellent teacher in Waynesboro City Public Schools in Virginia. Mrs. Calder McLellan and Ms. Carol Busching are excellent teachers in Charlottesville City Schools in Virginia. They are actively engaged in implementing Visible Learning into their classrooms. Their contributions to this book provide a clear example of how they have taken the Visible Learning research and translated the findings into their teaching and learning. We are forever grateful to these three teachers for sharing their journeys with us so that we could share these examples with you.

About the Authors

John Almarode, PhD, has worked with schools, classrooms, and teachers all over the world. John began his career in Augusta County, Virginia, teaching mathematics and science to a wide range of students. In addition to spending his time in preK–12 schools and classrooms, he is an associate professor in the Department of Early, Elementary, and Reading Education and the Co-Director of James Madison University's Center for STEM Education and Outreach. In 2015, John was named the Sarah Miller Luck Endowed Professor of Education. However, what really sustains John—and what marks his greatest accomplishment—is his family. John lives in Waynesboro, Virginia, with his wife, Danielle, a fellow educator; their two children, Tessa and Jackson; and their Labrador Retrievers, Angel and Forest. John can be reached at www.johnalmarode.com.

Douglas Fisher, PhD, is professor of educational leadership at San Diego State University and a teacher leader at Health Sciences High & Middle College. He is the recipient of a William S. Grey Citation of Merit and NCTE's Farmer Award for Excellence in Writing, as well as a Christa McAuliffe Award for Excellence in Teacher Education. Doug can be reached at dfisher@mail.sdsu.edu.

Kateri Thunder, PhD, served as an inclusive, early childhood educator, an Upward Bound educator, a mathematics specialist, an assistant professor of mathematics education at James Madison University, and site director for the Central Virginia Writing Project (a National Writing Project site at the University of Virginia). Kateri is a member of the Writing Across the Curriculum Research Team with Dr. Jane Hansen, co-author of *The Promise of Qualitative Metasynthesis for Mathematics Education,* and co-creator of *The Math Diet.* Currently, Kateri has followed her passion back to the classroom. She teaches in an at-risk preK program, serves as the preK–4 math lead for Charlottesville City Schools, and works as an educational consultant. Kateri is happiest exploring the world with her best friend and husband, Adam, and her family. Kateri can be reached at www.mathplusliteracy.com.

John Hattie, PhD, has been laureate professor of education and director of the Melbourne Education Research Institute at the University of Melbourne, Australia, since March 2011. He was previously professor of education at the University of Auckland, as well as in North Carolina, Western Australia, and New England. His research interests are based on applying measurement models to education problems. He has been president of the International Test Commission, has served as adviser to various ministers, chairs the Australian Institute for Teachers and School Leaders, and in the 2011 Queen's Birthday Honours was made "Order of Merit for New Zealand" for his services to education. He is a cricket umpire and coach, enjoys being a dad to his young men, is besotted with his dogs, and moved with his wife as she attained a promotion to Melbourne. Learn more about his research at www.corwin.com/visiblelearning.

Nancy Frey, PhD, is professor of literacy in the Department of Educational Leadership at San Diego State University. She is the recipient of the 2008 Early Career Achievement Award from the National Reading Conference and is a teacher leader at Health Sciences High & Middle College. She is also a credentialed special educator, reading specialist, and administrator in California.

Introduction

Ms. Adrien Paulson assembles her kindergarteners on the rug and engages them with a few questions to kick off her mathematics block. She asks her young learners what they are learning in mathematics this week. Without hesitation, they respond, "We are learning to represent and recognize numbers." She then asks the follow-up question, "Why are we learning to represent and recognize numbers?" Again, without hesitation, her learners call out, "So we can use them to solve problems." Finally, she asks her learners how they will know they can represent and recognize numbers. As before, they respond, "We can use our tens frames and show our friends how to solve problems." In Ms. Paulson's classroom, the learning for the day is visible to her students. They know the *why* behind their learning and what success will look like at the end of today's mathematics block.

Skipping ahead to the spring of the same academic year, we encounter a young learner named Tessa. Tessa is a quiet kindergartener who loves school, and mathematics is no exception. Over the span of 1 academic year, she has developed the skill and will to ask her friends to "give me a hard math problem." Eight plus seven, three times four, and five minus two are really no challenge for Tessa. She quickly rattles off the sum, product, and difference between two numbers.

Tessa demonstrates a high level of proficiency, or mastery, in procedural fluency and knowledge in the area of computation involving the basic operations with single-digit whole numbers (e.g., number combinations). However, there is more to Tessa's mathematics learning than her mastery of number facts. Tessa possesses a balance of conceptual understanding, procedural knowledge, and the ability to apply those concepts and thinking skills to different mathematics problems. By

Teaching Takeaway

Learners should expect at least 1 year's worth of growth in 1 year of formal school.

balance, we mean that no one dimension of mathematics learning is more important than the other two. Conceptual understanding, procedural knowledge, and the application of concepts and thinking skills are each essential aspects of learning mathematics. Tessa's prowess in addition, multiplication, and subtraction of single-digit numbers is not the result of her teachers implementing procedural knowledge, conceptual understanding, and application in isolation, but through a series of linked learning experiences and challenging mathematical tasks that result in her engaging in both mathematical content and processes.

If you were to engage in a conversation with Tessa about mathematics, you would quickly see that she is able to discuss the tools and strategies for tackling more complex and difficult problems. For example, Tessa decided to tackle a problem involving goats on a local farm. As Tessa travels to and from school, she passes a farm with goats. While waiting for the traffic light to turn green one day, she counted 23 goats in the field. Ms. Paulson recalls this particular experience because Tessa constructed a sentence about the 23 goats in her writing journal. The next day, she reported that she only observed 14 goats in the field. Tessa noted, "I can't do this with my fingers or in my head. Ms. Paulson, can I use the tens frames to figure out how many goats are missing?" Tessa recognizes that she can use tens frames as a tool to solve the goat problem. Furthermore, she applies a thinking strategy to identify how many goats were missing from the field ("I can make 23 with my tens frames and keep pulling out counters until I only have 14 counters left."). Her learning progression from recognizing and representing numbers to using tools and strategies to solve more complex and difficult mathematics problems comes from the purposeful, deliberate, and intentional decisions of Ms. Paulson. For example, Ms. Paulson makes sure that the learning is visible to her kindergarteners each and every day as they balance conceptual understanding, procedural knowledge, and the application of concepts and thinking. All of Ms. Paulson's decisions focus on the following:

- *What works best* and *what works best when* in the teaching and learning of mathematics, and
- Building and supporting assessment-capable visible learners in mathematics.

This book explores the components in mathematics teaching and learning for grades K–2, with the lens of *what works best* in student learning at the surface, deep, and transfer phases. We fully acknowledge that not every student in your classroom is like Tessa. Our students come to our classrooms with different background knowledge, levels of readiness, and learning needs. Our goal is to unveil what works best so that your learners develop the tools needed for successful mathematics learning.

What Works Best

Identifying what works best draws from the key findings from Visible Learning (Hattie, 2009) and also guides the classrooms described in this book. One of those key findings is that *there is no one way to teach mathematics or one best instructional strategy that works in all situations for all students*, but there is compelling evidence for certain strategies and approaches that have a greater likelihood of helping students reach their learning goals. In this book, we use the effect size information that John Hattie has collected and analyzed over many years to inform how we transform the findings from the Visible Learning research into learning experiences and challenging mathematical tasks that are most likely to have the strongest influence on student learning.

For readers less familiar with Visible Learning, we would like to take a moment to review what we mean by *what works best*. The Visible Learning database is composed of over 1,800 meta-analyses of studies that include over 80,000 studies and 300 million students. Some have argued that it is the largest educational research database amassed to date. To make sense of so much data, John Hattie focused his work on meta-analyses. A **meta-analysis** is a statistical tool for combining findings from different studies, with the goal of identifying patterns that can inform practice. In other words, a meta-analysis is a study of studies. The mathematical tool that aggregates the information is an effect size and can be represented by Cohen's *d*. An **effect size** is the magnitude, or relative size, of a given effect. Effect size information helps readers understand not only that something does or does not have an influence on learning but also the relative impact of that influence.

Our Learning Intention: To understand what works best in the mathematics classroom in grades K–2.

A meta-analysis is a statistical tool for combining findings from different studies, with the goal of identifying patterns that can inform practice.

Effect size represents the magnitude of the impact that a given approach has.

Video 1
What Is Visible Learning
for Mathematics?

To read a QR code, you must
have a smartphone or tablet with
a camera. We recommend that
you download a QR code reader
app that is made specifically for
your phone or tablet brand.

Videos can also be accessed at
*https://resources.corwin.com/
vlmathematics-k-2*

For example, imagine a hypothetical study in which playing Mozart in the background while learners are engaged in mathematics instruction results in relatively higher mathematics scores among first graders. Schools and classrooms around the country might feel compelled to devote significant resources to the implementation of "thinking music" in all first grade classrooms in a specific district. However, let's say the results of this hypothetical study also indicate that the use of Mozart had an effect size of 0.01 in mathematics achievement over the control group, an effect size pretty close to zero. Furthermore, the large number of students participating in the study made it almost certain there would be a difference in the two groups of students (those listening to Mozart versus those not listening to Mozart in the background during mathematics instruction). As an administrator or teacher, would you still devote large amounts of professional learning and instructional time on "thinking music"? How confident would you be in the impact or influence of your decision on mathematics achievement in your district or school?

This is where an effect size of 0.01 for the "thinking music effect" is helpful in discerning what works best in mathematics teaching and learning. Understanding the effect size helps us know how powerful a given influence is in changing achievement—in other words, the impact for the effort or return on the investment. The effect size helps us understand not just what works, but *what works best*. With the increased frequency and intensity of mathematics initiatives, programs, and packaged curricula, deciphering where to best invest resources and time to achieve the greatest learning outcomes for all students is challenging and frustrating. For example, some programs or packaged curricula are hard to implement and have very little impact on student learning, whereas others are easy to implement but still have limited influence on student growth and achievement in mathematics. This is, of course, on top of a literacy program, science kits, and other demands on the time and energy of elementary school teachers. Teaching mathematics in the Visible Learning classroom involves searching for those things that have the greatest impact and produce the greatest gains in learning, some of which will be harder to implement and some of which will be easier to implement.

As we begin planning for our unit on number combinations, equality, and addition and subtraction, knowing the effect size of different

THE BAROMETER OF INFLUENCE

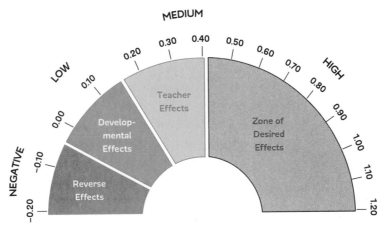

Source: Hattie, J. (2009). *Visible learning: A synthesis of over 800 meta-analyses relating to achievement.* Figure 2.4, page 19. New York, NY: Routledge.

Figure I.1

influences, strategies, actions, and approaches to teaching and learning proves helpful in deciding where to devote our planning time and resources. Is a particular approach (e.g., classroom discussion, exit tickets, use of manipulatives, a jigsaw activity, computer-assisted instruction, simulation creation, cooperative learning, instructional technology, presentation of clear success criteria, development a rubric, etc.) worth the effort for the desired learning outcomes of that day, week, or unit? With the average effect size across all influences measuring 0.40, John Hattie was able to demonstrate that influences, strategies, actions, and approaches with an effect size greater than 0.40 allow students to learn at an appropriate rate, meaning at least a year of growth for a year in school. Effect sizes greater than 0.40 mean more than a year of growth for a year in school. Figure I.1 provides a visual representation of the range of effect sizes calculated in the Visible Learning research.

Before this level was established, teachers and researchers did not have a way to determine an acceptable threshold, and thus we continued to use weak practices, often supported by studies with statistically significant findings.

EFFECT SIZE FOR ABILITY GROUPING (TRACKING/ STREAMING) = 0.12

THE BAROMETER FOR THE INFLUENCE OF CLASSROOM DISCUSSION

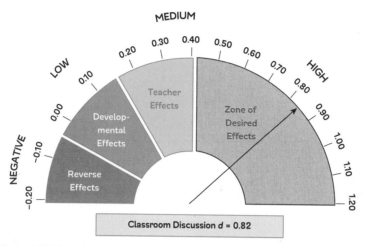

Classroom Discussion d = 0.82

Source: Adapted from Hattie, J. (2009). *Visible learning: A synthesis of over 800 meta-analyses relating to achievement.* Figure 2.4, page 19. New York, NY: Routledge.

Figure I.2

Ability grouping, also referred to as tracking or streaming, is the long-term grouping or tracking of learners based on their ability. This is different from flexibly grouping students to work on a specific concept, skill, or application or address a misconception.

Consider the following examples. First, let us consider classroom discussion or the use of mathematical discussions (see NCTM, 1991). Should teachers devote resources and time to planning for the facilitation of classroom discussion? Will this approach to mathematics provide a return on investment rather than "chalk talk," where we work out lots of problems on the board and students then complete worksheets? With classroom discussion, teachers intentionally design and purposefully plan for learners to talk with their peers about specific problems or approaches to problems (e.g., comparing and contrasting strategies for adding and subtracting large numbers versus small numbers, applying properties to find unknown values) in collaborative groups. Peer groups might engage in working to solve complex problems or tasks (e.g., determining the rule for a growing or shrinking pattern). Although they are working in collaborative groups, the students would not be **ability grouped**. Instead, the teacher purposefully groups

THE BAROMETER FOR THE INFLUENCE OF MANIPULATIVE MATERIALS ON MATHEMATICS

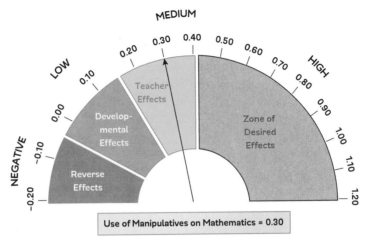

Source: Adapted from Hattie, J. (2009). *Visible learning: A synthesis of over 800 meta-analyses relating to achievement.* Figure 2.4, page 19. New York, NY: Routledge.

Figure I.3

learners to ensure that there is academic diversity in each group as well as language support and varying degrees of interest and motivation. As can be seen in the barometer in Figure I.2, the effect size of classroom discussion is 0.82, which is well above our threshold and is likely to accelerate learning gains.

EFFECT SIZE FOR CLASSROOM DISCUSSION = 0.82

Therefore, individuals teaching mathematics in the Visible Learning classroom would use mathematical discussions to understand mathematics learning through the eyes of their students and for students to see themselves as their own mathematic teachers.

Second, let us look at the use of manipulatives in mathematics and the many conversations about their use. For example, some teachers argue that students "have to learn to do this level of computation without counters." Other teachers may assert that "if they rely on manipulatives, how are they ever going to learn to do math without them?" Using a barometer as a visual representation of effect sizes, we see that the use

EFFECT SIZE OF MANIPULATIVE MATERIALS ON MATHEMATICS = 0.30

of manipulatives has an overall effect size of 0.30. The barometer for the use of manipulatives is shown in Figure I.3.

As you can see, the effect size of 0.30 is below the zone of desired effects of 0.40. The evidence suggests that the impact of the use of manipulative materials on mathematics achievement is low. However, closer examination of the six meta-analyses and the 274 studies that produced an overall effect size of 0.30 reveals a deeper story to the use of manipulatives. Mathematical manipulatives provide opportunities for learners to acquire understanding of mathematical concepts through the manipulation of concrete representations (i.e., counters, tens frames, number lines, fraction tiles, base ten blocks). As learners progress in their conceptual understanding and procedural knowledge, they rely less on these concrete representations because they have now developed fluency in this prior knowledge. In other words, manipulatives provide better learning benefits when used at the right time. This leads us into a second key finding from John Hattie's Visible Learning research: *We should not hold any influence, instructional strategy, action, or approach to teaching and learning in higher esteem than students' learning.*

What Works Best When

Visible Learning in the mathematics classroom is a continual evaluation of our impact on student learning. From the above example, the use of manipulatives is not really the issue and should not be our focus. Instead, our focus should be on the intended learning outcomes for that day and how manipulatives support that learning. Visible Learning is more than a checklist of dos and don'ts. Rather than checking influences with high effect sizes off the list and scratching out influences with low effect sizes, we should match the *best* strategy, action, or approach with learning needs of our students. In other words, is use of manipulatives the right strategy or approach for the learners at the right time, for this specific content? Clarity about the learning intention brings into focus what the learning is for the day, why students are learning about this particular piece of content and process, and how we *and* our learners will know they have learned the content. Teaching mathematics in the Visible Learning classroom is not about a specific strategy, but a location in the learning process.

Visible Learning in the mathematics classroom occurs when teachers *see* learning through the eyes of their students and students *see* themselves as their own teachers. How do teachers of mathematics see patterns, relational thinking, and the meanings of addition and subtraction through the eyes of their students? In turn, how do teachers develop assessment-capable visible learners—students who see themselves as their own teachers—in the study of numbers, operations, and relationships? Mathematics teaching and learning, where *teachers see learning through the eyes of their learners and learners see themselves as their own teachers*, results from specific, intentional, and purposeful decisions about each of these dimensions of mathematics instruction critical for student growth and achievement. Conceptualizing, implementing, and sustaining Visible Learning in the mathematics classroom by identifying *what works best* and *what works best when* is exactly what we set out to do in this book.

Over the next several chapters, we will show how to support mathematics learners in their pursuit of conceptual understanding, procedural knowledge, and application of concepts and thinking skills through the lens of *what works best when*. This requires us, as mathematics teachers, to be clear in our planning and preparation for each learning experience and challenging mathematics tasks. Using the guiding questions in Figure I.4, we will model how to blend what works best with what works best *when*. You can use these questions in your own planning. This planning guide is found also in Appendix B.

Through these specific, intentional, and purposeful decisions in our mathematics instruction, we pave the way for helping learners see themselves as their own teachers, thus making them assessment-capable visible learners in mathematics.

Teaching Takeaway

Using the right approach, at the right time increases our impact on student learning in the mathematics classroom.

HOW TO USE APPENDIX B
WHEN PLANNING FOR CLARITY

I have to be clear about what content and practice or process standards I am using to plan for clarity. Am I using only mathematics standards or am I integrating other content standards (e.g., writing, reading, or science)?

Rather than what I want my students to be doing, this question focuses on the learning. What do the standards say my students should learn? The answer to this question generates the **learning intentions** for this particular content.

Once I have clear learning intentions, I must decide when and how to communicate them with my learners. Where does it best fit in the instructional block to introduce the day's learning intentions? Am I going to use guiding questions?

As I gather evidence about my students' learning progress, I need to establish what they should know, understand, and be able to do that would demonstrate to me that they have learned the content. This list of evidence generates the **success criteria** for the learning.

ESTABLISHING PURPOSE

1 **What are the key content standards I will focus on in this lesson?**
Content Standards:

2 **What are the learning intentions (the goal and *why* of learning, stated in student-friendly language) I will focus on in this lesson?**
Content:
Language:
Social:

3 **When will I introduce and reinforce the learning intention(s) so that students understand it, see the relevance, connect it to previous learning, and can clearly communicate it themselves?**

SUCCESS CRITERIA

4 **What evidence shows that students have mastered the learning intention(s)? What criteria will I use?**

I can statements:

online resources ⬏ This planning guide is available for download at resources.corwin.com/vlmathematics-k-2.

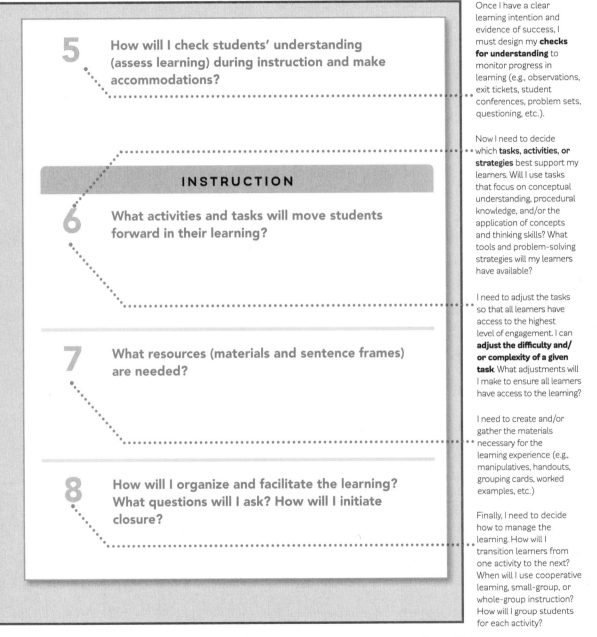

5 How will I check students' understanding (assess learning) during instruction and make accommodations?

Once I have a clear learning intention and evidence of success, I must design my **checks for understanding** to monitor progress in learning (e.g., observations, exit tickets, student conferences, problem sets, questioning, etc.).

INSTRUCTION

6 What activities and tasks will move students forward in their learning?

Now I need to decide which **tasks, activities, or strategies** best support my learners. Will I use tasks that focus on conceptual understanding, procedural knowledge, and/or the application of concepts and thinking skills? What tools and problem-solving strategies will my learners have available?

I need to adjust the tasks so that all learners have access to the highest level of engagement. I can **adjust the difficulty and/ or complexity of a given task**. What adjustments will I make to ensure all learners have access to the learning?

7 What resources (materials and sentence frames) are needed?

I need to create and/or gather the materials necessary for the learning experience (e.g., manipulatives, handouts, grouping cards, worked examples, etc.)

8 How will I organize and facilitate the learning? What questions will I ask? How will I initiate closure?

Finally, I need to decide how to manage the learning. How will I transition learners from one activity to the next? When will I use cooperative learning, small-group, or whole-group instruction? How will I group students for each activity?

Figure I.4

11

The Path to Assessment-Capable Visible Learners in Mathematics

Teaching mathematics in the Visible Learning classroom builds and supports assessment-capable visible learners (Frey, Hattie, & Fisher, 2018). With an effect size of 1.44, providing a mathematics learning environment that allows learners to see themselves as their own teacher is essential in today's classrooms.

Jackson is an energetic first grader who loves school. He loves school for all of the right reasons—gaining knowledge and having fun. From Jackson's perspective, these two characteristics are not mutually exclusive. During a spiral review to activate prior knowledge, Jackson is engaging in the deliberate practice of comparing two numbers between 0 and 110. During a discussion with his shoulder partner, Jackson talks about his areas of strength and areas for growth: "I am good at smaller numbers, you know, when they are single-digit or double-digit numbers. I get a little messed up when there are three digits and a zero, like 104 and 110. You see, 4 is greater than 0, but you should not look there." This is a characteristic of an assessment-capable learner in mathematics.

EFFECT SIZE FOR ASSESSMENT-CAPABLE VISIBLE LEARNERS = 1.44

Video 2
Creating Assessment-Capable Visible Learners

https://resources.corwin.com/vlmathematics-k-2

Assessment-capable visible mathematics learners are:

1. Active in their mathematics learning. Learners deliberately and intentionally engage in learning mathematics content and processes by asking themselves questions, monitoring their own learning, and taking the reins of their learning. They know their current level of learning.

Later on in the lesson, Jackson is working on solving story and picture problems using addition and subtraction with his cooperative learning group. His group has encountered a challenging problem, 55 + 60. However, they quickly recognize that they have the tools to solve this problem. One of the group members chimes in, "We can break 55 up into 50 and 5, right? These are more friendly numbers. I am going to do that! The number 55 feels unfriendly." This is a characteristic of an assessment-capable learner in mathematics.

Assessment-capable visible mathematics learners are:

2.   Able to plan the immediate next steps in their mathematics learning within a given unit of study or topic. Because of the active role taken by an assessment-capable visible mathematics learner, these students can plan their next steps and select the right tools (e.g., manipulatives, problem-solving approaches, and/or meta-cognitive strategies) to guide their learning. They know what additional tools they need to successfully move forward in a task or topic.

As Jackson's teacher begins to wrap up the day, she has the opportunity to conference with Jackson. His teacher takes time to individually conference with each student at least once a week. This allows her to provide very specific feedback on each learner's progress. Jackson begins the conference by stating, "The practice problems were hard for me." Jackson's teacher engages him in a discussion about how to compare two numbers. Rather than working through examples that Jackson understood, the two of them analyzed examples that Jackson missed on the spiral. He says, "I think I mixed up the places. So, tomorrow, I am going to pick the mathematics center during the morning work block so that I can try this process for finding which number again. You know, the one with the part-part-whole mat. I won't try and do it all in my head." This is a characteristic of an assessment-capable learner in mathematics.

Assessment-capable visible mathematics learners are:

3.   Aware of the purpose of the assessment and feedback provided by peers and the teacher. Whether the assessment is informal, formal, formative, or summative, assessment-capable visible mathematics learners have a firm understanding of the information behind each assessment and the feedback exchanged in the classroom. Put differently, these learners not only seek feedback, but they recognize that errors are opportunities for learning, monitor their progress, and adjust their learning (adapted from Frey et al., 2018) (see Figure I.5).

ASSESSMENT-CAPABLE LEARNERS:

 KNOW THEIR CURRENT LEVEL OF UNDERSTANDING

 KNOW WHERE THEY'RE GOING AND ARE CONFIDENT TO TAKE ON THE CHALLENGE

 SELECT TOOLS TO GUIDE THEIR LEARNING

 SEEK FEEDBACK AND RECOGNIZE THAT ERRORS ARE OPPORTUNITIES TO LEARN

 MONITOR THEIR PROGRESS AND ADJUST THEIR LEARNING

 RECOGNIZE THEIR LEARNING AND TEACH OTHERS

Source: Adapted from Frey, Hattie, & Fisher (2018).

Figure I.5

Over the next several chapters, we will explore how to create a classroom environment that focuses on learning and provides the best environment for developing assessment-capable visible mathematics learners who can engage in the mathematical habits of mind represented in one form or another in every standards document. Such learners can achieve the following:

1. Make sense of problems and persevere in solving them.

2. Reason abstractly and quantitatively.

3. Construct viable arguments and critique the reasoning of others.

4. Model with mathematics.

5. Use appropriate tools strategically.

6. Attend to precision.

7. Look for and make use of structure.

8. Look for and express regularity in repeated reasoning (© Copyright 2010. National Governors Association Center for Best Practices and Council of Chief State School Officers. All rights reserved.).

How This Book Works

As authors, we assume you have read *Visible Learning for Mathematics* (Hattie et al., 2017), so we are not going to recount all of the information contained in that book. Rather, we are going to dive deeper into aspects of mathematics instruction in grades K–2 that are critical for students' success, helping you to envision what a Visible Learning mathematics classroom like yours looks like. In each chapter, we profile three teachers who have worked to make mathematics learning visible for their students and have influenced learning in significant ways. Each chapter will do the following:

1. Provide effect sizes for specific influences, strategies, actions, and approaches to teaching and learning.

2. Provide support for specific strategies and approaches to teaching mathematics.

3. Incorporate content-specific examples from kindergarten, first grade, and second grade mathematics curricula.

4. Highlight aspects of assessment-capable visible learners.

Through the eyes of kindergarten, first grade, and second grade mathematics teachers, as well as the additional teachers and the instructional leaders in the accompanying videos, we aim to show you the mix and match of strategies you can use to orchestrate your lessons in order to help your students build their conceptual understanding, procedural fluency, and application of concepts and thinking skills in the most visible ways possible—visible to you and to them. If you're a mathematics specialist, mathematics coordinator, or methods instructor, you may be interested in exploring the vertical progression of these content areas across grades K–12 within Visible Learning classrooms and see how visible learners grow and progress across time and content areas. Although you may identify with one of the teachers from a content perspective, we encourage you to read all of the vignettes to get a full sense of the variety of choices you can make in your instruction, based on your instructional goals.

In Chapter 1, we focus on the aspects of mathematics instruction that must be included in each lesson. We explore the components of effective mathematics instruction (conceptual, procedural, and application) and note that there is a need to recognize that student learning has to occur at the surface, deep, and transfer levels within each of these components. Surface, deep, and transfer learning served as the organizing feature of *Visible Learning for Mathematics*, and we will briefly review them and their value in learning. This book focuses on the ways in which teachers can develop students' surface, deep, and transfer learning, specifically by supporting students' conceptual understanding, procedural knowledge, and application whether with equality or number combinations. Finally, Chapter 1 contains information about the use of checks for understanding to monitor student learning. Generating evidence of learning is important for both teachers and students in determining the impact of the learning experiences and challenging mathematical tasks on learning. If learning is not happening, then we must make adjustments.

Following this introductory chapter, we turn our attention, separately, to each component of mathematics teaching and learning. However, we will walk through the process, starting with the application of concepts and thinking skills, then direct our attention to conceptual understanding, and finally, procedural knowledge. This seemingly unconventional approach will allow us to start by making the ultimate goal or endgame visible: learners applying mathematics concepts and thinking skills to other situations or contexts.

Chapter 2 focuses on *application* of concepts and thinking skills. Returning to our three profiled classrooms, we will look at how we plan, develop, and implement challenging mathematical tasks that scaffold student thinking as they apply their learning to new contexts or situations. Teaching mathematics in the Visible Learning classroom means supporting learners as they use mathematics in a variety of situations. In order for learners to effectively apply mathematical concepts and thinking skills to different situations, they must have strong conceptual understanding and procedural knowledge. Returning to Figure I.4, we will walk through the process for establishing clear learning intentions, defining evidence of learning, and developing challenging tasks that, as you have already come to expect, encourage learners to see themselves as their own teachers. Each chapter will discuss how to differentiate mathematical tasks by adjusting their difficulty and/or complexity, working to meet the needs of all learners in the mathematics classroom.

Chapters 3 and 4 take a similar approach with conceptual understanding and procedural knowledge, respectively. Using Chapter 2 as a reference point, we will return to the three profiled classrooms and explore the conceptual understanding and procedural knowledge that provided the foundation for their learners applying ideas to different mathematical situations. For example, what influences, strategies, actions, and approaches support a learner's conceptual understanding of unknown values, part-part-whole relationship, and inverse operations? With conceptual understanding, what works best as we encourage learners to see mathematics as more than a set of mnemonics and procedures? Supporting students' thinking as they focus on underlying conceptual principles and properties, rather than relying on memory cues like "the alligator eats the larger number," also necessitates adjusting the difficulty and complexity of mathematics tasks. As in Chapter 2, we will talk about differentiating tasks by adjusting the difficulty and complexity of these tasks.

In this book, we do not want to discourage the value of procedural knowledge. Although mathematics is more than procedural knowledge, developing skills in basic procedures is needed for later work in each area of mathematics from solving algebraic equations to evaluating functions. As in the previous two chapters, Chapter 4 will look at what works best when supporting students' fluency in procedural knowledge. Adjusting the difficulty and complexity of tasks will once again help us meet the needs of all learners.

In the final chapter of this book, we focus on how to make mathematics learning visible through evaluation. Teachers must have clear knowledge of their impact so that they can adjust the learning environment. Learners must have clear knowledge about their own learning so that they can be active in the learning process, plan the next steps, and understand what is behind the assessment. What does evaluation look like so that teachers can use it to plan instruction and to determine the impact that they have on learning? As part of Chapter 5, we highlight the value of feedback and explore the ways in which teachers can provide effective feedback to students that is growth producing. Furthermore, we will highlight how learners can engage in self-regulation feedback and provide feedback to their peers.

This book contains information on critical aspects of mathematics instruction in grades K–2 that have evidence for their ability to influence student learning. We're not suggesting that these be implemented in isolation, but rather that they be combined into a series of linked learning experiences that result in students engaging in mathematics learning more fully and deliberately than they did before. Whether translating a pattern or solving a mental math problem, we strive to create a mathematics classroom where we *see* learning through the eyes of our students and students *see* themselves as their own mathematics teachers. As learners progress from combining quantities to solving for unknown addends, teaching mathematics in the Visible Learning classroom should build and support assessment-capable visible mathematics learners.

Please allow us to introduce you to Adrien Paulson, Adam Southall, Calder McLellan, and Carol Busching. These four elementary school teachers set out each day to deliberately, intentionally, and purposefully impact the mathematics learning of their students. Whether they teach kindergarten, first grade, or second grade, they recognize that:

- They have the capacity to select and implement various teaching and learning strategies that enhance their students' learning in mathematics.

- The decisions they make about their teaching have an impact on student learning.

- Each student can learn mathematics, and they need to take responsibility to teach all learners.

- They must continuously question and monitor the impact of their teaching on student learning. (Adapted from Hattie & Zierer, 2018)

Through the videos accompanying this book, you will meet additional elementary teachers and the instructional leaders who support them in their teaching. Collectively, the recognitions above—or their **mindframes**—lead to action in their mathematics classrooms and their actions lead to outcomes in student learning. This is where we begin our journey through *Teaching Mathematics in the Visible Learning Classroom.*

Mindframes are ways of thinking about teaching and learning. Teachers who possess certain ways of thinking have major impacts on student learning.

TEACHING WITH CLARITY IN MATHEMATICS

1

CHAPTER 1 SUCCESS CRITERIA:

(1) I can describe teacher clarity and the process for providing clarity in my classroom.

(2) I can describe the components of effective mathematics instruction.

(3) I can relate the learning process to my own teaching and learning.

(4) I can give examples of how to differentiate mathematics tasks.

(5) I can describe the four different approaches to teaching mathematics.

A **learning intention** describes what it is that we want our students to learn.

Success criteria specify the necessary evidence students will produce to show their progress toward the learning intention.

EFFECT SIZE FOR LEARNING INTENTION = 0.68 AND SUCCESS CRITERIA = 1.13

EFFECT SIZE FOR COOPERATIVE LEARNING = 0.40 AND COOPERATIVE LEARNING COMPARED TO COMPETITIVE LEARNING = 0.53

In Ms. Adrien Paulson's kindergarten class, students are learning to investigate and describe part-whole relationships for numbers up to 10 using multiple representations. Ms. Paulson starts the math block by walking her learners through the **learning intention** and **success criteria** she has provided on chart paper.

Learning Intention: I am learning about part-whole relationships with numbers.

Success Criteria:

1. I can identify ways to make a number.

2. I can use the terms *compose* and *decompose*.

3. I can represent the parts of a number in different ways.

To support her young learners, Ms. Paulson provides visuals to accompany each success criterion. For example, next to the first success criterion, she provides two examples of what this looks like (e.g., 6 and 4, 5 and 5, and 8 and 2 all make 10), labeling the examples with the words *compose* and *decompose* (the second criterion). With the third criterion, she holds up tens frames with two different color counters as examples that represent the parts of a number in different ways.

There are many different approaches for engaging learners in recognizing part-whole relationships and then describing those relationships. Given that the specific standard associated with today's learning emphasizes describing, representing, and investigating these relationships, Ms. Paulson provides her learners with a vast array of manipulatives (e.g., tens frames, part-to-whole mats, color cubes, tiles, squares, pattern blocks, snap cubes, and counters) to allow her kindergarteners to work with a partner and in a small group throughout the mathematics block.

During this particular unit, Ms. Paulson's learners will encounter part-whole relationships in literacy, science, and social studies (e.g., leveled readers, categorizing living things, and maps). Furthermore, she knows that they will progress toward the collecting, organizing, and representing of data in the first grade. Therefore, she incorporates a morning meeting and asks, "Last week, boys and girls, how many days out of the whole week were sunny?"

Today, learners are flexibly grouped for their table work based on Ms. Paulson's preassessment. For this assessment, she had asked learners to investigate a leaf and determine the number of ladybugs (part) compared to the total number of insects (whole) on the leaf. In addition, she had asked her learners how many ways they could make the number 5 (adapted from Kobett, Miles, & Williams, 2018). From this formative assessment, Ms. Paulson noted that there were learners who demonstrated surface knowledge about counting and one-to-one correspondence (e.g., they accurately identified the number of ladybugs). Other learners identified the number of ladybugs and the number of "other bugs," as well as one way to make the number 5. Previous checks for understanding provided evidence about her learners' proficiency in modeling and solving single-step story problems with sums and differences, an important piece of prior knowledge for this particular content. Today, Ms. Paulson provides each table with multiple containers of counters and two dice, the tools they will use to accomplish today's mathematics task. A folder contains laminated part-whole boards for each student at the table.

Teaching Takeaway

Formative evaluation that makes student thinking visible provides valuable information about where learners are in their learning progression.

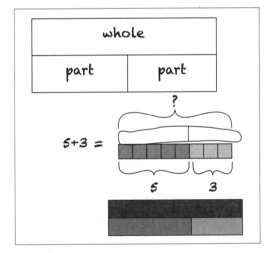

Ms. Paulson decides to provide a brief mini-lesson and direct/deliberate instruction on the decomposition of numbers. She says, "Good morning fellow mathematicians. Please get out your dry erase markers, a pair of dice, and your part-whole boards. Your part-whole board looks like this and can be found in the folder on your table." She walks students through the process of each table member picking a number.

Some table groups have the option of selecting a number between 1 and 5, other groups have the option of picking a number between 6 and 10, and a group of learners has the option of picking a number between 11 and 15. The other students in the group use their dry erase markers to record the number in the whole section of their part-whole boards. Then, each student rolls one die and records that number in one of the parts. Tessa goes first and selects the number 12. The other two students at the table record the number 12 in the whole section of their boards. Then they each roll their die and record that number in one of the smaller circles. Bryce says, "Tessa, I rolled a 2." Deandre jumps in, "I rolled a 5." Tessa rolls a 4 and records a 4 down on the smaller segment of the part-whole board. She says, "If I have 4, then I know the other part is 8. 8 and 4 make 12." The other learners follow the same process with their numbers, discussing their thinking and checking their answers with their peers.

Based on preassessment data and evidence gathered during the initial discussions in these tasks, Ms. Paulson provides the following different levels of support to adjust the difficulty of the task based on her learners' needs:

EFFECT SIZE FOR FINDING "RIGHT" LEVEL OF CHALLENGE = 0.74

- Laminated examples of decomposed numbers between 1 and 5
- A number strip containing the numbers 7 through 12 so that learners can scratch off the numbers as they are selected by fellow group members
- A list of strategies for finding the third number (e.g., tally marks, counters)
- The suggestion to use two dice and offer learners the opportunity to find more than two parts or addends (this also requires that they have a different part-whole board)

EFFECT SIZE FOR SCAFFOLDING = 0.82

Throughout the task, Ms. Paulson monitors her learners' progress, asking guiding questions and providing feedback and additional support as needed. She wants to give her learners an opportunity for productive struggle, but she carefully monitors this struggle to ensure her students do not get frustrated.

As Ms. Paulson monitors her learners during this task, she is making note of the specific mathematical discussions around the decomposing of numbers. She notices some students are using tally marks, their fingers, or counting forward to identify the second addend. Others are using the counters to determine the missing number. Still others are using known facts, such as doubles. Ms. Paulson uses the evidence gathered during these discussions to provide additional direct/deliberate instruction through a mini-lesson to specific groups of learners.

EFFECT SIZE FOR DIRECT/ DELIBERATE INSTRUCTION = 0.60

Before Ms. Paulson wraps up today's mathematics block, she asks students to complete an individual writing prompt in their mathematics notebooks.

> As you wrap up today's task, I want you to draw your own part-whole diagram on the right side of your notebook. Then select your favorite number from today and decompose that number. During our one-on-one conference this week, you will get to explain the diagram and we will write your thoughts on the left side of the interactive notebook.

Ms. Paulson is implementing the principles of Visible Learning in her kindergarten classroom. Our intention is to help you implement these principles in your own classroom. By providing her learners with a challenging task, a clear learning intention and success criteria, and direct/deliberate instruction where and when needed, Ms. Paulson's cooperative learning teams are developing conceptual understanding, gaining procedural knowledge, and applying their learning. She holds high expectations for her students in terms of both the difficulty and complexity of the task, as well as her learners' ability to deepen their mathematics learning by making learning visible to herself and each individual learner. As Ms. Paulson monitors the learning progress in each team, holding all students individually accountable for their own learning, she takes opportunities to provide additional instruction when needed. Although her learners are engaged in cooperative learning with their peers, she regularly assesses her students for

EFFECT SIZE FOR TEACHER CLARITY = 0.75

Visible Teaching	Visible Learning
Clearly communicates the learning intention	Understands the intention of the learning experience
Identifies challenging success criteria	Knows what success looks like
Uses a range of learning strategies	Develops a range of learning strategies
Continually monitors student learning	Knows when there is no progress and makes adjustments
Provides feedback to learners	Seeks feedback about learning

Figure 1.1

 This figure is available for download at **resources.corwin.com/ vlmathematics-k-2**.

Video 3
What Does Teacher
Clarity Mean in K–2
Mathematics?

*https://resources.corwin.com/
vlmathematics-k-2*

formative purposes. Ms. Paulson is mobilizing principles of Visible Learning through her conscious awareness of her impact on student learning, and her students are consciously aware of their learning through this challenge task. Ms. Paulson works to accomplish this through these specific, intentional, and purposeful decisions in her mathematics instruction. She had clarity in her mathematics teaching, allowing her learners to also have clarity and see themselves as their own teachers (i.e., assessment-capable visible mathematics learners). This came about from using the following guiding questions in her planning and preparation for learning:

1. What do I want my students to learn?

2. What evidence shows that the learners have mastered the learning or are moving toward mastery?

3. How will I check learners' understanding and progress?

4. What tasks will get my students to mastery?

5. How will I differentiate tasks to meet the needs of all learners?

6. What resources do I need?

7. How will I manage the learning?

Ms. Paulson exemplifies the relationship between Visible Teaching and Visible Learning (see Figure 1.1).

Now, let's look at how to achieve **clarity** in teaching mathematics by first understanding how components of mathematics learning interface with the learning progressions of the students in our classrooms. Then, we will use this understanding to establish learning intentions, identify success criteria, create challenging mathematical tasks, and monitor or check for understanding.

> Clarity in learning means that both the teacher and the student know what the learning is for the day, why they are learning it, and what success looks like.

Components of Effective Mathematics Learning

Mathematics is more than just memorizing fact families or mnemonics or following procedures for operating on whole numbers. Mathematics learning involves an interplay of conceptual understanding, procedural knowledge, and application of mathematical concepts and thinking skills. Together these compose rigorous mathematics learning, which is furthered by the Standards for Mathematical Practice that claim students should:

1. Make sense of problems and persevere in solving them.

2. Reason abstractly and quantitatively.

3. Construct viable arguments and critique the reasoning of others.

4. Model with mathematics.

5. Use appropriate tools strategically.

6. Attend to precision.

7. Look for and make use of structure.

8. Look for and express regularity in repeated reasoning (© Copyright 2010. National Governors Association Center for Best Practices and Council of Chief State School Officers. All rights reserved).

Teaching mathematics in the Visible Learning classroom fosters student growth through attending to these mathematical practices or processes. As highlighted by Ms. Paulson in the opening of this chapter, this comes from linked learning experiences and challenging mathematics tasks that make learning visible to both students and teachers.

THE RELATIONSHIP BETWEEN SURFACE, DEEP, AND TRANSFER LEARNING IN MATHEMATICS

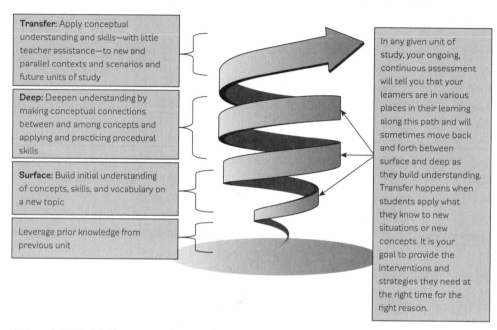

Transfer: Apply conceptual understanding and skills—with little teacher assistance—to new and parallel contexts and scenarios and future units of study

Deep: Deepen understanding by making conceptual connections between and among concepts and applying and practicing procedural skills

Surface: Build initial understanding of concepts, skills, and vocabulary on a new topic

Leverage prior knowledge from previous unit

In any given unit of study, your ongoing, continuous assessment will tell you that your learners are in various places in their learning along this path and will sometimes move back and forth between surface and deep as they build understanding. Transfer happens when students apply what they know to new situations or new concepts. It is your goal to provide the interventions and strategies they need at the right time for the right reason.

Source: Hattie et al. (2017). Spiral Image copyright EssentialsCollection/iStock.com

Figure 1.2

Surface, Deep, and Transfer Learning

Each school year, regardless of the grade level, students develop their mathematics prowess through a progression that moves from understanding the surface contours of a concept into how to work with that concept efficiently by leveraging procedural skills as well as applying concepts and thinking skills to an ever-deepening exploration of what lies beneath mathematical ideas. For example, kindergarteners transition from recognizing numbers, one-to-one correspondence, and number sentences to the addition, subtraction, and multiplication of those numbers. As another example, learners progress in their mathematics learning from kindergarten to second grade through an increased emphasis on using different representations of numbers to engage in problem solving. Understanding these progressions requires that teachers consider the levels of learning expected from students. We think of three levels, or phases, of learning: surface, deep, and transfer (see Figure 1.2).

Learning is a process, not an event. With some conceptual understanding, procedural knowledge, and application, students may still only understand at the surface level. We do not define surface-level learning as superficial learning. Rather, we define **surface learning** as the initial development of conceptual understanding and procedural skill, with some application. In other words, this is the learners' initial learning around what a part is and what a whole is, the various representations of part-whole relationships (e.g., color cubes, tiles, squares, fraction circles, rekenreks, snap cubes, and/or counters), and fundamental ideas about how to use part-whole relationships to solve problems. Surface learning is often misrepresented as rote rehearsal or memorization and is therefore not valued, but it is an essential part of the mathematics learning process. Students must understand how to represent the part-whole relationship with manipulatives, in words, in drawings, and in real-world applications to be able to connect these representations and use them in an authentic situation.

With the purposeful and intentional use of learning strategies that focus on how to relate and extend ideas, surface mathematics learning becomes deep learning. **Deep learning** occurs when students begin to make *connections* among conceptual ideas and procedural knowledge and apply their thinking with greater fluency. As learners begin to monitor their progress, adjust their learning, and select strategies to guide their learning, they more efficiently and effectively plan, investigate, elaborate on their knowledge, and make generalizations based on their experiences with mathematics content and processes.

If learners are to deepen their knowledge, they must regularly encounter situations that foster the transfer and generalization of their learning. The American Psychological Association (2015) notes that "student transfer or generalization of their knowledge and skills is not spontaneous or automatic" (p. 10) and **transfer learning** requires intentionally created events on the part of the teacher.

EFFECT SIZE FOR PRIOR ABILITY = 0.94 AND PRIOR ACHIEVEMENT = 0.55

Deep learning is a period when students consolidate their understanding and apply and extend some surface learning knowledge to support deeper conceptual understanding.

EFFECT SIZE FOR ELABORATION AND ORGANIZATION = 0.75

Transfer learning is the point at which students take their consolidated knowledge and skills and apply what they know to new scenarios and different contexts. It is also a time when students are able to think more meta-cognitively, reflecting on their own learning and understanding.

HIGH-IMPACT APPROACHES AT EACH PHASE OF LEARNING

Surface Learning		Deep Learning		Transfer Learning	
Strategy	ES	Strategy	ES	Strategy	ES
Integrating prior knowledge	0.93	Questioning	0.48	Extended writing	0.44
Leveraging prior knowledge	0.65	Concept mapping	0.64	Peer tutoring	0.53
Classroom discussion	0.82	Inquiry-based teaching	0.40	Problem-solving teaching	0.68
Vocabulary programs/ instruction	0.62	Self-questioning	0.55	Synthesizing information across texts	0.63
Imagery	0.45	Meta-cognitive strategy instruction	0.60	Formal discussions (e.g., debates)	0.82
Mnemonics	0.76	Reciprocal teaching	0.74	Transforming conceptual knowledge	0.85
Direct/deliberate instruction	0.60	Class discussion: discourse	0.82	Organizing conceptual knowledge	0.85
Process skill: summarization	0.79	Outlining and transforming notes	0.85	Identifying similarities and differences	1.32
Process skill: organizing	0.60	Cooperative learning 0.40			
		Small-group learning 0.47			
Process skill: record keeping	0.52				
Note taking	0.50				
Teacher expectations 0.43					
Teacher clarity 0.75					
Feedback 0.70					
Assessment-capable visible learner 1.33					

Source: Adapted from Almarode, Fisher, Frey, & Hattie (2018).

Figure 1.3

Figure 1.3 contains a representative list of strategies or influences organized by phase of learning. This is an updated list from *Visible Learning for Mathematics* (Hattie et al., 2017). Notice how many of these strategies and influences—clarity of learning goals, questioning, discourse, and problem solving—align with the Effective Teaching Practices outlined by the National Council for Teachers of Mathematics (2014) in *Principles to Actions: Ensuring Mathematical Success for All* (see Figure 1.4).

Establish mathematics goals to focus learning. Effective teaching of mathematics establishes clear goals for the mathematics that students are learning, situates goals within learning progressions, and uses the goals to guide instructional decisions.

Implement tasks that promote reasoning and problem solving. Effective teaching of mathematics engages students in solving and discussing tasks that promote mathematical reasoning and problem solving and allow multiple entry points and varied solution strategies.

Use and connect mathematical representations. Effective teaching of mathematics engages students in making connections among mathematical representations to deepen understanding of mathematics concepts and procedures and as tools for problem solving.

Facilitate meaningful mathematical discourse. Effective teaching of mathematics facilitates discourse among students to build shared understanding of mathematical ideas by analyzing and comparing student approaches and arguments.

Pose purposeful questions. Effective teaching of mathematics uses purposeful questions to assess and advance students' reasoning and sense making about important mathematical ideas and relationships.

Build procedural fluency from conceptual understanding. Effective teaching of mathematics builds fluency with procedures on a foundation of conceptual understanding so that students, over time, become skillful in using procedures flexibly as they solve contextual and mathematical problems.

Support productive struggle in learning mathematics. Effective teaching of mathematics consistently provides students, individually and collectively, with opportunities and supports to engage in productive struggle as they grapple with mathematical ideas and relationships.

Elicit and use evidence of student thinking. Effective teaching of mathematics uses evidence of student thinking to assess progress toward mathematical understanding and to adjust instruction continually in ways that support and extend learning.

Source: NCTM. (2014). *Principles to actions: Ensuring mathematical success for all.* Reston, VA: NCTM, National Council of Teachers of Mathematics. Reprinted with permission.

Figure 1.4

For the influences from the Visible Learning research, we placed them in a specific phase based on the evidence of their impact and the outcomes that researchers use to document the impact each has on students' learning. For example, we have included concept maps and graphic organizers under deep learning. Learners will find it hard to organize mathematics information or ideas if they do not yet understand that information, whether it is a procedure, concept, or application. Without a conceptual understanding of one-to-one correspondence and counting, first grade mathematics students may approach single-step and multistep problems based on surface-level features (e.g., this problem involves snap cubes, different color counters, or insects and ladybugs) instead of deep-level features (e.g., this problem requires me to compare two numbers or estimate). When students have sufficient surface learning about specific content and processes, they are able to see the connections between multiple ideas and connect their specific knowledge of properties to analyze problems based on these deep-level features (i.e., the commutative property is applicable across addition and multiplication), which allow for the generalization of mathematics principles. As a reminder, two key findings from the Visible Learning research are as follows:

1. There is no one way to teach mathematics or one best instructional strategy that works in all situations for all students; and

2. We should not hold any influence, instructional strategy, action, or approach in higher esteem than students' learning.

As teachers, our conversations should focus on identifying where students are in their learning journey and moving them forward in their learning. This is best accomplished by talking about learning and measuring the impact that various approaches have on students' learning. If a given approach is not working, change it. If you experienced success with a particular strategy or approach in the past, give it a try, but make sure that the strategy or approach is working in this context. Just because we can use a song to support our learning about pennies, nickels, dimes, and quarters, for example, does not mean those songs or rhymes will work for all students in your mathematics classroom—particularly if they lack understanding of the conceptual underpinnings of those procedures. Put differently, they can sing the song, but not solve the problem. Teachers have to monitor the impact that learning strategies have on students' mathematics learning and how they are progressing from surface, to deep, to transfer.

Moving Learners Through the Phases of Learning

The **SOLO Taxonomy** (Structure of Observed Learning Outcomes) (Biggs & Collis, 1982) conceptualizes the movement from surface to deep

---

> As teachers, our conversations should focus on identifying where students are in their learning journey and moving them forward in their learning.

> The SOLO Taxonomy is a framework that describes learners' thinking and understanding of mathematics. The taxonomy conceptualizes the learning process from surface, to deep, and then to transfer.

to transfer learning as a process of first branching out and then strengthening connections between ideas (Figure 1.5).

As you reflect on your own students, you can likely think of learners that have limited to no prior experiences with certain formal mathematics content (e.g., vocabulary and tools). They do, however, have significant informal prior knowledge. Take, for example, counting forward by ones to 100. Although learners have likely encountered real-world uses of these concepts (e.g., the number of pieces of candy they are allowed to have after dinner, the number of minutes they are allowed to play a video game), many have had no experience with the formal mathematics behind those real-world applications (e.g., numeric symbols, number charts, and the equal sign). Thus, they lack the formal mathematical language and tools to efficiently organize and communicate their thinking. This means they likely struggle to transfer their knowledge of sharing toys fairly to dividing to make equal groups.

Another example of this occurs with the use of number lines. Learners may know that a friend with five marbles has more than a friend with three marbles, but they are not able to place the numerals 3 and 5 on a number line and explain how the order of the numerals implies their value. This part of the SOLO Taxonomy is referred to as the prestructural level or prestructural thinking. At the prestructural level, learners may focus on irrelevant ideas, avoid engaging in the content, or not know where to start. In some cases, learners may ask about the color of the marbles or think the third marble is three. This requires the teacher to support the learner in acquiring and building background knowledge. When teachers clearly recognize that a learner or learners are at the

THE SOLO TAXONOMY

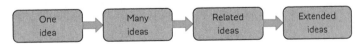

Source: Adapted from Biggs & Collis (1982).

Figure 1.5

prestructural level, the learning experience should aim to build surface learning around concepts, procedures, and applications.

Surface Learning in the Kindergarten Through Second Grade Mathematics Classroom

As learners progress in their thinking, they may develop single ideas or a single aspect related to a concept. Learners at this level can count one way starting at zero, identify and name attributes of shapes, follow simple procedures, highlight single aspects of a concept, and solve one type of problem (Hook & Mills, 2011). Consider three types of addition and subtraction problems: join result unknown, join change unknown, and join start unknown.

> Join Result Unknown: Zoey had 5 pipe pencils. Luke gave her 3 more pencils. How many pencils does Zoey have altogether?
>
> Join Change Unknown: Zoey had 6 crayons. Luke gave her some of the crayons. Now Zoe has 17 crayons. How many did Luke give her?
>
> Join Start Unknown: Zoey brought some crayons to her desk. Luke gave her 6 more crayons. Now Zoey has 17 crayons. How many crayons did Zoey start with?

With surface learning, students can only solve problems involving the exact type of problem provided in an in-class example. For example, some learners can solve a join result-unknown type of problem. Any variation to the problem, such as shifting to a join start-unknown type of problem, will pose a significant challenge to a learner at the surface level, requiring additional instruction (e.g., direct/deliberate instruction and practice). With the right strategy at the right time, learners will continue to build surface learning by acquiring multiple ideas about concepts, procedures, and applications. Learners can then solve problems involving different variations of addition and subtraction problems or from different perspectives, and they describe coherently how they approached each scenario. However, at this phase of their thinking and learning, learners see each variation of a problem as a distinct scenario that is not connected to the other types of addition and subtraction problems.

Like Ms. Paulson, all teachers should establish learning intentions and success criteria based on where students are in their learning progression.

Moving away from addition and subtraction and back to Ms. Paulson's classroom, let us look at how we can develop learning intentions and success criteria for conceptual understanding, procedural knowledge, and application for learners at these two levels (one idea and many ideas) (Figures 1.6 and 1.7).

SURFACE-PHASE LEARNING INTENTIONS FOR EACH COMPONENT OF MATHEMATICS LEARNING

Learning Intentions	Conceptual Understanding	Procedural Knowledge	Application of Concepts and Thinking Skills
Unistructural (one idea)	I am learning that a number can be decomposed into two numbers.	I am learning that I can represent a single number as a combination of two numbers.	I am learning that I can use the "parts" of a number to solve a problem.
Multistructural (many ideas)	I am learning that there are different ways to decompose numbers.	I am learning that I can represent numbers as multiple combinations of two numbers.	I am learning that different problems may use a different combination of a number.

Figure 1.6

SURFACE-PHASE SUCCESS CRITERIA FOR EACH COMPONENT OF MATHEMATICS LEARNING

Success Criteria	Conceptual Understanding	Procedural Knowledge	Application of Concepts and Thinking Skills
Unistructural (one idea)	I can describe how to decompose a number.	I can decompose a number into two parts.	I can decompose a number to solve a problem.
Multistructural (many ideas)	I can describe how different combinations make the same number.	I can list different ways to decompose a number.	I can describe the process for solving problems using parts of a number.

Figure 1.7

Teaching Takeaway

Learners in the deep phase can identify relationships between concepts and draw connections between concepts, procedures, and applications.

Deep Learning in the Kindergarten Through Second Grade Mathematics Classroom

Biggs and Collis (1982) conceptualize deep learning as identifying relationships between concepts or ideas. Learners at the deep level of the learning process focus on relationships and relational thinking about concepts, procedures, and applications. Returning to just some of the types of addition and subtraction problems mentioned previously, learners are able to compare and contrast the procedure for finding the solutions to each of these problems. Relating this to part-whole relationships in kindergarten, conceptually, learners deepen their understanding of composition, decomposition, part-whole, and the relationship to each of these types of problems. In other words, learners see the relationship between decomposing a number and the separate result-unknown type of problem. Learners can analyze a specific situation and determine the best approach to finding the solution, with minimal guidance on which approach is most efficient and effective. The development of relational thinking paves the way for transferring these concepts and thinking, or as Biggs and Collis (1982) call it, *extending thinking*. The learning intentions and success criteria should reflect this level of thinking or readiness for our learners (see Figures 1.8 and 1.9).

DEEP-PHASE LEARNING INTENTIONS FOR EACH COMPONENT OF MATHEMATICS LEARNING

Learning Intentions	Conceptual Understanding	Procedural Knowledge	Application of Concepts and Thinking Skills
Relational (related ideas)	I am learning that the specific context of the situation determines how to best represent a number (e.g., composition or decomposition).	I am learning the relationship between the parts of a number and the type of problem.	I am learning that the specific mathematics problem influences the way I represent a number and the unknown part.

Figure 1.8

DEEP-PHASE SUCCESS CRITERIA FOR EACH COMPONENT OF MATHEMATICS LEARNING

Success Criteria	Conceptual Understanding	Procedural Knowledge	Application of Concepts and Thinking Skills
Relational (related ideas)	I can explain the relationship(s) between the mathematics problem and the way I decompose the number.	I can justify the way I decomposed a number.	I can use different ways to represent numbers as a strategy for solving mathematics problems.

Figure 1.9

Transfer Learning in the Kindergarten Through Second Grade Mathematics Classroom

The next step in the SOLO progression is for the learner to transfer learning to different contexts. At the extended level of thinking, learners formulate big ideas and generalize their learning to a new domain. For example, an extended abstract thinker might predict how to solve a problem based on the type of question posed in the problem (e.g., identifying the action and the role of the unknown value). Learners at this level may begin to generalize this to other scenarios or contexts, recognizing that they can generate their own mathematics problems. Learners will begin to extend their thinking by using procedures in very different situations.

Being clear about the learning intentions and success criteria is just as important in extending student ideas as with the previous levels of thinking (Figures 1.10 and 1.11).

With clear learning intentions and success criteria in place, we must design learning experiences and challenging mathematics tasks that result in students engaging in both mathematical content and processes at the right level of thinking. This brings us to the question of rigor.

Teaching Takeaway

Learners at the transfer phase begin to transfer their conceptual and procedural knowledge to different contexts and situations.

TRANSFER-PHASE LEARNING INTENTIONS FOR EACH COMPONENT OF MATHEMATICS LEARNING

Learning Intentions	Conceptual Understanding	Procedural Knowledge	Application of Concepts and Thinking Skills
Extended abstract (extending ideas)	I am learning that numbers are represented multiple ways in everyday situations.	I am learning how numbers can be represented and unknown values can be found in everyday situations.	I am learning how I can use numbers to solve everyday problems.

Figure 1.10

TRANSFER-PHASE SUCCESS CRITERIA FOR EACH COMPONENT OF MATHEMATICS LEARNING

Success Criteria	Conceptual Understanding	Procedural Knowledge	Application of Concepts and Thinking Skills
Extended abstract (extending ideas)	I can represent numbers to solve problems in my life.	I can change the action and the unknown value to focus on a specific question.	I can explain the process for solving different mathematics problems.

Figure 1.11

Differentiating Tasks for Complexity and Difficulty

As we have noted, there are three phases to student learning: surface, deep, and transfer. Teachers have to plan tasks that provide students opportunities to learn and progress through these stages, as well as the flexibility to return to different phases of the learning when necessary. When students experience a "Goldilocks" challenge, the effect size is 0.74. A Goldilocks challenge is not too hard and not too boring. For example, if learners need additional surface learning around some aspect of procedural knowledge or conceptual understanding, we have the flexibility to go back, provide that instructional support, and then continue in the learning. The type of task matters as students

EFFECT SIZE FOR "RIGHT" LEVEL OF CHALLENGE = 0.74

move along in their thinking from surface to deep to transfer. In *Visible Learning for Mathematics*, we shared the Common Core State Standards for Mathematics definition of rigor as the balance of conceptual learning, procedural skills and fluency, and application. This is a good definition when applied to mathematics instruction, curricula, and learning as a whole. But we also want to address the appropriate challenge of any individual mathematical *task*. In this book, we are using the term **rigor** to mean the balance of complexity and difficulty of a mathematical task.

As soon as someone mentions "rigorous tasks," we mentally formulate what those are in our own classrooms. Is rigor completing a cut-and-paste worksheet 50 times during morning work? Is rigor engaging in a mathematics brainteaser? To effectively design rigorous mathematics tasks that align with our learning intentions and success criteria, we have to better understand what is meant by difficulty and complexity. *Difficulty* is the amount of effort or work expected of the student, whereas *complexity* is the level of thinking, the number of steps, or the abstractness of the task. We can differentiate by adjusting the level of difficulty and/or complexity for any task regardless of whether the task focuses on conceptual understanding, procedural knowledge, or application. Think back to Ms. Paulson's classroom and the example in which she expects learners to describe and investigate part-whole relationships in numbers. For these specific success criteria, recall how Ms. Paulson adjusted the difficulty of the task, while maintaining the level of complexity set by the success criteria, by providing learners with different levels of scaffolding. As learners develop greater procedural fluency and conceptual understanding, the level of difficulty can be increased by gradually removing the scaffolding.

We do not believe that teachers can radically impact student learning by making them do a lot more work. Practicing hundreds of addition and subtraction problems (increased difficulty) will not extend their thinking. Similarly, asking students to engage in a task that is far too complex or not complex enough for their current level of thinking can also reduce the impact on student learning. Instead, we should balance difficulty and complexity in the design of learning tasks. Throughout this book, we will return to the concepts of difficulty and complexity as we discuss the various strategies and tasks our three profiled teachers use and share how they can adjust the difficulty and complexity of those tasks to meet the needs of all learners.

Rigor is the level or balance of difficulty and complexity of any given mathematical task.

With clear learning intentions and success criteria in place, we must design learning experiences and challenging mathematics tasks that result in students engaging in both mathematical content and processes at the right level of thinking.

Teaching Takeaway

We can differentiate mathematics tasks by adjusting the difficulty and complexity of the task.

Teaching Takeaway

Learning tasks should balance conceptual understanding, procedural knowledge, and application in our mathematics classrooms. We should differentiate those tasks by adjusting the difficulty and complexity.

EFFECT SIZE FOR DIRECT/ DELIBERATE INSTRUCTION = 0.60

Guided practice involves the teacher and the students collaboratively engaged in problem solving. This helps the teacher and learners determine when students are ready to work independently.

Approaches to Mathematics Instruction

Just as task design is an important consideration in the Visible Learning classroom, learners need to experience a *wide range* of tasks if they are going to become assessment-capable visible learners. They need opportunities to work with their teacher, with their peers, and independently so that they develop the social and academic skills necessary to continue to learn on their own. Ms. Paulson decided to use a combination of direct/deliberate instruction and peer-led dialogic approaches, which are two of four approaches to mathematics instruction. Two additional approaches are teacher- or student-led dialogic instruction and independent learning.

Direct/Deliberate Instruction. Direct/deliberate instruction, commonly referred to as direct instruction, has a negative reputation in education. This approach is mistakenly assumed to be synonymous with lecture. That is not the case. Direct/deliberate instruction involves the following:

- Activation of prior knowledge
- Introduction of the new concept or skill
- Guided practice of the concept of skill
- Feedback on the guided practice
- Independent practice

To limit one's understanding of direct/deliberate instruction to highly scripted programs or lecture is to overlook the practices that make it highly effective for developing surface-level knowledge. With an effect size of 0.60, direct/deliberate instruction offers a pedagogical pathway that provides students with the modeling, scaffolding, and practice they require when learning new concepts and skills, as further explained by Hattie (2009):

> When we learn something new . . . we need more skill development and content; as we progress, we need more connections, relationships, and schemas to organize these skills and content; we then need more regulation or self-control over how we continue to learn the content and ideas. (p. 84)

Teacher-Led Dialogic. As learners develop the skills to engage in deepening dialogue, teacher-led dialogue allows the teacher to be present in student discussions about mathematics, facilitating the process to scaffold student conversation. In the end, the teacher will fade his or her support as students develop the necessary skills to take over and lead the conversations on their own. Teacher-led dialogic instruction does not require direct/deliberate instruction, first. Instead, this approach requires learners to possess the surface knowledge necessary to engage in deeper dialogue. For example, a teacher may utilize a teacher-led dialogic approach as she introduces the reasoning necessary to recognize any type of triangle in any orientation. Over time, after modeling the type of questioning and reasoning, the teacher's role in this dialogue will lessen, gradually releasing the students to more independent work (i.e., less dependent on the teacher).

Student-Led Dialogic. Children have a way of making themselves understood by their peers. In other words, students' thoughts and explanations can propel the learning of their peers. Whether solving problems, providing feedback, or engaging in reciprocal teaching, the collaborative act of peer-assisted learning in mathematics benefits all students in the exchange. In student-led dialogic learning, the role of the teacher is to organize and facilitate, but it is the students who lead the discussion.

Independent. The learning continues, and in fact deepens, when students are able to employ what they have been learning. This can occur in three possible ways (Fisher & Frey, 2008):

- Fluency building
- Spiral review
- Extension

Fluency building is especially effective when students are in the surface learning phase and need spaced practice opportunities to strengthen automaticity. For instance, students who play online mathematics games, or engage in independent practice, are engaged in fluency-building independent learning.

Spiral review is one in which learners connect previous content to current learning intentions as a way to activate prior knowledge or target their specific needs.

EFFECT SIZE FOR
SCAFFOLDING
= 0.82

EFFECT SIZE
FOR DELIBERATE
PRACTICE = 0.79

EFFECT SIZE FOR
FEEDBACK = 0.70

Teaching Takeaway

These approaches are in no particular order. Using the right approach, at the right time increases our impact on student learning in the mathematics classroom.

EFFECT SIZE FOR
QUESTIONING
= 0.48

EFFECT SIZE
FOR SELF-
VERBALIZATION
AND SELF-
QUESTIONING
= 0.55

EFFECT SIZE FOR
HELP SEEKING
= 0.83

Extension promotes transfer and occurs when learners are asked to use what they have learned in a new way. Independent learning through extension includes writing about mathematics, teaching information to peers, and engaging in mathematics investigations.

Checks for Understanding

There is no one way to teach mathematics. We should not hold any influence, instructional strategy, action, or approach to teaching and learning in higher esteem than students' learning.

Checks for understanding offer both teachers and learners the opportunity to monitor the learning process as students engage in challenging tasks and progress toward the learning intention. To ensure the learning is visible in our mathematics classroom, we must have the necessary information about student progress so that we provide effective feedback. In addition, learners must also have the necessary information about their progress so that they can effectively monitor progress and adjust their learning. Using the success criteria as a guide, checks for understanding include any strategies, activities, or tasks that make student thinking visible and allow both the teacher and learner to observe learning progress. When we are planning, developing, and implementing checks for understanding, two essential questions should guide our thinking:

Guiding Questions for Creating Opportunities to Respond

1. What checks for understanding will tell me and my learners how they are progressing in their learning related to the Learning Intention(s) and Success Criteria?

2. What are we going to do with this information that will help students with their next steps in learning this content?

Teaching Takeaway

Unless we, as teachers, have clear success criteria, we are hardly likely to develop good checks for understanding for our learners.

Checks for understanding give us feedback about the impact of our teaching and should be driven by the learning intention and success criteria for that particular lesson or learning experience. For example, if the success criteria say, *describe*, the check for understanding should focus on or provide deliberate practice in *describing*. Someone teaching mathematics in the Visible Learning classroom should focus on assessment for the purpose of informing instructional decisions and providing feedback to learners. The following assumptions inform our collective understanding about teaching and learning:

1. Assessment occurs throughout the academic year, and the results are used to inform the teacher and the learner. Each period, time is set aside to understand students' mathematics learning progress and provide feedback to learners.

2. A meaningful amount of time is dedicated to developing mathematics content and processes. Across every unit, students engage in sustained, organized, and comprehensive experiences with all of the components: conceptual understanding, procedural knowledge, and application of concepts and thinking skills.

3. Solving problems and discussing tasks occurs every class period. These events occur with the teacher, with peers, and independently.

Profiles of Three Teachers

In addition to the videos accompanying each chapter of this book, we will follow the practices of three teachers throughout the remaining chapters. Just as we have provided specific examples throughout this chapter and in the videos, we will devote more time to take an in-depth look into the classrooms of three elementary mathematics teachers. We will give you a front-row seat as they make specific, intentional, and purposeful decisions in teaching mathematics in the Visible Learning classroom.

Adam Southall

Adam Southall is a kindergarten teacher in Virginia. Although he has taught first grade, Mr. Southall finds that the opportunity to work with kindergarteners as they engage in mathematics, many for the first time, is incredibly satisfying: "For many of my learners, this is their first experience with formal mathematics learning. I love engaging in them in challenging mathematical thinking; thinking that most people, including their parents, don't think is possible." His prior experience in teaching first grade has allowed him to better frame his learners experiences to where they are headed next year. He says, "In addition to building their conceptual understanding and procedural skills, I have an eye toward first grade. This helps me be more purposeful in how I ask them to apply their concepts and thinking." Mr. Southall has spent 9 years in this small, urban district. This year, he has 27 learners and they stay with him all day, with the exception of specials (i.e., music, art, and physical education). Approximately 16% of Mr. Southall's learners speak a language in addition to English. His school qualifies as a school-wide Title I school, with 94% of the students qualifying for free lunch (a measure of poverty). In addition, 16% of the students receive special education services. Mr. Southall is unique in that he is licensed to teach preK through third grade and general education and to provide special education services for students from birth to age 8 years. As he notes, "Having attended a university that offered an inclusive early childhood program equipped me with the tools to ensure all of my learners make gains in their learning."

Calder McLellan

Calder McLellan teaches first grade in Nebraska. She is in her third year of teaching in this small, rural district. On the surface, there appears to be little diversity in the community or in the classroom. However, she has learned that the diversity in learners is in their prior experiences and exposure to mathematics outside of the school. That is, most of her learners speak English, but they differ greatly in terms of socioeconomic status. Approximately 60% of the students in the school qualify for free lunch, and 13% of the students receive special education services. Ms. McLellan had to make quick adjustments to her classroom to ensure all learners had access to mathematics concepts and thinking at the right level of rigor. She says,

> For example, James has spent his entire life on the farm, under the mentoring of his father and grandfather. He is incredibly fluent in computation and estimation, measurement, and spatial reasoning. He has grown up doing that type of mathematical thinking on the farm. I have to not only keep him engaged, but provide the right level of challenge for him. He knows so much about the application of mathematics.

Ms. McLellan works very hard to emphasize mathematical thinking each and every day, pushing back against a focus only on procedures (e.g., memorizing algorithms or mnemonics). There are about 24 students in her first grade classroom. She is the only first grade teacher in the building.

Carol Busching

Carol Busching is a second grade teacher in Idaho. She is part of a three-person grade-level team that meets regularly as a professional learning network to discuss student progress in learning. The team also includes an instructional coach who provides support to all teachers in the primary school. The 24 learners in Ms. Busching's classroom are diverse, with 83% of them qualifying for free or reduced school lunch. Fifty-two percent of her students are female, 48% are Latino/Hispanic, 40% are African American, and the remaining students identify as Caucasian or other. Of Ms. Busching's 24 students, 7 are students with disabilities. Overall, her learners have a wide range of instructional needs, and she collaborates well with the instructional coach to ensure she builds her skills to meet each student's instructional needs. Ms. Busching says, "I noticed that I was not having an impact on my students learning, yet. So I meet with the instructional coach on a regular basis to look at the evidence of my impact and make adjustments to my teaching." Ms. Busching is entering her 23rd year as a teacher, having only taught second grade. Although she is very comfortable with the Common Core State Standards, she pays very close attention to her impact on student learning. She says, "In addition to meeting with my grade-level team, I spend a lot of time looking at student work. I want to know exactly what they get and don't get so that I can use the instructional time as effectively as possible. Plus, if I cannot connect with them, I have to find another way."

These three teachers, although in different regions and contexts, operate under three important assumptions:

1. There is no one way to teach mathematics or one best instructional strategy that works in all situations for all students, but there is compelling evidence for tools that can help students reach their learning goals.

2. We should not hold any influence, instructional strategy, action, or approach to teaching and learning in higher esteem than students' learning.

3. Effective teaching and learning requires establishing clear learning intentions and success criteria, designing learning experiences and challenging mathematics tasks, monitoring student progress, providing feedback, and adjusting lessons based on the learning of students.

In the chapters that follow, you will encounter these three teachers and view the lesson plans they have developed for themselves. In order to establish a predictable pattern for displaying this information, we will use the Planning for Clarity questions (see Figure I.4). Lessons based on these guiding questions are not meant to be delivered in a strictly linear fashion; rather, they are intended to serve as a way to guide your thinking about the elements of the lesson. In addition, through the videos accompanying this book, you will more briefly meet a number of teachers from other grade levels whose practices illustrate the approaches under discussion. Although no book on lesson planning could ever entirely capture every context or circumstance you encounter, we hope that the net effect is that we provide a process for representing methods for incorporating Visible Learning for mathematics consistently in your classroom.

Reflection

Mathematics instruction that capitalizes on Visible Learning is established upon principles of learning. Recognizing that learners develop procedural knowledge, improve conceptual understanding, and apply concepts and thinking by engaging in surface, deep, and transfer learning allows us to intentionally and purposefully foster increasingly deeper and more sophisticated types of thinking in mathematics. This focus on the individual learner makes this approach inclusive of all learners, including those with language or additional learning needs. Teaching mathematics in the Visible Learning classroom means leveraging high-impact instruction to accelerate student learning through surface, deep, and transfer phases of learning by engaging them in strategies, actions, and approaches to learning at the right time and for the right content. These challenging learning tasks have clear learning intentions and success criteria that allow students to engage in those tasks in a variety of ways and with a variety of materials. Learning becomes visible for the teacher and the students. In other words, an assessment-capable visible mathematics learner notices when he or she is learning and is proactive in making sure that learning is obvious. As we engage in discussions about mathematics learning in this book, we will return to these indicators that students are visible mathematics learners to explore how they might look in the classroom.

1. Take a moment and develop your own explanation of teacher clarity. What does teacher clarity look like in your mathematics classroom?

2. Using an upcoming lesson plan as an example, what components of mathematics instruction are you focusing on in the lesson? How does your lesson incorporate all or some of the following?

   a. Making sense of problems and persevering in solving them

   b. Reasoning abstractly and quantitatively

   c. Constructing viable arguments and critiquing the reasoning of others

   d. Modeling with mathematics

   e. Using appropriate tools strategically

   f. Attending to precision

   g. Looking for and making use of structure

   h. Looking for and expressing regularity in repeated reasoning

3. Using that same lesson plan, how will you or could you adjust the difficulty and/or complexity of the mathematics tasks to meet the needs of all learners?

4. Give some examples of learners engaged in surface learning, deep learning, and transfer learning. What are the observed learning outcomes of these students? What learning experiences best support learners at each level?

TEACHING FOR THE APPLICATION OF CONCEPTS AND THINKING SKILLS

2

CHAPTER 2 SUCCESS CRITERIA:

(1) I can describe what teaching for the application of concepts and thinking skills in the mathematics classroom looks like.

(2) I can apply the Teaching for Clarity Planning Guide to teaching for application.

(3) I can compare and contrast different approaches to teaching for application.

(4) I can give examples of how to differentiate the complexity and difficulty of mathematics tasks designed for application.

Assessment-capable visible learners in the mathematics classroom use mathematics in situations that require the application of mathematics concepts and thinking skills. How efficiently and effectively this occurs depends on the learners' conceptual understanding and procedural knowledge. When planning for clarity (see Figure I.4), we begin with the end in mind and we ask ourselves, "What do I want my students to learn?"

In this chapter, we take the same approach. Mr. Southall, Ms. McLellan, and Ms. Busching focus on the end goal for each of their learners. All three teachers expect their learners to apply mathematics concepts and thinking skills to authentic situations. Thus, our journey begins with how these three teachers, by design, teach for this purpose. The QR codes in the margin provide video examples of application in action from other mathematics classrooms. In Chapters 3 and 4, we will go back in time and look at how these classrooms got here.

The nature of the application of concepts and thinking skills differs *across* the three classrooms and *within* the three classrooms. How each teacher approaches this purpose depends on the learning needs of the students in his or her classroom. Therefore, you will see that Mr. Southall, Ms. McLellan, and Ms. Busching adjust the rigor—or complexity and difficulty—of the application task, depending on where their learners currently are in the learning process (e.g., surface, deep, or transfer). For example, Mr. Southall adjusts the rigor of his application task for learners that need additional surface learning around the specific application task. Likewise, Ms. McLellan and Ms. Busching adjust the rigor of their application task to support learners who have gaps in their conceptual understanding. In all three classrooms, learners apply concepts and thinking skills to authentic scenarios. As we journey through these three classrooms, pay special attention to how each teacher differentiates the complexity and difficulty of the mathematics tasks so that all learners have access and the opportunity to apply concepts and thinking skills.

Mr. Southall and Number Combinations

A mathematician, like a painter or a poet, is a maker of patterns.

—G. H. Hardy

This quote hangs above the math bulletin board where students select and display work they are proud of. Mr. Southall's kindergarteners have covered the bulletin board with their pattern creations, including number chart patterns, patterned stories retold with images, season symbol patterns, and song patterns.

Mr. Southall knows patterns are important to mathematicians as a vehicle for problem solving and understanding the number system. Therefore, he focuses on a unifying big idea: *Mathematicians use patterns to problem solve.* He also knows the brain learns best when it can compare and contrast (Almarode & Miller, 2013). Therefore, his unit includes repeating, growing, *and* shrinking patterns. He wants his students to think flexibly about and apply each of these types of patterns to the number system.

Mr. Southall does not teach solely repeating patterns. This could lead to the misconception that all patterns repeat. Also, this would be too easy for most kindergarteners. Typically, kindergarteners already have some level of informal and formal knowledge about recognizing, duplicating, and extending repeating patterns (Clements & Sarama, 2014). Mr. Southall relies on learning trajectories to pinpoint a "just-right" spot along the trajectories of composing numbers counting, and patterning to focus the content of his unit.

After spending time developing conceptual understanding and procedural knowledge of what patterns are and how patterns can help solve problems, Mr. Southall's students are ready to apply these concepts and skills to number combinations. To facilitate his students' successful transfer of knowledge, Mr. Southall returns to familiar contexts, play, and student-initiated inquiries. Today, he structures his work-time tasks into two categories: must-do tasks and may-do tasks. He wants all students to tackle a number combination problem that aligns with today's big idea while having time to continue unfinished tasks of interest (Thunder & Demchak, 2017). The must-do task is based on their class pets (Figure 2.1):

> EFFECT SIZE FOR IDENTIFYING SIMILARITIES AND DIFFERENCES = 1.32

> EFFECT SIZE FOR "RIGHT" LEVEL OF CHALLENGE = 0.74

THE HAMSTER CAGE PROBLEM

Our class has five hamsters. There are two cages connected by a tube.

The **nest cage** has food, water, and nests.

The **play cage** has ramps and a running wheel.

In the morning, there are five hamsters in the nest cage and zero hamsters in the play cage. As the hamsters wake up, they eat and then

(Continued)

(Continued)

go play. First, one hamster is playing. Then two hamsters. Then three hamsters. Eventually, all the hamsters are awake and playing.

Describe the pattern.

How many hamsters could be in each cage?

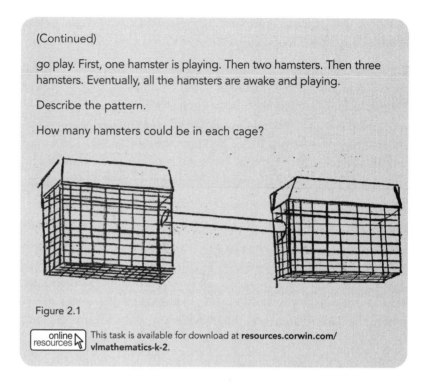

Figure 2.1

online resources — This task is available for download at **resources.corwin.com/vlmathematics-k-2.**

Mr. Southall knows from formative assessments that his students are ready to fluently work with different-sized numbers. He creates three versions or parallel tasks to reflect the three readiness levels of his students and matches his students to the right task (Thunder, 2014): 5 hamsters, 10 hamsters, and 15 hamsters.

The may-do tasks include two student-initiated inquiries into patterns: the Rug Pattern Challenge (building an ABACA pattern around the class rug) and Naming Shapes (building and naming two- and three-dimensional shapes based on the growing number of sides or faces). One may-do task is an extension of the Hamster Cage problem (Figure 2.2).

The final may-do task is a class favorite: Mystery Numbers (on number charts and number lines). Mr. Southall will mathematize the wealth of informal knowledge his students bring to each task by explicitly connecting these familiar contexts, play, and inquiries with formal mathematical language, notation, and materials (Thunder, 2011).

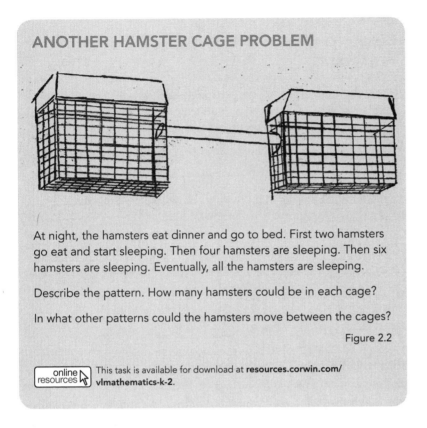

ANOTHER HAMSTER CAGE PROBLEM

At night, the hamsters eat dinner and go to bed. First two hamsters go eat and start sleeping. Then four hamsters are sleeping. Then six hamsters are sleeping. Eventually, all the hamsters are sleeping.

Describe the pattern. How many hamsters could be in each cage?

In what other patterns could the hamsters move between the cages?

Figure 2.2

online resources ☞ This task is available for download at **resources.corwin.com/vlmathematics-k-2.**

What Mr. Southall Wants His Students to Learn

In Mr. Southall's unit-planning process, he uses the Virginia Standards of Learning and searches for connections across content areas and standards. By using both standards resources, he notices that some standards build upon each other, some are subskills of broader skills, and some reveal the purpose for learning the content.

For today's application lesson, Mr. Southall identifies two Virginia Mathematics Standards of Learning that explicitly detail how and why mathematicians use numeric patterns to problem solve. He uses these to create his content big idea for the lesson: *Benchmarks of 5 and 10 help us decompose and compose numbers.*

EFFECT SIZE FOR TEACHER CLARITY = 0.75

> ## VIRGINIA MATHEMATICS STANDARDS OF LEARNING
>
> K.4. The student will (a) recognize and describe with fluency part-whole relationships for numbers up to 5; and (b) investigate and describe part-whole relationships for numbers up to 10.
>
> K.13. The student will identify, describe, extend, create, and transfer repeating patterns.
>
> **Mr. Southall is helping his learners develop the following Standards for Mathematical Practice:**
>
> - Make sense of problems and persevere in solving them.
> - Look for and express regularity in repeated reasoning.
> - Look for and make use of structure.

Mr. Southall wants his students to learn the what, why, and how of mathematics. He uses these to create his practice big idea for the lesson: *Mathematicians make sense of and use mathematical structures to problem solve.*

Learning Intentions and Success Criteria

Informed by the content and practice standards, Mr. Southall creates learning intentions. These are the end goals for today's lesson and stepping stones toward the profile of an end-of-year kindergartener. His approach is to develop learning intentions for content, language, and social dimensions of this application experience. Dividing learning intentions into *content*, *language*, and *social* varieties can provide teachers and students alike a clearer sense of the day's expectations. **Content learning intentions** answer the question "What is the math I am supposed to use and learn today?" **Language learning intentions** give teachers a space to lay out the language demands of the day: Are students developing new academic or content vocabulary, are they practicing recently developed vocabulary within proper linguistic structures,

EFFECT SIZE FOR TEACHER CLARITY = 0.75

Content learning intentions: What is the math I am supposed to use and learn today?

Language learning intentions: How should I communicate my mathematical thinking today?

or are they utilizing those structures toward their actual communicative functions? This is not limited to verbal communication and can include written or visual representations of mathematical thinking. **Social learning intentions** allow teachers to develop and leverage social and sociomathematical norms within their classroom culture.

Mr. Southall's learning intentions for this lesson are as follows:

> *Content Learning Intention:* I am learning the ways to decompose and compose numbers using benchmarks of fives and tens.
>
> *Language Learning Intention:* I am learning to apply the language of patterns to number combinations and number patterns.
>
> *Social Learning Intention:* I am learning to give and receive feedback about mathematical thinking.

Mr. Southall also knows his students will be better equipped to meet his instructional goals and evaluation criteria if he makes the success criteria transparent and accessible. The success criteria for the day are as follows:

> ☐ I can decompose and compose numbers to find all the combinations.
>
> ☐ I can use number patterns to find all the number combinations.
>
> ☐ I can record the combinations to show the number pattern.
>
> ☐ I can make suggestions and use suggestions to make revisions.

As always, Mr. Southall presents the learning intentions and success criteria in child-friendly language with images. However, today, he plans to broadly introduce the learning goals for the day and then specifically introduce them mid-way through work time. This will allow students to examine number combinations using informal language first. Then, Mr. Southall will explicitly connect their informal language with the formal language of the learning intentions and success criteria, and he

Social learning intentions: How should I interact with my learning community today?

Teaching Takeaway

Success criteria should articulate the evidence learners must show to demonstrate if they have met the learning intentions or their growth toward the learning intentions.

will model this language throughout the remainder of the lesson in his think-alouds, explanations, questions, and reflections.

Activating Prior Knowledge

Mr. Southall's students are slowly putting their thumbs up, holding them at chest level while sitting on the carpet in the middle of his room. They are engaged in a math routine called quick images. Quick images are flashed images of quantities that are organized in a way that makes them easy to quickly recognize without counting (Clements & Sarama, 2007). Mr. Southall says, "Remember, you're thinking about how many empty spaces you see on the ten-frame. I will flash the image again so you can revise or confirm your thinking in 3, 2, 1." He flips the enlarged ten-frame so it is visible again.

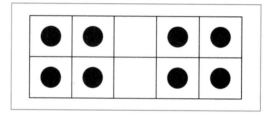

After 3 seconds, he lays the ten-frame down again. More thumbs are up. He says, "Turn and tell a partner how many empty spaces there are and how you know."

After 1 minute of talk, Mr. Southall asks for someone to share how they saw the quick image or how their partner saw it.

"I saw one empty in the top row and one empty in the bottom row, so that's two empty," says Brant.

"I know there are two rows, and I saw both were missing going straight down both rows," Pemba explains.

"I saw four dots and then empty spaces and then four more dots. I know four and four is eight. And then I counted up to 10 to figure out the empty spaces: 9, 10," adds Xavier.

Mr. Southall says, "I notice some people are thinking about both empty and full spaces to figure out the empty spaces. I'm going to make a table

Teaching Takeaway

Asking learners to share their thinking and reasoning makes their learning visible.

to record how many spaces are empty and how many are full." He models noticing and making a table to record their thinking. Then he continues with the next two quick images:

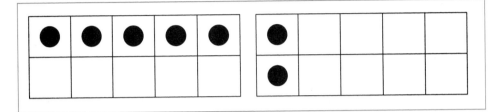

Similarly, he flashes each ten-frame for 3 seconds. He gives students about 20 seconds of think time and then reflashes the image so students can confirm or revise their thinking. Students think-pair-share how many spaces were empty and how they knew. Mr. Southall records their findings in the table.

Meredyth notices that the first image (Object a) has eight dots and two empty spaces while the last image has two dots and eight empty spaces. Mr. Southall highlights this noticing and wonders aloud if that might happen with other ten-frames. Through this math routine, the students' prior knowledge related to the language, notation, and visual models for combinations of 10 is activated. Now, they are ready to examine today's application task.

EFFECT SIZE
FOR PRIOR
ACHIEVEMENT
= 0.55

To introduce the learning intentions and success criteria, Mr. Southall uses an anchor chart with the headings, "Benchmark of 5" and "Benchmark of 10," as an advance organizer, or a visual to help students organize the big ideas in advance of engaging in the learning task.

Video 4
Activating Prior Knowledge in an Application Lesson

https://resources.corwin.com/ vlmathematics-k-2

> Today, we are continuing to work as mathematicians who use patterns to help us problem solve. One important pattern for our number system is the way every number has a relationship with the numbers 5 and 10. We call them benchmarks. Our work is to search for patterns so that we can describe every number's relationship with 5 and 10. We did some of this work with quick images. We looked at dots organized into ten-frames and figured out how many dots there were and how many spaces were empty because of the relationship with 10.

Then we recorded our findings in this table. I'm going to draw an empty five-frame under "Benchmark of 5" and an empty ten-frame under "Benchmark of 10" to remind you what these phrases mean.

Mr. Southall is now ready to introduce the must-do task and make sure his students understand the problem. He is using a familiar context and has an image and manipulatives to support their independent work. But Mr. Southall knows that acting out the problem will go a long way toward supporting students' visualization and comprehension of the problem.

First, Mr. Southall reads the story problem. Everyone is familiar with the pet hamsters and their connecting cage. The teacher says, "We're going to act out this story problem. Let's pretend this area is the nest cage and this area is the play cage. These carpet squares can be the tube that connects them." Mr. Southall has used tape to make two large rectangles on the ground and placed carpet squares to connect them. He says, "We need five hamsters." Immediately, hands jump into the air, and Mr. Southall choses five students to act as hamsters: "I will reread the story as you act it out, hamsters." As Mr. Southall reads the story context, the children act out waking up, eating, and crawling across the carpet to the play cage. The class applauds their peers.

Mr. Southall says, "Describe the pattern. Turn knee-to-knee, eye-to-eye with your neighbor." After 1 minute of talk, he has heard enough descriptions to know they understand the problem and are ready to work.

> As you think about how many hamsters could be in each cage, you might use cubes, tiles, five-frames or ten-frames, or a table, like the one we made for keeping track of the quick images. When you have found all the solutions to this problem, you may work on a task from our list. I am adding one new task called *Back to the Hamster Cage*, in case you want to solve more hamster cage problems.

Mr. Southall points to the may-do task list with images next to each title. He pairs students based on the size number they are ready to work with (5, 10, 15) and the may-do tasks they are already working on together. Students spread out around the room.

Scaffolding, Extending, and Assessing Student Thinking

Mr. Southall works with two pairs of students who are unsure of how to get started. He models using cubes and the cage picture. He asks them scaffolding questions: "Describe what you see happening. How is this similar to what we acted it out? How many hamsters are in each cage? How could we record that? What happens next?" After modeling a few moves, the pairs are ready to work.

With his observation chart in hand, Mr. Southall monitors and confers with students while taking notes. Students' names are grouped on the chart by the size number they are working with. Alma and Valerie are problem solving with 10 hamsters. They are drawing ten-frames under each cage to show how many hamsters could be on each side. They have 10 and 0, 9 and 1, 8 and 2, and 7 and 3 when Mr. Southall checks in. "What kind of pattern is this?" Mr. Southall asks.

"It's growing. One more hamster wakes up each time and starts to play," replies Alma.

"Show me what will happen next," Mr. Southall uses an in-the-moment Show Me move (Fennell, Kobett, & Wray, 2017) to formatively assess their thinking.

"One will wake up and move, so six are on this side and four on this side," says Valerie.

"And we'll draw six here and then four here," adds Alma.

"How will you know when you've found all the ways the hamsters could be in each cage?" Mr. Southall asks.

"When all the hamsters are awake," Alma says.

"What will that look like?" Mr. Southall asks them to make a jump in their thinking.

"All of the hamsters will be here and none will be here," Alma points to each cage.

"So 10 hamsters will be awake and zero hamsters will be sleeping," Valerie says.

"I can hear and see you applying what you know about growing patterns and ten-frames to solve this problem," Mr. Southall summarizes as he makes notes in his observation chart.

EFFECT SIZE FOR
SCAFFOLDING
= 0.82

EFFECT SIZE FOR
QUESTIONING
= 0.48

Teaching Takeaway

As teachers, we must record evidence of student learning if we are going to determine our impact.

He pauses to observe the class and notes that Xavier and Halima have drawn a table. Mr. Southall confers with Nayquon and Kaitlin, who are acting out 15 hamsters with cubes but keep losing track and recounting. They decide to make a stack of cubes instead of a pile, and they record their work in a table. Again, Mr. Southall makes notes in his chart.

It is mid-way through work time, and Mr. Southall wants to introduce the technical language of number combinations. He has students pause their work and join him in a circle, where he introduces the learning intentions and success criteria. To model composing and decomposing, he acts out moving the "hamster" cubes again. He uses Nayquon and Kaitlin's idea of stacking the cubes and models breaking one off to reconnect it with the stack in the other cage. "This is decomposing and composing numbers," Mr. Southall says. "Every time, we are breaking the number 5 into parts and describing those parts. I am thinking about the benchmark of five. All those parts have relationships with five because we can combine them or compose them to make five. And the list we can make in a table, like Nayquon and Kaitlin's table, shows the number combinations." This mini-lesson lasts just 5 minutes. Then Mr. Southall releases the students to work again.

During the second half of work time, many pairs begin selecting may-do tasks. Mr. Southall continues to monitor and confer while asking scaffolding, extending, and assessing questions. After intentionally sequencing tasks that develop conceptual understanding before developing procedural knowledge and fluency, Mr. Southall is excited to see his students transfer their knowledge and understanding of patterns to number combinations (Thunder & Demchak, 2016).

Teaching for Clarity at the Close

Mr. Southall highly values sharing time and works to include it each day. This is when his class comes together as a learning community of mathematicians to share and celebrate their successes, mistakes, and questions. Mr. Southall strategically chooses when to focus on the content, craft, process, or progress in students' sharing (Thunder & Demchak, 2012). Based on his anticipation of strategies and mistakes, Mr. Southall makes plans to monitor, select, and sequence specific content, craft, process, or progress aligned with the day's learning intentions (Smith & Stein, 2011). He also plans questions to help students make meaningful connections among what is shared.

EFFECT SIZE FOR RECORD KEEPING = 0.52

EFFECT SIZE FOR DIRECT/ DELIBERATE INSTRUCTION = 0.60

Teaching Takeaway

Direct/deliberate instruction is a very effective approach to acquiring and consolidating mathematics learning. This can occur as a mini-lesson at any time during the instructional block.

EFFECT SIZE FOR VOCABULARY INSTRUCTION = 0.62

EFFECT SIZE FOR COGNITIVE TASK ANALYSIS = 1.29

EFFECT SIZE FOR STRONG CLASSROOM COHESION = 0.44

Today, students are sharing their craft: the representations they created to keep track of all possible number combinations. Pemba and Meredyth share their two-colored ten-frames. They used one color for sleeping hamsters and one color for playing hamsters. Mr. Southall has them draw one sample ten-frame under "Benchmark of 10." Xavier and Halima share their table, on which they draw the anchor chart for "Benchmark of 5." Mr. Southall then asks connecting questions: "How are these representations similar? How do we know if Xavier and Halima found every possible combination? How do we know if Pemba and Meredyth found every possible combination? How did they use a pattern to help them problem solve?"

Mr. Southall directs students toward self-evaluation and reflection:

> We're going to close today's work with some personal reflection time. This time is for you as a mathematician and learner. Let's return to our learning intentions and success criteria. Remember, the success criteria let you know that you've met the learning intentions of our lesson. Take a sticky note and put your initials on it. As you put away your math folder, place your sticky note on the target. Remember the green circle in the middle with the tooth-smiley face means "I've got it!" The yellow ring with the smiley face is "I need a little more time. I'm just starting to get it." The red outer ring with the straight face is "I'm stuck. I don't understand."

He is interested in comparing his observation checklist and conference notes with students' self-evaluation and student work. With regular practice, Mr. Southall's students' self-evaluations are more frequently matching his evaluation of their work. When they do not match, he confers with the student and is often surprised by the student's self-awareness and reasoning. Tomorrow, students will extend their thinking about the benchmark of 10 to engage in surface-level thinking about place value and numbers composed of 10 ones and several ones. They will continue to apply their understanding and knowledge of patterns to this analysis and exploration. Figure 2.3 shows how Mr. Southall made his planning visible so that he could then provide an engaging and rigorous learning experience for his learners.

Teaching Takeaway

Closure is an important aspect of a learning experience. Closure helps to consolidate student learning.

> EFFECT SIZE FOR EVALUATION AND REFLECTION = 0.75

Teaching Takeaway

Self-regulation feedback is an essential characteristic of an assessment-capable visible learner.

Mr. Southall's Teaching for Clarity PLANNING GUIDE

ESTABLISHING PURPOSE

1 What are the key content standards I will focus on in this lesson?

Content Standards:

Virginia Mathematics Standards of Learning

K4. The student will (a) recognize and describe with fluency part-whole relationships for numbers up to 5; and (b) investigate and describe part-whole relationships for numbers up to 10.

K.13. The student will identify, describe, extend, create, and transfer repeating patterns.

Standards for Mathematical Practice:

- Make sense of problems and persevere in solving them.
- Look for and express regularity in repeated reasoning.
- Look for and make use of structure.

2 What are the learning intentions (the goal and *why* of learning stated in student-friendly language) I will focus on in this lesson?

- Content: I am learning the ways to decompose and compose numbers using benchmarks of fives and tens.
- Language: I am learning to apply the language of patterns to number combinations and number patterns.
- Social: I am learning to give and receive feedback about mathematical thinking.

3 When will I introduce and reinforce the learning intention(s) so that students understand it, see the relevance, connect it to previous learning, and can clearly communicate it themselves?

- Advance organizer: anchor chart of benchmarks of 5 and 10
- Conference questions

- Catch and release mini-lesson with modeling
- Connecting questions

SUCCESS CRITERIA

4 What evidence shows that students have mastered the learning intention(s)? What criteria will I use?

I can statements:

- I can decompose and compose numbers to find all the combinations.
- I can use number patterns to find all the number combinations.
- I can record the combinations to show the number pattern.
- I can make suggestions and use suggestions to make revisions.

5 How will I check students' understanding (assess learning) during instruction and make accommodations?

Formative Assessment Strategies:

- Conference/observation notes
- Show Me tasks during conferences
- Student work
- Bull's-eye self-evaluation

Differentiation Strategies:

- Differentiate the process by readiness and personal interest: purposeful pairings based on size of numbers and ongoing tasks

- Differentiate the process by situational interest: choice of materials
- Differentiate the content by readiness: tiered or parallel tasks
- Differentiate the content by situational interest: must-do and may-do tasks

INSTRUCTION

6   What activities and tasks will move students forward in their learning?

- Quick images: ten-frames
- Must-do task: Hamster Cage problem
- May-do tasks: Rug Pattern Challenge, Naming Shapes, Mystery Numbers, Back to the Hamster Cage problem
- Sharing craft

7   What resources (materials and sentence frames) are needed?

- Quick images: ten-frames
- Anchor chart of benchmarks of 5 and 10
- Math folders
- Hamster Cage and Back to the Hamster Cage problems
- Taped rectangles on the floor with connecting carpet squares
- Rug Pattern Challenge
- Naming Shapes
- Mystery Numbers
- Tiles
- Cubes
- Paper tiles
- Five-frames

- Ten-frames
- Number charts
- Number lines
- Markers
- Scissors
- Glue
- Two- and three-dimensional shape pieces

8 How will I organize and facilitate the learning? What questions will I ask? How will I initiate closure?

Instructional Strategies:

- Quick images: ten-frames
- Advance organizer: anchor chart of benchmarks of 5 and 10
- Acting out the Hamster Cage problem
- Must-do task: Hamster Cage problem
- May-do tasks: Rug Pattern Challenge, Naming Shapes, Mystery Numbers, Back to the Hamster Cage problem
- Catch and release: modeling mini-lesson
- Conferences
- Show Me tasks
- Sharing craft
- Bull's-eye self-evaluation
- Talk knee-to-knee, eye-to-eye

Scaffolding Questions:

- Describe what you see happening.
- How is this similar to what we acted out?

- How many hamsters are in each cage?
- How could we record that?
- What happens next?
- What kind of pattern is this?
- What is the pattern's rule?

Extending Questions:

- How will you know when you've found all the ways the hamsters could be in each cage? What would that look like?
- How could you record that more efficiently?
- How could you organize your recording to prove you found every combination?
- How are you using a pattern to problem solve?
- How could this pattern be growing and shrinking?

Connecting Questions:

- How are these representations similar?
- How do we know if _____ found every possible combination?
- How did they use a pattern to help them problem solve?

Self-Reflection and Self-Evaluation Questions:

- The green circle in the middle with the tooth-smiley face means "I've got it!"
- The yellow middle ring with the smiley face is "I need a little more time. I'm just starting to get it."
- The red outer ring with the straight face is "I'm stuck. I don't understand."

 This lesson plan is available for download at **resources.corwin.com/vlmathematics-k-2**.

Figure 2.3   Mr. Southall's Application Lesson on Number Combinations

Ms. McLellan and Unknown Measurement Values

Ms. McLellan has mixed things up this year. She noticed a trend in her previous students' data. Throughout first grade and into second grade, they struggled with relational thinking, including finding unknown values in equations, understanding and applying the concept of equality, making meaning of mathematical notation, and transferring the properties of operations to develop fluent strategies. As a result, Ms. McLellan took 1 week from the end of her addition and subtraction unit and 1 week from the beginning of her measurement unit to create a mini-unit on relational thinking. She is bringing the meaning and power of equality to the forefront of her students' thinking through a targeted 2 weeks of rich tasks, classroom discourse, and questioning.

Today's task will close this unit and transition students to the measurement unit, followed by another addition and subtraction unit expanding to numbers within 100. Students will apply their equality concepts and skills to find unknown weights and lengths. This application lesson will focus on the big idea: *Relationships between known values help determine unknown values and the reasonableness of the values.* Students will work in teams of three on two similar tasks (Figure 2.4).

> **EFFECT SIZE FOR FORMATIVE EVALUATION = 0.48**
>
> **Teaching Takeaway**
>
> Teaching mathematics in the Visible Learning classroom involves us, as teachers, evaluating our impact and making changes to our teaching when what we have done is no longer working.

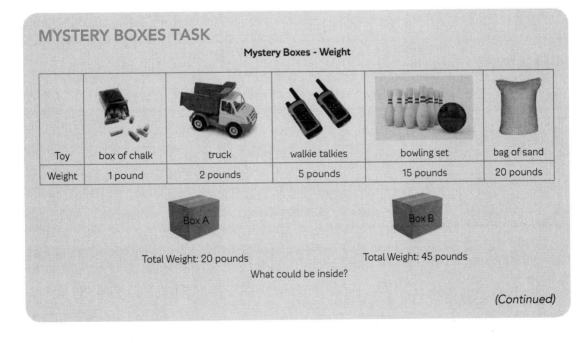

MYSTERY BOXES TASK

Mystery Boxes - Weight

Toy	box of chalk	truck	walkie talkies	bowling set	bag of sand
Weight	1 pound	2 pounds	5 pounds	15 pounds	20 pounds

Box A

Box B

Total Weight: 20 pounds   Total Weight: 45 pounds

What could be inside?

(Continued)

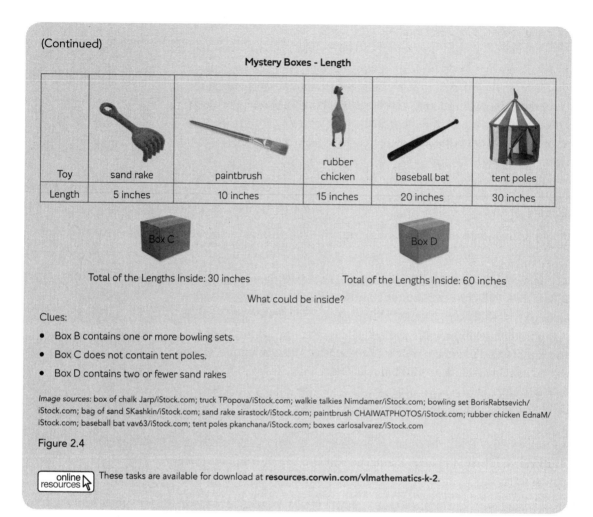

(Continued)

Mystery Boxes - Length

Toy	sand rake	paintbrush	rubber chicken	baseball bat	tent poles
Length	5 inches	10 inches	15 inches	20 inches	30 inches

Total of the Lengths Inside: 30 inches

Total of the Lengths Inside: 60 inches

What could be inside?

Clues:

- Box B contains one or more bowling sets.
- Box C does not contain tent poles.
- Box D contains two or fewer sand rakes

Image sources: box of chalk Jarp/iStock.com; truck TPopova/iStock.com; walkie talkies Nimdamer/iStock.com; bowling set BorisRabtsevich/iStock.com; bag of sand SKashkin/iStock.com; sand rake sirastock/iStock.com; paintbrush CHAIWATPHOTOS/iStock.com; rubber chicken EdnaM/iStock.com; baseball bat vav63/iStock.com; tent poles pkanchana/iStock.com; boxes carlosalvarez/iStock.com

Figure 2.4

online resources ↖ These tasks are available for download at **resources.corwin.com/vlmathematics-k-2**.

Teaching Takeaway

Sharing the big idea with students enhances the clarity of the learning intentions and success criteria for both the teacher and the students.

Each team member will be given one Mystery Box clue:

- Box B contains one or more bowling sets.
- Box C does not contain tent poles.
- Box D contains two or fewer sand rakes.

Ms. McLellan knows her students have a lot of prior knowledge about weight and length from their home lives and kindergarten. She built on this throughout the relational thinking unit as students used weight models (weights and scales, number balances) and length models (Cuisenaire rods, bar models, and number lines) to solve equality problems. Today, her students will apply these concepts and skills to find unknown weight and length values and to determine if those values are reasonable. The size of the numbers in the tasks provides students with additional opportunities to practice combining sums within 20 as well as extending to sums within 100.

What Ms. McLellan Wants Her Students to Learn

There are many possible sequences of topics, and Ms. McLellan relies on her division pacing guide to provide the scope and sequence of mathematical units in first grade. Ms. McLellan uses application tasks to build meaningful bridges between mathematical topics and units of study. She selects and creates tasks accessible to all of her learners to make these connections visible to students (Boaler, 2016). In this lesson, Ms. McLellan accomplishes three goals:

1. Engaging students in transfer of prior knowledge about equality and basic facts.

2. Engaging students in surface learning about measurement as well as multidigit addition strategies.

3. Helping students connect relational thinking to weight and length contexts.

In today's lesson, Ms. McLellan will continue to emphasize the unit's unifying standard (MA 1.2.1.a) and she will also begin to address three new standards.

NEBRASKA MATHEMATICS STANDARDS

MA 1.2.1.a. Use the meaning of the equal sign to determine if equations are true and give examples of equations that are true (e.g., $4 = 4$, $6 = 7 - 1$, $6 + 3 = 3 + 6$, and $7 + 2 = 5 + 4$).

MA 1.3.3.d. Order three objects by directly comparing their lengths, or indirectly by using a third object.

MA 1.1.2.d. Mentally find 10 more or 10 less than a two-digit number without having to count and explain the reasoning used (e.g., 33 is 10 less than 43).

(Continued)

EFFECT SIZE FOR TEACHER EXPECTATIONS = 0.43

EFFECT SIZE FOR TRANSFER STRATEGIES = 0.86

Teaching Takeaway

The application of concepts and thinking requires learners to detect similarities and differences between concepts, thinking, and situations.

Teaching Takeaway

Low-floor/high-ceiling tasks ensure all learners have access to the application of concepts and thinking.

(Continued)

MA 1.1.2.e. Add within 100, which may include adding a two-digit number and a one-digit number, and adding a two-digit number and a multiple of 10 using concrete models, drawings, and strategies which reflect understanding of place value.

Ms. McLellan is helping her learners develop the following Nebraska Mathematical Processes:

- Solves mathematical problems.
- Makes mathematical connections.

Teaching Takeaway

Standards are the starting point for ensuring clarity in learning: What do we want our students to know, understand, and be able to do?

Learning Intentions and Success Criteria

Ms. McLellan uses learning intentions and success criteria each day to help her students practice self-monitoring, self-evaluation, and goal setting. When students evaluate their progress toward the learning intentions, find evidence of the success criteria in their work, and make plans for next steps, their learning becomes visible to themselves and others. The learning intentions integrate the relational thinking standards with the new measurement standards to tell students what and why they are learning today:

Content Learning Intention: I am learning to understand how relationships between known values can help find unknown values and decide if values are reasonable.

Language Learning Intention: I am learning to understand the language of equality and comparisons in measurement situations (*heavier, lighter, longer, shorter, the same length/weight as*).

Social Learning Intention: I am learning to understand everyone contributes to our learning and to appreciate the connections among our reasoning.

The success criteria break down what it will look like and sound like when they have mastered the learning intentions:

☐ I can find unknown values and decide if a value is reasonable.

☐ I can mathematically model a real-life measurement problem.

☐ I can make connections between strategies and representations.

☐ I can use what I know about equality to solve new problems.

Ms. McLellan will introduce the learning intentions and success criteria after activating students' prior knowledge about measurement and equality, since these terms are significant to making sense of the success criteria. She will return to the learning intentions and success criteria as students share their many strategies and solutions and again as students begin to assemble their math portfolios.

Activating Prior Knowledge

Before launching into the main task, Ms. McLellan asks students to analyze the following image:

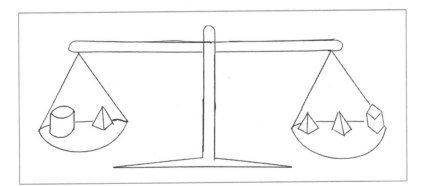

Students talk in pairs: "We know each side is the same because it's balanced." "The square pyramids are all the same weight." This is a regular math routine called a math talk. Ms. McLellan uses math talks to activate prior knowledge or to bring closure and consolidate learning each day. This 2- to 5-minute routine brings important math vocabulary, tools, representations, and strategies to the surface of students' thinking so they can easily apply them to the main task.

Ms. McLellan brings the students back together and says, "We know so much about these weights without knowing any values! Now, I'm going to label each weight." She labels the square pyramids "6 pounds" and

Teaching Takeaway

Learning Intentions and Success Criteria should serve as guides for teaching and learning. Both teachers and learners should refer to them throughout the entire instructional block.

EFFECT SIZE FOR STRATEGY TO INTEGRATE WITH PRIOR KNOWLEDGE = 0.93

EFFECT SIZE FOR COOPERATIVE LEARNING VERSUS INDIVIDUALISTIC = 0.55

Video 5
Differentiation and Choice in an Application Lesson

https://resources.corwin.com/vlmathematics-k-2

the cube "1 pound." She leaves the cylinder blank and says, "The cylinder is the unknown value. Turn and tell your neighbor: What would be a reasonable value for the cylinder weight?"

After 2 minutes, she asks, "What are reasonable values for the cylinder weight?" Ms. McLellan records all responses: 6, 7. "Could the cylinder weigh both 6 or 7 pounds in this situation?"

"Not in this problem. There is just one weight we don't know and the balance is straight, not tipped," responds James. Sometimes the students work on open-ended tasks in which more than one answer is correct. Ms. McLellan wants to draw the students' attention to why this task has one solution.

"Which answer would you like to defend first?" Ms. McLellan asks.

Kanice chooses seven and explains, "We saw the doubles-fact six and six. We know that's 12 and one more is 13. So that side of the scale is 13 pounds and the other side has to be the same. So then we thought, six and what is 13? And it's seven. So the cylinder has to be 7 pounds." As Kanice shares her thinking, Ms. McLellan records her work in mathematical notation:

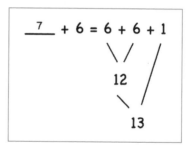

"What's another way to prove seven is the cylinder's weight?" Ms. McLellan asks.

Justin makes a connection to a rule the class developed for comparing two values without combining and says,

> I saw the square pyramid on both sides and those are the same weight so I could ignore them. It's like in Double Compare if you both flip one card that's the same. So then I just compared the other weights. I knew the cylinder had to be the same as the square pyramid and the cube together. That's six and one, which is seven. So the cylinder is seven.

Ms. McLellan records his thinking:

$$\underline{}^{7} + \boxed{6} = \boxed{6} + 6 + 1$$

$$\diagdown \diagup$$

$$7$$

Ms. McLellan knows her students have many mental math strategies but they are learning how to record them efficiently. She often uses math routines as an opportunity to model mathematical notation.

"Who would like to defend 6 pounds?" she asks

"Six was reasonable because I know the doubles-fact six and six is 12. But the right side of the scale is one more than 12, so six isn't the exact answer," Quintus explains.

"Yes. Six was a reasonable estimate but not the exact answer," summarizes Ms. McLellan. "We have been working a lot with weight models and length models to show equality. Today, we're going to work with larger numbers where there will be more than one correct answer."

Ms. McLellan posts an enlarged copy of the Mystery Boxes tasks. She reads the task aloud and asks students to think about what information they need to solve the problem. She is using the instructional strategy called **Bansho** (Curriculum Services Canada, 2011; Kuehnert, Eddy, Miller, Pratt, & Senawongsa, 2018). Bansho, or board writing, emphasizes the comparison of strategies to synthesize big ideas. The Mystery Boxes tasks are open questions (Small, 2012), which means they are open middled (many strategies) and open ended (many solutions). With so many possible strategies and solutions, Ms. McLellan wants to target the synthesis of big ideas, which will facilitate students' transfer of concepts.

Bansho is a strategy for recording and making mathematics vocabulary, learning, and strategies visible throughout the instructional block.

After some think time, Ms. McLellan records students' noticings and important vocabulary (such as *total weight* and *total lengths inside*). These notes, along with the recordings from the math talk, remain on the board as a reference for students. She says, "You will each receive one clue about a Mystery Box. You must share this clue with your team to help you with your problem solving." Ms. McLellan also points out

EFFECT SIZE FOR
RECORD KEEPING
= 0.52

the materials available to students: number balances, Cuisenaire rods, weights and balance scales, rulers and yardsticks, number lines, graph paper, colored pencils, scissors, and glue.

The class discussion lets Ms. McLellan hear that her students understand the task and are ready to problem solve. She says, "We will use four success criteria to evaluate our work today." She reads the four success criteria and adds the following:

> As you work, keep these success criteria in mind. At the end of our work time, you will evaluate your process and product using these success criteria, and you will have to identify evidence to prove you've met each. I will also be meeting with teams as you work in order to hear about your process.

Scaffolding, Extending, and Assessing Student Thinking

Ms. McLellan has purposefully created the teams based on the size numbers students are ready to work with, levels of representation they typically use, language needs of her students, and specific pairings she knows to be productive. Her goal is to create teams in which no two students are "too far apart" to communicate productively yet they bring unique strengths of conceptual understanding and procedural knowledge. In this way, her creation of the small group task and teams reflects the social learning intention. In addition, each team member holds one requirement, which means the team must communicate and collaborate in order to include each.

Ms. McLellan's observation/conference chart is a checklist of the four success criteria with space for notes (Figure 2.5). Students on the same team are clustered together but each student has his or her own row. This allows Ms. McLellan to check for evidence of each individual's learning and to note trends within and across teams.

Ms. McLellan also uses her chart as a resource for herself. She includes a list of resources to scaffold students who are struggling and her list of planned questions to extend and assess student thinking. Before

Teaching Takeaway

As teachers, we must ensure that we are collecting evidence of learning for individual students so that we can make adjustments to our teaching.

OBSERVATION/CONFERENCE CHART

Mystery Box Tasks - Date _____

Observation/Conference Checklist

Name	SC #1: I can find unknown values and decide if a value is reasonable.	SC #2: I can mathematically model a real life measurement problem.	SC #3: I can make connections between strategies and representations.	SC #4: I can use what I know about equality to solve new problems in new contexts.	Notes

Overall Patterns:

Questions:

- How could you represent the total weight/length?
- Which toys cannot fit in the mystery box? Why?
- Why is this value reasonable? What other values are reasonable?
- How does your clue change the possible solutions?
- How can you represent this with an equation?
- How can you use what you know to figure out what you don't know?

Materials:

number balances

Cuisenaire rods

weights and balance scales

rulers and yardsticks

number lines

graph paper

colored pencils

scissors and glue

Figure 2.5

teaching the lesson, she anticipates student strategies. Anticipating enables Ms. McLellan to plan her conference chart for monitoring student learning and to identify scaffolding strategies, materials, and questions that will support students without removing them from productive struggle (Smith & Stein, 2011). Ms. McLellan knows that effective, differentiated instruction requires intentional planning. The time spent planning in advance of the lesson maximizes her instructional time and students' growth toward the learning intentions.

With 2 minutes left to work, Ms. McLellan reviews her chart to select and sequence student sharers. Three of the strategies are those she anticipated and knew in advance she wanted to highlight. One group used a strategy she did not anticipate: building lengths with overlapping rulers and comparing the total length to yardsticks. Ms. McLellan sees the power of this strategy for making sense of Cuisenaire rods and bar models as well as applying their work to measuring length.

Teaching for Clarity at the Close

In the consolidation phase of Bansho, Ms. McLellan displays the student strategies she selected in sequence from left to right on the board, next to the notes from activating prior knowledge. The strategy furthest left relies on concrete and familiar representations, while more abstract strategies and new representations are posted to the right. Each group of students presents their work:

1. Neil, Autumn, and Tobias apply what they know about Cuisenaire rods to model two possible solutions for Mystery Boxes C and D. They built each total length using the longest rods and then built equivalent lengths. They recorded their concrete representations using bar models labeled with lengths and names of toys.

2. Justin, Harmony, and DeAndre built the total lengths of Mystery Boxes C and D using overlapping yardsticks. Then they lined up

rulers to find the lengths of the objects. They also recorded a sketch of each of their builds using bar models.

3. Sinai, Lyric, and Ann represented each possible total weight for Mystery Boxes A and B using weights and scales. During Ms. McLellan's conference with the team, she modeled how they could create a table to organize their list of solutions. They made one table of solutions for each mystery box.

4. Summer, Mahammed, and Zimir used open number lines. The hops show the lengths of each object, and the total distance on the number line shows the total lengths inside each mystery box. Sometimes they hopped forward to reach the target total, and sometimes they hopped backward from the target total to zero.

Students in the audience ask clarifying questions. Ms. McLellan annotates next to each with important math vocabulary and concise explanations: "Counting by 10 was fastest." "The total length is the same as all the toy lengths lined up." "We visualized to see what rod would fit in the empty space."

> EFFECT SIZE FOR SUMMARIZATION = 0.79

After all four groups share, Ms. McLellan facilitates the class discussion to highlight key ideas, strategies, models, and properties. She records these to the right of the student work. Ms. McLellan begins by asking, "What do you notice is the same across all of the strategies and representations?"

"We all showed the total is the same as adding together the smaller lengths or weights," Justin notes.

"Everyone used what they knew to find out what they didn't know. Like they looked at the empty spaces on their bar models or open number lines and figured out what was missing to make the total," says Yah'Meen.

"This reminds me of our big ideas from addition and subtraction. We talked a lot about the relationship between parts and wholes. Who can describe this connection?" Ms. McLellan asks.

"Adding is combining the parts to make the whole. We wrote that on our anchor chart. We combined the little lengths to find the total length," Raoul connects.

"When we figured out the unknown values to make the total, that's like thinking addition to subtract," Heidi says.

"It's like finding the missing part of the whole," adds Sinai.

"With your team, look at each group's work and see if you can find evidence of this part-whole relationship," Ms. McLellan directs. She records this big idea and listens as teams talk and point to students' posted work.

She continues, "One of the important skills of our next unit is about measuring length: You can repeatedly line up a unit to measure length, or you can find the distance between two units to measure length." Ms. McLellan writes these on the board and says, "Look at each group's work. Where do you see people using these skills already? Turn and talk with your team." After 1 minute, she asks two teams to share their analysis.

"We saw Harmony's team line up the rulers over and over to find equal the total length," says one team.

"We saw Mahammed's team find the distance between numbers by hopping on the number line and counting hops," says the other team.

Ms. McLellan brings closure to that discussion by making the transfer of their knowledge and skills explicit.

> Earlier Yah'Meen noticed that everyone used what they knew to figure out what they didn't know. This was one of our success criteria. And it's a one of our year-long goals. We know so much now about equality and finding unknown values. We will use all of this in measurement, addition, and subtraction.

Ms. McLellan moves the class into the final phase of Bansho: the practice problems. She says, "We're going to practice applying these big ideas and strategies to problems that focus on length. I have three bar models. Two are true and one is not. You and your team should talk and decide which two are true and which is a lie." This is a favorite game of the class and an engaging way to deliberately practice a transferred skill in a short period of time. Ms. McLellan displays three bar models, and immediately her students begin constructing arguments about why each is true or false.

EFFECT SIZE FOR DELIBERATE PRACTICE = 0.79

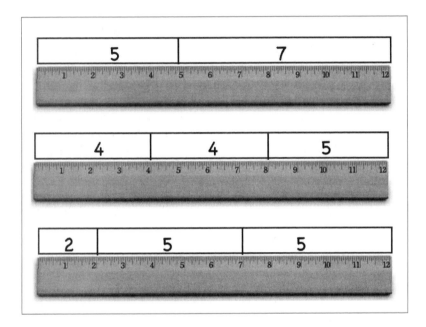

After 3 minutes, the class shares which bar model is the lie and explains why.

To make sure each student is accountable for the learning intentions, Ms. McLellan transitions to the final reflection.

> For each of the four success criteria, you need one sticky note—red, yellow, or green. Put your initials on the sticky note and record your evidence to support the color you chose. Place your sticky note on your work in your math binder or posted on the board from today. If you have work from a previous day that addresses the success criteria, you can place a sticky note on that in your math binder as well.

The students flip through their math binders, study their work, and write on colored sticky notes. This is one step toward creating their math portfolios for the quarter. They will use their portfolios to reflect on their long-term learning across units and to set goals for learning in the next quarter. Ms. McLellan is excited for her students to physically see their growth. In this way, her students become their own teachers, continually transferring and applying concepts and skills; her students also become her teachers, helping Ms. McLellan analyze data to find out if her mini-unit on relational thinking was an effective change in her instruction. Figure 2.6 shows how Ms. McLellan made her planning visible so that she could then provide an engaging and rigorous learning experience for her learners.

Ms. McLellan's Teaching for Clarity PLANNING GUIDE

ESTABLISHING PURPOSE

1 What are the key content standards I will focus on in this lesson?

Content Standards:

Nebraska Mathematics Standards

MA 1.2.1.a. Use the meaning of the equal sign to determine if equations are true and give examples of equations that are true (e.g., 4 = 4, 6 = 7 - 1, 6 + 3 = 3 + 6, and 7 + 2 = 5 + 4).

MA 1.3.3.d. Order three objects by directly comparing their lengths, or indirectly by using a third object.

MA 1.1.2.d. Mentally find 10 more or 10 less than a two-digit number without having to count and explain the reasoning used (e.g., 33 is 10 less than 43).

MA 1.1.2.e. Add within 100, which may include adding a two-digit number and a one-digit number, and adding a two-digit number and a multiple of 10 using concrete models, drawings, and strategies which reflect understanding of place value.

Nebraska Mathematical Processes:

- Solves mathematical problems.
- Makes mathematical connections.

2 What are the learning intentions (the goal and *why* of learning stated in student-friendly language) I will focus on in this lesson?

Content: I am learning to understand how relationships between known values can help find unknown values and decide if values are reasonable.

Language: I am learning to understand the language of equality and comparisons in measurement situations (heavier, lighter, longer, shorter, the same length/weight as).

Social: I am learning to understand everyone contributes to our learning and to appreciate the connections among our reasoning.

3 When will I introduce and reinforce the learning intention(s) so that students understand it, see the relevance, connect it to previous learning, and can clearly communicate it themselves?

- *Turn and tell*
- *Conference questions*
- *Sticky note self-evaluation*

SUCCESS CRITERIA

4 What evidence shows that students have mastered the learning intention(s)? What criteria will I use?

I can statements:

- *I can find unknown values and decide if a value is reasonable.*
- *I can mathematically model a real-life measurement problem.*
- *I can make connections between strategies and representations.*
- *I can use what I know about equality to solve new problems.*

5 How will I check students' understanding (assess learning) during instruction and make accommodations?

Formative Assessment Strategies:

- *Conference/observation notes*
- *Student work*
- *Practice problems*
- *Sticky note self-evaluation*

Differentiation Strategies:

- *Differentiate the process and product by readiness: open questions*
- *Differentiate the process and product by interest: choice of materials*
- *Differentiate the process by readiness: purposeful small groups*

INSTRUCTION

6   **What activities and tasks will move students forward in their learning?**

- *Math talk: visualizing an unknown weight on a balance scale*
- *Mystery Box tasks*
- *Practice problems: Two Truths and a Lie*

7   **What resources (materials and sentence frames) are needed?**

Math binders

Math talk: sketch of a balance scale with weights

Mystery Box tasks with clues

Cuisenaire rods

Number balances

Number lines

Weights and balance scales

Rulers and yardsticks

Graph paper

Colored pencils

Scissors

Glue

Practice problems: Two Truths and a Lie

---

8 How will I organize and facilitate the learning? What questions will I ask? How will I initiate closure?

Instructional Strategies:

- Math talk
- Bansho
- Conferences/observations
- Turn and talk
- Sticky note self-reflection

Scaffolding Questions:

- How could you represent the total weight/length?
- Which toys cannot fit in the mystery box? Why?
- Why is this value reasonable? What other values are reasonable?
- How can you use what you know to figure out what you don't know?

Extending Questions:

- How does your clue change the possible solutions?
- How can you represent this with an equation?

Connecting Questions:

- *What do you notice is the same across all of the strategies and representations?*

- *How is this work related to our work with part-part-whole relationships in addition and subtraction?*

- *One of the important skills of our next unit is about measuring length: You can repeatedly line up a unit to measure length or you can find the distance between two units to measure length. Where do you see people using these skills already?*

Self-Reflection and Self-Evaluation Questions:

- *Green sticky note: met the success criteria*

- *Yellow sticky note: don't see evidence, need to make a revision*

- *Red sticky note: not sure how to meet the success criteria*

 This lesson plan is available for download at **resources.corwin.com/vlmathematics-k-2**.

Figure 2.6   Ms. McLellan's Application Lesson on Unknown Measurement Values

Ms. Busching and the Ever-Expanding Number System

Ms. Busching's second graders are ready to apply their conceptual understanding and procedural knowledge to a new context. The class has worked with numbers within 100 to answer the unit's essential questions: What is addition? What is subtraction? How are they related? How do we engage in the work of mathematicians?

Teaching Takeaway

Guiding or essential questions help frame learning and enhance the clarity in that learning.

EFFECT SIZE FOR INTEGRATED CURRICULA PROGRAMS = 0.47

Along the way, students have posed their own questions to which they have pursued answers:

Can you ever take away a larger number from a smaller number? What happens if you regroup two tens or three tens? If you can you add to solve a subtraction problem, can you subtract to solve an addition problem? Can you decompose the subtrahend to make subtraction more efficient? How do you compensate if you adjust three or four addends?

In literacy, the class is studying nonfiction texts, including comprehending nonfiction text features like tables, charts, and graphs. Ms. Busching has created a contextualized problem that will garner her students' interest by extending this study into mathematics (Figure 2.7).

LIFE SPANS TASK

Life Spans

What do you notice?   What do you wonder?

Animal	Maximum Life Span (in years)
Koi	226
Giant Tortoise	225
Bowhead Whale	210
Red Sea Urchin	200
Tuatara	150
Lobster	140
Box Turtle	123
Human	122
Crocodile	100
Carp	100
Cockatoo	92
Tarantula	49
Dog	29

1. Create your own addition and subtraction problems using this data. Consider all the unknown values and actions possible in problems.

2. Test strategies you know from the anchor charts to solve the problems you create.

3. Research and share new data to include and ask questions about.

 This task is available for download at **resources.corwin.com/vlmathematics-k-2**.

Figure 2.7

Using the Life Spans task, the class will explore the unit's essential questions for transfer: How can we use what we know about adding and subtracting small numbers to add and subtract large numbers? How can we apply the properties (associative, commutative, and identity) to problems with large numbers?

A challenging and fascinating quality of mathematics is the ever-expanding number system. Ms. Busching knows this quality can make some students (and teachers) feel overwhelmed, as though the rules are always changing and the quantity of things to learn in math is always growing. She embraces this quality of math by creating explicit opportunities for her students to transfer what they already know to new situations—new operations, new sizes of numbers, and new types of numbers. She also centers her instruction on vertical mathematical truths and big ideas rather than narrow facts that lead to misconceptions. In forming essential questions for transfer, Ms. Busching intentionally creates an opportunity for students to return to concepts and skills that remained at the surface or deep level earlier in the unit. The application task engages students in exploring multidigit addition and subtraction within 1,000 while also providing additional and different experiences to reach mastery with single digits.

> EFFECT SIZE
> FOR TRANSFER
> STRATEGIES
> = 0.86

What Ms. Busching Wants Her Students to Learn

To create her unit, Ms. Busching puts groups of related standards in order so that each is a building block to the next. Overall, she begins with one-digit numbers and single-step, single-operation contextualized problems and then moves onto multidigit, multistep, multioperation contextualized problems. This sequence mirrors the SOLO Taxonomy model, beginning with one or a few aspects of the concept (unistructural), then several aspects (multistructural), then integrating all aspects into a meaningful whole (relational), and finally, generalizing and transferring that whole to new contexts (extended abstract) (Biggs & Collis, 1982).

Three Common Core State Standards for second grade align with her transfer essential questions and specify what this application of addition and subtraction will look like within 1,000.

EFFECT SIZE FOR
THE "RIGHT" LEVEL
OF CHALLENGE
= 0.74

MATHEMATICS CONTENT AND PRACTICE STANDARDS

2.NBT.B.7. Add and subtract within 1,000, using concrete models or drawings and strategies based on place value, properties of operations, and/or the relationship between addition and subtraction; relate the strategy to a written method. Understand that in adding or subtracting three-digit numbers, one adds or subtracts hundreds and hundreds, tens and tens, ones and ones; and sometimes it is necessary to compose or decompose tens or hundreds.

2.NBT.B.8. Mentally add 10 or 100 to a given number 100–900, and mentally subtract 10 or 100 from a given number 100–900.

2.NBT.B.9. Explain why addition and subtraction strategies work, using place value and the properties of operations.

Ms. Busching is helping her learners develop the following Standards for Mathematical Practice:

- Construct viable arguments and critique the reasoning of others.

- Look for and make use of structure.

Learning Intentions and Success Criteria

The learning intentions integrate the essential questions and standards to tell students their focus for learning today:

Content Learning Intention: I am learning to understand how strategies for adding and subtracting small numbers can be transferred and revised to add and subtract large numbers.

Language Learning Intention: I am learning to understand how mathematical properties can be used to describe and defend addition and subtraction strategies.

Social Learning Intention: I am learning to understand that collaborating as a team means mathematical disagreement and debate are valued and resolved respectfully.

The success criteria communicate to students how they will know when they have mastered the learning intentions.

EFFECT SIZE FOR SUCCESS CRITERIA = 1.13

- ☐ I can make sense of the magnitude of large numbers by noticing, wondering, and representing their values.
- ☐ I can decompose and compose quantities to efficiently add and subtract.
- ☐ I can apply the commutative and associative properties to addition of large numbers.
- ☐ I can transfer and revise efficient strategies for addition and subtraction of large numbers.

Ms. Busching's students will engage in making sense of the learning intentions and success criteria before engaging in the Life Spans task. As a class, they will use the success criteria to evaluate a worked example of a similar task. In this way, Ms. Busching ensures her students have a vision for processes and products that demonstrate mastery of the learning intentions.

EFFECT SIZE FOR TEACHER CLARITY = 0.75

Activating Prior Knowledge

Today, Ms. Busching begins class by engaging in a math talk centered on oral counting. Students are counting by tens starting at five while Ms. Busching records their count. At several planned points,

Ms. Busching pauses for students to reason and talk about what number would come next and why.

Ms. Busching draws a box under 185 and asks, "What number will go here? Turn and talk for 1 minute."

> **5, 15, 25, 35, 45, 55, 65, 75, 85, 95**
> **105, 115, 125, 135, 145, 155, 165, 175, 185, 195**
> **205, 215, 225, 235, 245, 255**   ☐

Gyaltsen begins the sharing, "285. Sammy and I counted by tens three more times: 265, 275, 285."

"We looked at it differently. We noticed a pattern counting by hundreds down the columns. For example, 15, 115, 215. So we counted by hundreds starting at 85, 185, 285," Hailey shares.

Ms. Busching fills 285 into the box and the class continues. She pauses the count and draws a box three rows below 245.

> **5, 15, 25, 35, 45, 55, 65, 75, 85, 95**
> **105, 115, 125, 135, 145, 155, 165, 175, 185, 195**
> **205, 215, 225, 235, 245, 255, 265, 275, 285, 295**
> **305, 315**
>
>   ☐

"Based on the pattern, what number will go here? Share your conjecture with a partner and defend it." This time, Ms. Busching hears some debate.

"What numbers did you decide could go here?" Ms. Busching purposefully allows for multiple answers to her question. Bringing mistakes and misconceptions to light through discussion is important to all her students' learning. Often, other students are thinking the same way or may in the future. Like in a number talk, Ms. Busching asks for all solutions first (545, 645, 745) and then has students defend the various solutions.

Zoe defends 645. "We used Gyaltsen's pattern. We counted by hundreds from 245: 345, 445, 545, 645. Wait. Can I come point?" Zoe points as she counts and this time stops at 545. "I think we counted one too many rows. It should be 545."

"How did pointing help you realize your mistake?" Ms. Busching asks probing questions to scaffold metacognitive thinking.

"Imani and I were trying to point with our eyes and fingers from far away but we couldn't keep track of exactly how many rows down we needed to count," Zoe explains.

"I agree with Zoe," Megan adds. "We need three more rows, so that's 300. Then 245 and 300 is 545 because 2 and 3 is 5, so 200 + 300 is 500."

Through this classroom routine, Ms. Busching is able to activate students' prior knowledge related to groups of tens and hundreds, place value patterns within 1,000, and three-digit number notation and language.

Next, Ms. Busching spends time engaging the class in a discussion to be sure the task is understood and the expectations are clear (Van de Walle, Karp, & Bay-Williams, 2018).

> In our reading workshop, we're reading nonfiction texts with tables, charts, graphs, and timelines. Today, you're going to work in teams of four to read a table of nonfiction information. Each of your team members will be responsible for creating a problem to solve based on the information in the table.
>
> Our learning intentions are focused on taking what you already know about addition and subtraction problems, strategies, and models and applying that knowledge to numbers through 1,000. Let's read the learning intentions.

Ms. Busching asks students to think-pair-share what they notice and what they wonder about the learning intentions. When they share as a whole group, Sonam wonders what the associative and commutative properties are; Adric points to several labels on anchor charts and says, "It's the rules we've labeled that help us add numbers in any order or switch them to add."

Sonam makes the connection: "Oh, like 6 + 3 is the same as 3 + 6."

Next, Ms. Busching shares the success criteria: "To get ready for our work today, we're going to look at data presented in a table. Take a moment to study this table about Earth's Fastest Animals and think about what you notice and what you wonder" (Figure 2.8).

EFFECT SIZE FOR ELABORATIVE INTERROGATION = 0.42

EARTH'S FASTEST ANIMALS TASK

What do you notice?   What do you wonder?

Animal	Speed (miles per hour)	Does the animal travel in the air, on land, or in water?
Peregrine falcon	200	air
Spine-tailed swift	105	air
Sailfish	68	water
Cheetah	64	land
Free-tailed bat	60	air
Pronghorn antelope	55	land
Ostrich	40	land
Dolphin	25	water
Human	23	land
Gentoo penguin	22	water

1. Create your own addition and subtraction problems using this data. Consider all the unknown values and actions possible in problems.

2. Test strategies you know from the anchor charts to solve the problems you create.

3. Research and share new data to include and ask questions about.

Figure 2.8

 This task is available for download at **resources.corwin.com/vlmathematics-k-2.**

Teaching Takeaway

Wait time increases student engagement.

Ms. Busching waits 2 minutes. The wait time conveys that everyone should be noticing and wondering thoughtfully, not just superficially. She says, "Now turn and talk with a partner about what you notice and what you wonder." Students turn and share animatedly with a partner. An image or table paired with the open questions of noticings and wonderings allows for every student to access the task, whether they are at the surface, deep, or transfer levels of learning. After 1 minute, each pair shares one noticing or wondering with the whole class. Ms. Busching provides the following instructions:

> During our work time today, you will use your noticings and wonderings from a different data set to create at least one addition or subtraction problem for your team to solve. You will have to solve your problem first to make sure it's reasonable and makes sense. After you get feedback from your team, you will make revisions and final problem-and-solution pages. We'll post these problems on our bulletin board outside for other school members to solve.

Before beginning their work, Ms. Busching engages the class in using the success criteria to evaluate a worked example. This gives students a clear vision for the expectations of their final product. She says, "First, let me show you a problem and its solution page that Ms. Gatesman's class created based on the Fastest Animal data" (Figure 2.9).

WORKED EXAMPLE OF THE EARTH'S FASTEST ANIMAL TASK

The spine-tailed swift flies 105 miles per hour. It's swift but it's not the fastest bird.

A peregrine falcon flies 200 miles per hour.

How much slower is a swift than a falcon?

Answer: The swift is 95 miles per hour slower than a falcon.

Explanation: 200-100=100

100-5=95

We adjusted one number to make an easier problem.

We subtracted 100. Then we subtracted 5 more.

Figure 2.9

**Teaching
Takeaway**

Classroom
dialogue, through
either questioning
or discussion
strategies,
provides feedback
to the teacher
about student
thinking and
learning.

Ms. Busching continues, "Let's look at each success criterion and evaluate this work. First, 'I can make sense of the magnitude of large numbers by noticing, wondering, and representing their values.' Where do you see evidence of this?"

Emma begins, "They noticed the difference between the two birds' speeds and wondered how much slower the swift is than the peregrine."

"I don't see a representation. Well, they have equations. Is that a representation?" asks Cory.

"Our Mathematical Toolbox has equations listed, so I think it counts as a representation," says D'angelo.

"Okay. Then they met the first success criterion," concludes Cory.

"D'angelo reminds us of a great resource, our Mathematical Toolboxes. If you're wondering what might be a representation or strategy to use, you can refer to your toolbox to get ideas," Ms. Busching highlights this connection. "How about the second success criterion? What evidence do you see of them decomposing and composing quantities to efficiently add and subtract?"

"I don't see any addition," Mateo says.

"How could they address that part of the success criteria?" Ms. Busching probes.

"Well, they could use a second strategy to subtract. Maybe think addition. Or they could write a second problem and use addition to solve it," Mateo suggests.

"I see they decomposed 105 into 100 and 5. I don't see them composing any numbers. That would look like combining and they don't combine," analyzes Luciana.

"I agree with Luciana. But if they do Mateo's suggestion, they might compose when they use a different strategy or problem," adds David.

Ms. Busching summarizes this point:

> Mateo and David are saying we need more evidence to be sure these mathematicians can efficiently add and use composing strategies. They are arguing that Ms. Gatesman's class needs

to solve the problem two ways or create another problem
to solve. That's something to consider as you create and
solve your problems. How many strategies or problems and
solutions do you need in order to demonstrate mastery of the
success criteria? Should you use every opportunity to show
what you know about addition and subtraction, or should you
only show what is comfortable and easy for you?

Megan explains, "Well if it's comfortable and easy, then we already
know it. But I don't think we already know everything about addition
and subtraction with large numbers or we wouldn't be working on it
today." She continues,

> I think we should work on showing multiple strategies that
> are hard for us. We could also label and explain our work. The
> third success criterion says, "I can apply the commutative
> and associative properties to addition of large numbers." You
> would have to label when you used the properties to really
> prove you know what it is.

With this comment, Ms. Busching transitions the class to discussing the
third success criterion. Eventually, the class has unpacked each success
criterion by evaluating the worked example of the Earth's Fastest Animal
problem and solution.

EFFECT SIZE
FOR GOAL
COMMITMENT
= 0.40

Before she sends students to start their teamwork, Ms. Busching
points out a difference between the worked example and today's task:
"Ms. Gatesman's class created problems based on the Earth's Fastest
Animal table, but you will be using the Life Span data. A life span is
how long something lives, or the entire length of their life measured
in years." She then reminds her students of today's task and the roles
of the four team members.

> This task will take us multiple days of work. At the end of
> our work time today, we will practice evaluating one team's
> problem-and-solution pages in order to give them feedback for
> revisions and additions. Tomorrow, we will continue working
> on this task. Remember the resources you have available to
> help you with problem solving and modeling.

Teaching Takeaway

Alternate ranking is a flexible grouping strategy that is supported by assessment data and based on students' instructional needs for specific content. Learners are then grouped for collaborative learning based on that specific need and not a general label or ability.

Ms. Busching points to the manipulatives, graph paper, calculators, colored pencils, and anchor charts. She continues, "Also remember this task will take perseverance and attention to the structures of addition, subtraction and place value. Rely on your team members' mathematical reasoning and questioning, and check in with the success criteria and the Fastest Animal problem for support."

Scaffolding, Extending, and Assessing Student Thinking

Ms. Busching knows purposefully engaging students in collaborative problem-solving tasks provides students opportunities to teach and learn from each other; to practice communicating effectively as mathematicians, learners, and friends; and to examine multiple strategies and representations. She knows that labeling students has negative results for each group: the "gifted" group avoids taking risks because they perceive themselves as being expected to be capable of everything, and the "not gifted" group avoids taking risks because they perceive themselves as already being incapable of challenge.

Instead, Ms. Busching uses a variety of flexible groupings throughout each unit. Today's task relies on students solving each other's problems and giving each other feedback. Ms. Busching has intentionally created teams of four using a heterogeneous grouping strategy called alternate group ranking (Frey et al., 2018). She ordered a recent Show Me formative assessment (Fennell et al., 2017) on addition and subtraction strategies with 100 from highest score to lowest and then split the list in half. Two students from the first half of the list were paired with the corresponding two students on the second half of the list. This resulted in the groups shown in Figure 2.10.

Ms. Busching strives to create groups with a moderate range of skills but without a broad gap that prevents students from truly collaborating effectively. She wants students to rely on everyone in their group for input. The Show Me formative assessment (Fennell et al., 2017) is one piece of data that helps her create these initial groups that reflect heterogeneous *current* abilities. Then she makes adjustments based on the language needs of her students, specific pairings she knows to be productive, and social concerns.

ALTERNATE GROUP RANKING

Team 1		Team 2		Team 3	
Student 1	Student 13	Student 3	Student 15	Student 5	Student 17
Student 2	Student 14	Student 4	Student 16	Student 6	Student 18
Team 4		**Team 5**		**Team 6**	
Student 7	Student 19	Student 9	Student 21	Student 11	Student 23
Student 8	Student 20	Student 10	Student 22	Student 12	Student 24

Figure 2.10

During the 40 minutes of work time, Ms. Busching is able to confer with four of six teams. She records notes from each conference in her observation chart. The chart is organized by team, with individual boxes for each student. Each box has space to record the student's choice of problem type, strategy, and representation as well as any strengths or needs.

Ms. Busching identifies one team to share their in-progress problem-and-solution pages during the whole-group share today. She also notes an overall pattern in students' confusion: "What do you do when there is a zero in the tens place?" This will guide her mini-lesson focus for tomorrow. Ms. Busching also notes the two teams she still needs to confer with during work time tomorrow.

Teaching for Clarity at the Close

Ms. Busching dings her chime. Students assemble on the carpet with their mathematician's journals and colored pencils in hand. Ms. Busching says, "We worked hard as mathematicians today. We are working to use what we know about adding and subtracting two-digit numbers to add and subtract three-digit numbers. As we share, remember to listen to and respond to each other's ideas and questions in ways that move us all forward as learners." Ms. Busching gestures to the dialogue bubbles with language frames around her board, as shown in Figure 2.11.

EFFECT SIZE FOR STRONG CLASSROOM COHESION = 0.44

LANGUAGE FRAMES

- I agree with _____ because . . .
- I disagree with _____ because . . .
- I still have questions about . . .
- To clarify, you're saying . . .
- I was thinking about what _____ said, and I was wondering, what if . . .
- I don't know what you mean by . . .
- I want to go back to what _____ said . . .
- I want to add on to what _____ said about . . .

Figure 2.11

Teaching Takeaway

Teaching mathematics in the Visible Learning classroom involves getting feedback from our learners about where to go next.

Video 6
Exploration and Closure During an Application Lesson

https://resources.corwin.com/vlmathematics-k-2

Her students have internalized some of these frames and use them throughout sharing conversations, while others are a reference as students search for how to say what they want to say.

Similar to the mini-lesson, the team shares one problem-and-solution draft and the class discusses each success criterion, looking for "Gems and Opportunities." As a community, students look for evidence of mastery to celebrate (gems) and offer suggestions for revisions and additions (opportunities). Ms. Busching records each on sticky notes, modeling how students will provide feedback via gems and opportunities independently during a future lesson. This process not only provides the sharing team with timely, specific feedback aligned to the success criteria, but it also gives all teams an opportunity to reflect on their work through comparison and analysis.

Ms. Busching passes out a two-column chart with the following headings: Gems (Great! Keep doing this!) and Opportunities (Make a change. Be sure to add.).

From evaluating Tashi, Adric, Phoebe, and Bryant's draft, you should also be thinking about your own draft and what you did well and what you need to revise. Take 3 minutes to discuss this with your team, and make notes of gems and opportunities for your own draft based on the success criteria. You will use these notes as a plan for your work tomorrow.

Each team sits talking, looking at their drafts, referring to the success criteria, and recording their gems and opportunities.

Ms. Busching says, "Now, flip over your Gems and Opportunities chart. There are three questions for you to discuss with your team. As you discuss, take turns recording your responses. Be specific." The three questions are as follows:

1. Compare your problem context to the sharing team's context. How is the action of your context similar to or different from the sharing team's context? Where do you see this action in your representations?

2. Compare your strategy to the sharing team's strategy. How did operating with three-digit numbers affect your strategies in similar ways? Where do you see place value being used?

3. Compare your representation to the sharing team's representation. How does the efficiency of the representation change with three-digit numbers?

As teams discuss, Ms. Busching joins each group and makes additional notes on her conference chart. She will collect their work and use it to plan her mini-lesson, conference questions, and sharing tomorrow. This student work will also guide her planning and differentiation of other tasks within the next phase of her addition and subtraction unit as she analyzes who is at the surface, deep, and transfer levels of learning related to three-digit numbers.

Ms. Busching notices some students flipping back to the gems and opportunities side of the paper to make additional notes. This gives Ms. Busching important feedback about her questions; these self-monitoring and analysis questions are successfully making students' learning visible to both the teacher and students. Figure 2.12 shows how Ms. Busching made her planning visible so that she could then provide an engaging and rigorous learning experience for her learners.

Teaching Takeaway

As part of the closure to a lesson, linking back to the learning intentions and success criteria enhances the clarity in the learning for students, which supports the building of assessment-capable learners.

EFFECT SIZE FOR TEACHING COMMUNICATION SKILLS AND STRATEGIES = 0.43

EFFECT SIZE FOR EVALUATION AND REFLECTION = 0.75

EFFECT SIZE FOR FEEDBACK = 0.70

Ms. Busching's Teaching for Clarity PLANNING GUIDE

ESTABLISHING PURPOSE

1

What are the key content standards I will focus on in this lesson?

Content Standards:

2.NBT.B.7. Add and subtract within 1,000, using concrete models or drawings and strategies based on place value, properties of operations, and/or the relationship between addition and subtraction; relate the strategy to a written method. Understand that in adding or subtracting three-digit numbers, one adds or subtracts hundreds and hundreds, tens and tens, ones and ones; and sometimes it is necessary to compose or decompose tens or hundreds.

2.NBT.B.8. Mentally add 10 or 100 to a given number 100-900, and mentally subtract 10 or 100 from a given number 100-900.

2.NBT.B.9. Explain why addition and subtraction strategies work, using place value and the properties of operations.

Standards for Mathematical Practice:

- Construct viable arguments and critique the reasoning of others.
- Look for and make use of structure.

2

What are the learning intentions (the goal and *why* of learning stated in student-friendly language) I will focus on in this lesson?

- Content: I am learning to understand how strategies for adding and subtracting small numbers can be transferred and revised to add and subtract large numbers.

- Language: I am learning to understand how mathematical properties can be used to describe and defend addition and subtraction strategies.

- Social: I am learning to understand that collaborating as a team means mathematical disagreement and debate are valued and resolved respectfully.

3 When will I introduce and reinforce the learning intention(s) so that students understand it, see the relevance, connect it to previous learning, and can clearly communicate it themselves?

- Essential questions
- Turn and talk
- Worked-example group evaluation
- Conferences
- Sharing: group Gems and Opportunities chart
- Reflection plan and Gems and Opportunities chart

SUCCESS CRITERIA

4 What evidence shows that students have mastered the learning intention(s)? What criteria will I use?

I can statements:

- I can make sense of the magnitude of large numbers by noticing, wondering, and representing their values.
- I can decompose and compose quantities to efficiently add and subtract.
- I can apply the commutative and associative properties to addition of large numbers.
- I can transfer and revise efficient strategies for addition and subtraction of large numbers.

5 How will I check students' understanding (assess learning) during instruction and make accommodations?

Formative Assessment Strategies:

- Conference/observation chart
- Student work and reflection in the mathematician's journal
- Reflection plan and Gems and Opportunities chart

Differentiation Strategies:

- Differentiate the process by readiness: alternate rank grouping
- Differentiate the process by situational interest: choice of materials, strategies
- Differentiate the product by situational interest: create contextualized problem

INSTRUCTION

6 What activities and tasks will move students forward in their learning?

- Worked-example analysis: Earth's Fastest Animals
- Life Spans task
- Gems and Opportunities chart sharing
- Gems and Opportunities chart reflection and plan

7 What resources (materials and sentence frames) are needed?

Mathematician's journal

Mathematical Toolbox

Life Spans task

Earth's Fastest Animal task and worked example

Gems and Opportunities chart reflection and plan

Sticky notes

Base-ten blocks

Cuisenaire rods

Number charts

Number lines and whiteboard markers

Graph paper

Highlighters

Colored pencils

Language frames

---

8 How will I organize and facilitate the learning? What questions will I ask? How will I initiate closure?

Instructional Strategies:

- Worked example
- Open task
- Peer feedback
- Gems and Opportunities chart

Scaffolding Questions:

- What do you notice about life spans?
- What do you wonder about life spans? How could this become an addition or subtraction strategy?
- How could you use your Mathematical Toolbox to select a representation?

- How could you use the anchor charts for addition and subtraction strategies to select a strategy?

Extending Questions:

- How is this story represented in your work? What does the answer mean?
- How could you use addition and subtraction to solve this problem?
- Will this strategy always work? Why or why not?
- For what numbers would this strategy be inefficient?
- How does this representation show why the strategy works?

Connecting Questions:

- Compare your problem context to the sharing team's context. How is the action of your context similar or different to the sharing team's context? Where do you see this action in your representations?
- Compare your strategy to the sharing team's strategy. How did operating with three-digit numbers affect your strategies in similar ways? Where do you see place value being used?
- Compare your representation to the sharing team's representation. How does the efficiency of the representation change with three-digit numbers?

Self-Reflection and Self-Evaluation Questions:

- Gems and Opportunities chart

 This lesson plan is available for download at **resources.corwin.com/vlmathematics-k-2**.

Figure 2.12   Ms. Busching's Application Lesson for the Ever-Expanding Number System

Reflection

The three examples from Mr. Southall, Ms. McLellan, and Ms. Busching exemplify what teaching mathematics for application of concepts and thinking skills in the Visible Learning classroom looks like. Using what you have read in this chapter, reflect on the following questions:

1. In your own words, describe what teaching for the application of concepts and thinking skills looks like in your mathematics classroom.

2. How does the Teaching for Clarity Planning Guide support your intentionality in teaching for the application of concepts and thinking skills?

3. Compare and contrast the approaches to teaching taken by the classroom teachers featured in this chapter.

4. How did the classroom teachers featured in this chapter adjust the difficulty and/or complexity of the mathematics tasks to meet the needs of all learners?

TEACHING FOR CONCEPTUAL UNDERSTANDING 3

CHAPTER 3 SUCCESS CRITERIA:

(1) I can describe what teaching for conceptual understanding in the mathematics classroom looks like.

(2) I can apply the Teaching for Clarity Planning Guide to teaching for conceptual understanding.

(3) I can compare and contrast different approaches to teaching for conceptual understanding with teaching for application.

(4) I can give examples of how to differentiate mathematics tasks designed for conceptual understanding.

In Chapter 2, we visited the three classrooms as they engaged in the application of concepts and thinking skills. As you recall, this application of mathematics to counting hamsters in cages, using weight and length to solve mystery boxes, or analyzing life span data required learners to have foundational knowledge in conceptual understanding and procedural knowledge. In this chapter, we will turn back time to see how each of the three teachers supported their learners as they developed conceptual understanding in their mathematics learning. We will also share videos of what conceptual learning looks like in the K–2 mathematics classroom.

If learners are to see mathematics as more than algorithms and mnemonics, we must provide learning experiences that focus on the underlying properties and principles. For Mr. Southall, Ms. McLellan, and Ms. Busching, the end goal is for students to understand the meaning behind mathematical practices or processes rather than relying on shortcuts and memory jingles. As in Chapter 2, each of these teachers will differentiate the mathematics tasks by providing varying degrees of complexity and difficulty to their learners. Although every learner will be actively engaged in a challenging mathematical task that builds conceptual understanding of key concepts, Mr. Southall, Ms. McLellan, and Ms. Busching will adjust the complexity and difficulty of the task to ensure all learners have access to these concepts.

Mr. Southall and Patterns

Mr. Southall knows all children bring rich, experiential mathematical knowledge to school. There is no difference in children's informal mathematical knowledge based on socioeconomic status, race, ethnicity, or gender (Tudge & Doucet, 2004). His role is to create learning experiences to scaffold and extend his students' thinking and to connect informal with formal or school mathematical knowledge through language, materials, content, and instructional strategies (National Association for the Education of Young Children, 2009). As a result, Mr. Southall often builds mathematical tasks from his students' interests, play, and inquiries, and this boosts his **teacher credibility**.

His kindergarteners have done a lot of work counting, sorting, and counting and comparing collections. Now, Mr. Southall wants his students

Teacher credibility: involves competence, trustworthiness, and caring.

EFFECT SIZE
FOR TEACHER
CREDIBILITY = 0.90

to see numbers in a different way. He wants them to see numbers and counting as a way to problem solve, to make sense of the structure of the number system, and to describe and represent patterns. At recess, his students are working individually and in teams to create hopscotch paths that go around the entire playground. Each hopscotch path is a unique combination of one-foot hops and two-feet hops. This is Mr. Southall's inspiration for a math task (Figure 3.1).

THE GIANT HOPSCOTCH CHALLENGE

We want to make a giant hopscotch path around the playground.

Kevin starts with one foot, two feet, one foot, two feet, one foot, two feet. What should come next? For how many hops can you extend the hopscotch path?

Ollie draws one foot, two feet, one foot, one foot, two feet, one foot, one foot, one foot, two feet. What should come next? How long can you extend the hopscotch path?

Valerie makes a different hopscotch path. It begins one foot, two feet, one foot, two feet, two feet, one foot, two feet, two feet, two feet. What should come next? How long can you extend the hopscotch path?

Kevin's Hopscotch Path

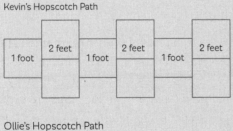

Ollie's Hopscotch Path

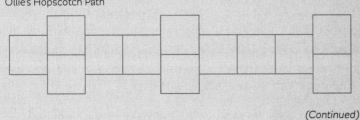

(Continued)

Teaching Takeaway

Supporting learners' conceptual understanding requires that we link mathematics content and processes to authentic situations.

Teaching Takeaway

Teacher clarity includes structures, routines, and expectations, as well as learning intentions and success criteria.

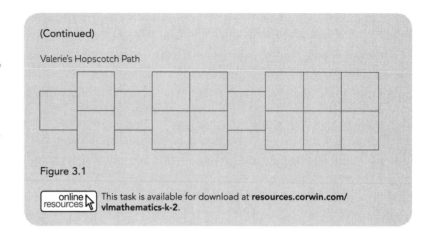

(Continued)

Valerie's Hopscotch Path

Figure 3.1

online resources ⟋ This task is available for download at **resources.corwin.com/ vlmathematics-k-2.**

To mathematize his students' informal mathematical knowledge (Clements, 2004), Mr. Southall explicitly connects their ongoing problem-solving work with the work of mathematicians. He looks for opportunities to teach his students about the language, tools, representations, and practices of mathematicians and to connect these to their everyday play and work. Through the Giant Hopscotch Challenge, Mr. Southall will connect the natural pattern seeking of his students to the pattern seeking of mathematicians for problem solving. He states this as a big idea: *Mathematicians look for patterns in order to problem solve.* Mr. Southall will also use this task to engage his students in exploring two content big ideas:

- Patterns repeat, grow, or shrink in predictable ways.

- The core of a repeating pattern is the part that repeats in the same way over and over. The rule of a changing pattern describes how to grow or shrink each step of the pattern.

In this way, he will explicitly teach them the concepts and procedures of patterns.

What Mr. Southall Wants His Students to Learn

Mr. Southall begins his instructional planning with the end in mind. He and his grade-level team created a profile of a kindergartener. This description is made up of success criteria for what an end-of-year kindergartener can do in the categories of content knowledge, learning and language practices across content areas, and socioemotional growth.

As Mr. Southall plans each math unit, he considers what structures, routines, and expectations he needs to communicate to his students so they can focus on making connections with the content and developing the mathematical practices or practices.

Mr. Southall pays special attention to his language. He knows the way he speaks to his students, the vocabulary and sentence structure he uses, and the explicit instruction he provides can communicate either high or low expectations to his students (Denton, 2013). Mr. Southall consistently uses teacher language that models high expectations, because language development is pivotal for all his 5-year-olds as they connect familiar concepts and skills to mathematical language (Thunder, 2011). He makes time to teach his kindergarteners how to speak as mathematicians and to allow them to practice this math talk frequently with in-the-moment feedback.

VIRGINIA MATHEMATICS STANDARDS OF LEARNING

K.13. The student will identify, describe, extend, create, and transfer repeating patterns.

K.3. The student will (a) count forward orally by ones from 0 to 100; (b) count backward orally by ones when given any number between 1 and 10; (c) identify the number after, without counting, when given any number between 0 and 100 and identify the number before, without counting, when given any number between 1 and 10; and (d) count forward by tens to determine the total number of objects to 100.

Mr. Southall is helping his learners develop the following Standards for Mathematical Practice:

- Look for and express regularity in repeated reasoning.
- Model with mathematics.
- Construct viable arguments and critique the reasoning of others.

The entire unit will be based on the first Standard for Mathematical Practice ("Look for and express regularity in repeated reasoning."), which Mr. Southall translates into his practice big idea that unites the unit: *Mathematicians look for patterns to problem solve.*

Video 7
A Model for Structuring a
Conceptual Lesson

*https://resources.corwin.com/
vlmathematics-k-2*

Learning Intentions and Success Criteria

Several months into the school year, Mr. Southall's students now expect to know, discuss, and reflect on the learning intentions and success criteria for each lesson. They know Mr. Southall creates three types of learning intentions. The first learning intention communicates to his students the new mathematical content they are learning. The second learning intention delineates the new language they will use. This deliberate focus on language learning supports the many English learners in Mr. Southall's class as well as all of the students as they mathematize their informal language (Thunder, 2011). The third learning intention makes explicit the social learning process that is ongoing as a classroom community.

> *Content Learning Intention:* I am learning the predictable ways patterns repeat, grow, and shrink.
>
> *Language Learning Intention:* I am learning the mathematical language to identify, describe, and extend patterns.
>
> *Social Learning Intention:* I am learning to understand each other's ideas by listening, looking, and thinking.

Mr. Southall then uses the learning intentions to create the success criteria that he and the students can use to know whether they mastered the learning intentions.

> ☐ I can identify repeating, growing, and shrinking patterns.
> ☐ I can describe the core or unit of a repeating pattern and the rule for a changing pattern.
> ☐ I can predict what comes next and extend a pattern.
> ☐ I can explain how I used a pattern to solve a problem.

Mr. Southall unpacks the content and language learning intentions to create the first three success criteria. The social learning intention is translated into the last success criterion. He plans to introduce the learning intentions and success criteria after he activates students' prior knowledge and before they examine the Giant Hopscotch Challenge.

EFFECT SIZE
FOR PRIOR
ACHIEVEMENT
= 0.55

Activating Prior Knowledge

Mr. Southall's students are sitting in a circle, creating a rhythm: clap, clap, pat, clap, clap, pat, clap, clap, pat. After a few repetitions of the pattern, Mr. Southall matches words to his actions and the students chant with him. Then he says, "Find my new pattern." Mr. Southall changes to: snap, clap, pat, snap, clap, pat, snap, clap, pat. As he changes, the students change their hand pattern to match. After a moment, they synchronize their words with their actions. He changes the pattern two more times and his students follow.

Mr. Southall clasps his hands in his lap and the class does the same. To make the **classroom cohesion** explicit, he says,

> Wow! You guys did a lot of looking, listening, and thinking to figure out my patterns. Those patterns were all repeating patterns. We did the same action over and over, like clap, clap, pat. We do another type of pattern with our clapping sometimes. If you can hear me, clap your hands one time.

> EFFECT SIZE
> FOR STRONG
> CLASSROOM
> COHESION = 0.44

Everyone claps once.

He continues, "If you can hear me, clap your hands two times."

Everyone claps twice.

Mr. Southall stops after four claps and says, "What do you predict I would say next?"

Aujha says, "If you can hear me, clap your hands five times."

"How did you know that would be next?" probes Mr. Southall.

"Because five comes after four," replies Aujha.

"And then what would I say?"

"If you can hear me, clap your hands six times."

"What if we went backwards? What if I started with: If you can hear me, clap your hands 10 times. And then nine times. And then eight times. Then what would I say next?"

"If you can hear me, clap your hands seven times."

"How did you know that would be next?"

Classroom cohesion: exists when there is a sense that all, teachers and learners, are working toward positive learning gains.

"Seven is before eight."

Mr. Southall explains, "We just used our hands to make three kinds of patterns. Patterns that repeat: snap, clap, snap, clap, snap, clap; patterns that grow: Clap your hands one time, two times, three times, four times; and patterns that shrink: Clap your hands ten times, nine times, eight times, seven times." He models the mathematical language to identify the patterns. He connects the words to familiar games and routines to activate and mathematize their prior knowledge. Then he transitions to introducing the learning intentions and success criteria.

He begins by saying, "Today, we are mathematicians looking for patterns to help us solve problems." He reads each learning intention and then says, "We will know when we have met these learning goals when we can say and show the success criteria." Each success criterion has an image next to it of a child working with a pattern and a speech bubble with the child's words.

> EFFECT SIZE FOR IMAGERY = 0.45

Mr. Southall notes, "I heard some new words in our learning intentions and success criteria for our word wall!" He has blank index cards ready to make "word wall" cards for the new vocabulary words: *repeating pattern*, *growing pattern*, *shrinking pattern*, *core* or *unit*, and *rule*. He glues pictures of the actions for one repeating pattern on the corresponding card: clap, snap, clap, snap, clap, snap. Then he glues pictures of the actions for the growing pattern on the corresponding card: 1 clap, 2 claps, 3 claps. Next he glues pictures of the actions for shrinking pattern on the corresponding card: 5 claps, 4 claps, 3 claps. Finally, he holds up the card that says "core or unit" and asks if anyone has heard of those words before.

> EFFECT SIZE FOR VOCABULARY INSTRUCTION = 0.62

"An apple has a core."

"So does a pear."

"The core has seeds in it. I don't eat that part."

Mr. Southall uses this connection to help students make sense of the new mathematical term. He holds the repeating pattern card and offers the following explanation:

> The core of an apple or pear is where the seeds are stored.
> It's the center of the apple. From those seeds, more apple
> trees grow and then more apples. The core of a pattern works

similarly. The core of a repeating pattern tells us what part of the pattern will be repeated. For this repeating pattern, we repeated two actions over and over. Those two actions are the core. What two actions did we repeat over and over?

"Clap and snap," the class responds.

Clap, snap is the core of the repeating pattern. We clap, snap, clap, snap, clap, snap without end. When a pattern grows or shrinks, there is a rule (instead of a core) that describes how the pattern changes. Think about the growing and shrinking patterns we made. Turn knee-to-knee, eye-to-eye with a partner and talk about the rule for how the growing pattern grows and how the shrinking pattern shrinks.

Mr. Southall holds up the two vocabulary cards with examples. He also listens to students' conversations. Some students are speaking in their heritage language. They know Mr. Southall values their words and ideas. Students are counting forward and backward, using words like *one more* and *one less*. Students share their rules with the whole class. Mr. Southall records the sample core and rule on the word wall cards.

Mr. Southall says, "Outside at recess, there are a lot of kids using chalk to make hopscotch paths. They're trying to extend the paths all the way around the playground. Here are three of the paths." Mr. Southall displays the Giant Hopscotch Challenge images. He has Kevin, Valerie, and Ollie pretend to hop their paths on carpet squares while the class says the matching words for their actions. As they hop and chant, Mr. Southall uses tiles to build a replica of the paths. He asks for student ideas to extend each pattern and then presents the expectations for today's work: "Your challenge is to figure out which kinds of patterns Kevin, Valerie, and Ollie have made, extend their patterns, and then create your own. You will work with a partner. You can use markers, tiles, cubes, construction paper, paper tiles, and glue." Mr. Southall answers questions, pairs students, and passes out the tasks to the pairs. He intentionally pairs students who have been working together outside on their hopscotch paths so they can continue making this connection to their play, and he pairs students who speak the same heritage language so they can continue making sense of the new mathematical language of patterns.

EFFECT SIZE FOR "RIGHT" LEVEL OF CHALLENGE = 0.74

Teaching Takeaway

Visible Learning in the mathematics classroom requires that we have clarity about what learners are expected to know, understand, and be able to do in their learning.

Teaching Takeaway

Visible Learning in the mathematics classroom involves the gathering of evidence about the impact we have on our students' learning.

Scaffolding, Extending, and Assessing Student Thinking

Math class follows a predictable structure in Mr. Southall's room: whole-group mini-lesson, work time, and whole-group sharing and closure. The math learning time begins or ends with one of several math routines (e.g., quick images, math talks, number talks, and "Which One Doesn't Belong?"). This predictable structure creates classroom cohesion and communicates consistent expectations to students about what, where, with whom, and when they will engage in different types of mathematical learning. This structure also reduces students' cognitive load so they can focus on the rigorous mathematical content and processes within each lesson.

As students work, Mr. Southall is rarely stationary. He moves among the groups of students, sitting to confer and teach for 5 to 10 minutes at a time, asking questions, observing students' work, and providing specific, timely feedback. Mr. Southall carries a clipboard with his conference chart. He uses his conference notes to document students' progress toward the learning intentions by listening and looking for evidence of the success criteria. Today, Mr. Southall uses an open conference chart, where each student's name is listed with space for notes. His students are engaged in surface learning, and he knows his students will surprise him with what they know, notice, ask, and try. The openness of his conference chart allows Mr. Southall to document both what he has anticipated and what he has not.

Mr. Southall looks for three strategies while conferring who he will select for sharing (Smith & Stein, 2011): someone who used a concrete representation of a pattern, a student who used a pictorial representation, and another student who used an abstract representation. The learning intentions and success criteria are listed at the top of his chart. His planned scaffolding and extending questions are listed at the bottom of his chart for quick reference and to keep his notes and questioning focused on the goals of the lesson.

Teaching for Clarity at the Close

After the students have cleaned up and returned to their carpet squares, Mr. Southall asks each pair that he selected to share their products. He reminds everyone of the success criteria first and directs students to be looking, listening, and thinking about where they see evidence of each pair working toward the success criteria. Adar and Wasiq used cubes to represent and extend the pattern, traced and colored their cubes, and finally, wrote word labels to describe the pattern. Kaitlin and Brant glued paper tiles to copy and extend each pattern. Their labels include numbers and words to show how many of each were needed. Rodrigo and Alma extended the patterns by sketching the boxes. They circled the core of the repeating pattern and used words to describe how the growing patterns changed.

As each pair shares, Mr. Southall creates an anchor chart (entitled "I can represent a pattern using. . .") and uses words and pictures to record the list of possible representations. He thinks aloud about where he sees each pair demonstrating the success criteria. Mr. Southall also asks questions to facilitate the class discussion and students' connections: "How are the cubes similar to the paper tiles? What numbers could you use to describe this pattern? How do you know what kind of pattern this is? Where do you see the core in the cubes and tiles?" This class discussion models how students share work, explain thinking, and actively listen to each other.

EFFECT SIZE
FOR CLASSROOM
DISCUSSION = 0.82

Next, students turn knee-to-knee, eye-to-eye with a person they did not work with and take turns sharing their work. Giving every student a chance to share with a partner is another way the class works toward the third learning intention: "I am learning to understand each other's ideas by listening, looking, and thinking."

As they finish sharing, the pairs put their work in their math folders in the "finished" or "not finished" pocket. They return to the circle, where Mr. Southall is singing a familiar song with both a growing and shrinking pattern: B-I-N-G-O. As the class sings, Mr. Southall represents the letters with five, four, three, two, one, and finally, zero snapping cubes. He brings closure to the lesson by summarizing their work:

> Mathematicians use patterns to help them solve problems.
> We used repeating, growing, and shrinking patterns to help us make our hopscotch paths longer. I wonder which hopscotch paths can be extended all the way around the playground. I'm excited to see what happens outside at recess today!

Figure 3.2 shows how Mr. Southall made his planning visible so that he could then provide an engaging and rigorous learning experience for his learners.

Mr. Southall's Teaching for Clarity PLANNING GUIDE

ESTABLISHING PURPOSE

1 What are the key content standards I will focus on in this lesson?

Content Standards:

Virginia Mathematics Standards of Learning

K.13. The student will identify, describe, extend, create, and transfer repeating patterns.

K.3. The student will (a) count forward orally by ones from 0 to 100; (b) count backward orally by ones when given any number between 1 and 10; (c) identify the number after, without counting, when given any number between 0 and 100 and identify the number before, without counting, when given any number between 1 and 10; and (d) count forward by tens to determine the total number of objects to 100.

Standards for Mathematical Practice:

- Look for and express regularity in repeated reasoning.
- Model with mathematics.
- Construct viable arguments and critique the reasoning of others.

2 What are the learning intentions (the goal and *why* of learning stated in student-friendly language) I will focus on in this lesson?

- Content: I am learning the predictable ways patterns repeat, grow, and shrink.
- Language: I am learning the mathematical language to identify, describe, and extend patterns.
- Social: I am learning to understand each other's ideas by listening, looking, and thinking.

3 When will I introduce and reinforce the learning intention(s) so that students understand it, see the relevance, connect it to previous learning, and can clearly communicate it themselves?

- Introduction of task
- Conference questions
- Think-aloud during sharing

SUCCESS CRITERIA

4   What evidence shows that students have mastered the learning intention(s)? What criteria will I use?

I can statements:

- I can identify repeating, growing, and shrinking patterns.
- I can describe the core or unit of a repeating pattern and the rule for a changing pattern.
- I can predict what comes next and extend a pattern.
- I can explain how I used a pattern to solve a problem.

5   How will I check students' understanding (assess learning) during instruction and make accommodations?

Formative Assessment Strategies:

- Conference/observation notes
- Student work

Differentiation Strategies:

- Differentiate the process by readiness and personal interest: purposeful pairings based on heritage language and outside tasks
- Differentiate the process and product by situational interest: choice of materials

INSTRUCTION

6   What activities and tasks will move students forward in their learning?

- Rhythm patterns
- Giant Hopscotch Challenge
- Sharing representations

7 What resources (materials and sentence frames) are needed?

Word wall index cards and pictures
Anchor chart of representations
Math folders
Giant Hopscotch Challenge
Tiles
Cubes
Paper tiles
Number charts
Number lines
Markers
Scissors
Glue

8 How will I organize and facilitate the learning? What questions will I ask? How will I initiate closure?

Instructional Strategies:

- Rhythm patterns
- Word wall words
- Acting out and building hopscotch paths
- Giant Hopscotch Challenge
- Whole-group sharing representations
- Partner-sharing representations
- Anchor chart of representations
- BINGO pattern
- Talk knee-to-knee, eye-to-eye

Scaffolding Questions:

- How could the tiles represent the hopscotch path?
- How could you use words to describe and point to the pattern?
- What would you predict comes next? Why?
- How will you record your thinking on paper?
- What kind of pattern is each?
- What is the core of the repeating pattern?
- What is the rule for changing the growing pattern?

Extending Questions:

- How are the three hopscotch paths similar? Different?
- How would you write a description of the core?
- How would you write a description of the rule for changing the growing pattern?
- What if I changed this? How would that change the pattern?

Connecting Questions:

- How are the cubes similar to the paper tiles?
- What numbers could you use to describe this pattern?
- How do you know what kind of pattern this is?
- Where do you see the core in the cubes and tiles?

Self-Reflection and Self-Evaluation Questions:

- Where do you see this pair working toward the success criteria?
- Where do you see evidence of you working toward the success criteria?

 This lesson plan is available for download at **resources.corwin.com/vlmathematics-k-2**.

Figure 3.2   Mr. Southall's Conceptual Lesson on Patterns

Ms. McLellan and the Meaning of the Equal Sign

Ms. McLellan believes her first grade mathematicians are capable of grappling with big mathematical truths. Relational thinking—understanding that the values on the right and left sides of the equal sign are the same—is a significant, vertical mathematical concept. She also knows that operational thinking—translating the equal sign to "the answer comes next"—can lead to misconceptions that will negatively impact her students' conceptual understanding through calculus. In order to form a solid foundation, Ms. McLellan wants to ensure her students deeply understand why the equal sign means "the same as." Her targeted mini-unit on relational thinking will engage students in making equality misconceptions visible and explicitly correcting and self-monitoring these misconceptions by developing deep, accurate conceptual understanding and procedural knowledge. In this way, Ms. McLellan incorporates **conceptual change programs** into her mini-unit.

Ms. McLellan's class has spent several weeks exploring the meanings of addition and subtraction, the relationship between the operations, and developing number sense with combinations to 20. Her students are at varying levels of understanding, from surface to deep to transfer. This unit on relational thinking will provide her students with another opportunity in a new context with new experiences to extend and deepen these concepts.

Depending on the size of the numbers with which her students need more practice, Ms. McLellan will assign students one of three variations of a comparing problem. The three tiered problems (Thunder, 2014) are as follows:

- *Low-Readiness Task:* Heidi has 2 blue, 5 red, and 3 yellow matchbox cars. Lyric has 6 purple, 2 orange, 1 green, and 1 black matchbox cars. Who has more matchbox cars?

- *Mid-Readiness Task:* Neil has 6 blue, 6 red, 4 yellow, and 4 brown matchbox cars. Justin has 5 purple, 7 orange, 3 green, and 5 black matchbox cars. Who has more matchbox cars?

- *High-Readiness Task:* Quintus has 5 blue, 9 red, 3 yellow, and 3 brown matchbox cars. Kanice has 6 purple, 3 orange, 4 green, and 7 black matchbox cars. Who has more matchbox cars?

EFFECT SIZE FOR CONCEPTUAL CHANGE PROGRAMS = 0.99

Conceptual change programs: focus on changing misguided or inaccurate student knowledge of important concepts. Research has found that conceptual change programs have a strong effect on changing the misconceptions that students bring with them.

EFFECT SIZE FOR COGNITIVE TASK ANALYSIS = 1.29

The low-readiness task uses sums of 10. The mid-readiness task uses sums to 20 and the numbers support doubles facts and sums of 10. The high-readiness task uses sums to 20 and the numbers support near-doubles facts and making 10. All of the students will be working toward the same learning intentions based on the same standards.

What Ms. McLellan Wants Her Students to Learn

When Ms. McLellan reviews her previous student data, she notes that relational thinking is typically a weakness for her students and she wants to change this. While unpacking standards to plan this unit, she realizes that she usually teaches the relational thinking standards in support of other overarching standards, like addition and subtraction. The big idea of equality is never the star of the show, and unintentionally, her students implicitly learn misconceptions about the equal sign and the meaning of equations. This year, Ms. McLellan chooses to make the meaning of the equal sign the big idea of her unit and to use other standards as supports in order to develop the rich relational thinking her students will need far into the future.

As a result, every lesson of the unit will focus on the following standards.

> **EFFECT SIZE FOR LEARNING GOALS = 0.68**

> **EFFECT SIZE FOR FORMATIVE EVALUATION = 0.48**

Teaching Takeaway

Teaching mathematics in the Visible Learning classroom requires teachers to focus on where learners are in their progression and move them forward in their learning.

NEBRASKA MATHEMATICS STANDARDS

MA 1.2.1.a. Use the meaning of the equal sign to determine if equations are true and give examples of equations that are true (e.g., $4 = 4$, $6 = 7 - 1$, $6 + 3 = 3 + 6$, and $7 + 2 = 5 + 4$).

MA 1.2.2.a. Decompose numbers and use the commutative and associative properties of addition to develop addition and subtraction strategies including (making tens and counting on from the larger number) to add and subtract basic facts within 20 (e.g., decomposing to make 10, $7 + 5 = 7 + 3 + 2 = 10 + 2 = 12$; using the commutative property to count on $2 + 6 = 6 + 2$; and using the associative property to make 10, $5 + 3 + 7 = 5 + (3 + 7) = 5 + 10$).

MA 1.2.3.b. Solve real-world problems that include addition of three whole numbers whose sum is less than or equal to 20 by

(Continued)

(Continued)

using objects, drawings, and equations with a symbol to represent the unknown number in the problem.

Ms. McLellan is helping her learners develop the following Nebraska Mathematical Processes:

- Solves mathematical problems.

- Communicates mathematical ideas effectively.

Learning Intentions and Success Criteria

Ms. McLellan knows that teacher clarity is important to her students' success. She creates three learning intentions that encompass the content and process standards:

Content Learning Intention: I am learning to understand the meaning of the equal sign.

Language Learning Intention: I am learning to understand the language and notation to describe equality.

Social Learning Intention: I am learning to understand the quality of work we expect from ourselves and others.

Based on these learning intentions, Ms. McLellan creates success criteria so that her students can see themselves learning and evaluate their movement along the path to success. Her success criteria communicate to students what they will be able to do and why this matters.

- ☐ I can use the equal sign to mean "the same as."
- ☐ I can find and compare the values on each side of the equal sign.
- ☐ I can represent and describe equal values.
- ☐ I can evaluate the quality of my work.

Ms. McLellan uses mathematically accurate and important language in her learning intentions and success criteria while also making them concise and child friendly. She knows her first graders are always learning new vocabulary. In order for this language to become part of their receptive and expressive vocabulary, her students need multiple and various exposures to mathematical language and experiences and to connect the new words to nonlinguistic representations (National Reading Panel, 2000). The learning intentions and success criteria are one opportunity to make this vocabulary instruction explicit. The task, discourse, and teacher questioning within the lesson are additional opportunities.

During her lesson, Ms. McLellan plans to share the learning intentions and success criteria with her students after activating their prior knowledge. As students are engaging in surface learning, she will reconnect them with familiar addition and subtraction language, notation, and representations through problem solving, think-alouds, and purposeful questioning.

Activating Prior Knowledge

Around the room, there are three large posters spread out on the floor. Each one has a large word, a smaller question beneath it, and a word or picture drawn by Ms. McLellan.

- When: When do you compare?

- Words: What words do you use to compare?

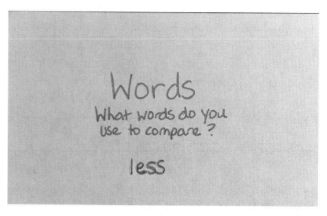

- Tools: What tools help you compare?

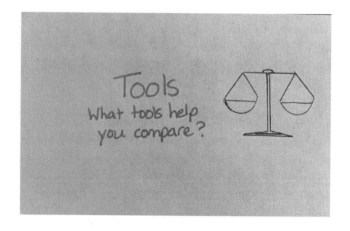

EFFECT SIZE FOR
STRATEGIES TO
INTEGRATE WITH
PRIOR KNOWLEDGE
= 0.93

EFFECT SIZE FOR
COOPERATIVE
LEARNING = 0.40

Teaching Takeaway

Gaining insight into our learners' thinking requires us to make their thinking visible.

Ms. McLellan uses this Graffiti activity to activate her students' prior knowledge related to the entire relational thinking unit. Each student is given a marker. The student may draw, list, label, write sentences, or choose another approach as long as they do not write over anyone else's ideas and keep the marker to the paper the whole time. Seven or eight students kneel at each poster. Ms. McLellan has them rotate every minute. They finally return to their starting poster; in pairs or trios, they read the poster in order to develop a one- to two-sentence answer to the question. After 2 minutes of reading and talking time, each group shares their word, question, and answer.

Next, Ms. McLellan transitions the class to the task at hand by introducing today's learning intentions and success criteria. Her students are in the habit of reading the learning intentions and success criteria and explaining to a partner what they think each means, describing when they have done something similar, and asking each other clarifying questions.

Then Ms. McLellan shares a version of the tiered problems that is numberless and does not present the specific question yet (Figure 3.3).

NUMBERLESS WORD PROBLEM

Ms. McLellan has some blue, some red, some yellow and some brown matchbox cars.

Ms. Lowe has some purple, some orange, some green, and some black matchbox cars.

Figure 3.3

A numberless word problem helps students focus on the meaning of the context and all the possible mathematics within it before considering calculations (Bushart, 2014). This format also allows Ms. McLellan to engage the whole class in a discussion around comprehending the context, while she adjusts the actual numbers to her students' readiness levels. She uses guided questioning to help her students apply literacy comprehension strategies to this task (Thunder & Demchak, 2012). She refers to an anchor chart that her students use in both literacy and math.

> EFFECT SIZE FOR QUESTIONING = 0.48

> Close your eyes and visualize the matchbox cars. Can you see my set of cars? I've sorted them by color so you can see my four piles. Some are blue and some are red, some are yellow and some are brown. Can you see Ms. Lowe's cars? She also sorted her cars by color. She has four piles too. Some are purple, some are orange, some are green, and some are black. Now, you know Ms. Lowe and I love to work together. We also love to think about math even when we are playing. Do you have friends like that?

Video 8
Student Modeling
Through a Think-Aloud

https://resources.corwin.com/
vlmathematics-k-2

Her students shake their heads in agreement and make comments that show they are making connections. Ms. McLellan often uses her students' and other familiar people's names in their problem-solving contexts in order to engage her students.

"What kind of math questions might we ask about Ms. Lowe's and my cars?" Ms. McLellan poses.

"How many cars do you have?"

"Who has more?"

"Maybe you lost some or broke some, then how many do you have?"

"You could make a trade and give each other some and then figure out how many you have now."

"If you lined the cars up, how long would they be?"

"What patterns could you make with them?"

"Which car travels the furthest when you roll them down a ramp?"

Ms. McLellan records questions as students share. She has a long list, and she wants to highlight some of the vocabulary and concepts she has heard.

> I hear you asking questions about counting, combining, and taking away cars. That reminds me of the work we've done with adding and subtracting. I hear questions about patterns. I wonder if you could make repeating and growing patterns with the cars. I hear questions about measuring length. And I hear a lot of questions about comparing: Who has more? Which car is fastest? Which car travels furthest? Those sound like times when you would compare and words that help us compare, just like our Graffiti.

Ms. McLellan points back to the large posters where students wrote "faster" and "longer" and drew a ruler. "Today, we're going to work on answering the question: Who has more matchbox cars? We have many tools we could use to solve this problem." Ms. McLellan writes the question under the numberless word problem. Then she points to the materials at the front of the circle and the anchor chart of mathematical tools.

There are tiles, cubes, Cuisenaire rods, number balances, number charts, number lines, graph paper, colored pencils, scissors, and glue. She asks, "What are some strategies you might use to solve this problem? Turn and talk with your neighbor."

After 2 minutes of talk, Ms. McLellan says, "I can hear you have many ideas for ways you might use these tools to solve the problem. After we work, friends will share their strategies so we can learn from each other." Then she poses a question to facilitate predicting reasonable solutions, "What might your answer or solution sound like?"

"You could have more," Maliyah suggest.

"Or Ms. Lowe could have more," Zimir counters.

Ms. McLellan waits and then says, "There is another possibility. What else could happen when you compare the cars?"

"You could have less or Ms. Lowe could have less."

"True. If I have less, then Ms. Lowe has more. And if Ms. Lowe has less, then I must have more." Ms. McLellan makes the connections between the language of *less* and *more* explicit.

"I guess you could have the same number of cars. But the question is who has more, so I thought someone has to have more," Autumn says.

"That's an interesting point, Autumn. I wonder if the question is, 'Who has more?' if the answer can be 'No one. They have the same.' What do you think? Turn and talk to your neighbor." Ms. McLellan hears mathematical debate, which lets her know that all her students are accessing the task and using the mathematical language of comparison. They are ready to problem solve.

Her last literacy comprehension strategy is summarizing: "Before we begin our problem solving, who will summarize what we are trying to figure out?" Several students volunteer.

> EFFECT SIZE FOR SUMMARIZATION = 0.79

The students' prior knowledge is activated and the task is understood. Ms. McLellan's final step with the whole class is to make expectations clear for what this problem-solving time will look and sound like as well as what students should be ready to share afterward (Van de Walle et al., 2018). She says,

As you problem solve, you should be collaborating with your partner. That means you will be talking, sharing materials, and making decisions together. Remember all the tools available to you. You should be sharing ideas and coming to consensus while also recording your thinking and models on your own paper. I will be conferring with partners as they work. I will ask some pairs to share their strategies when we come back together.

Ms. McLellan passes out the tiered problems with numbers, allows a few moments for final questions, and then lets the pairs go work.

Scaffolding, Extending, and Assessing Student Thinking

Ms. McLellan grabs her clipboard with her observation checklist and pencil. Over time, she has developed several formats for observation checklists that she selects and revises depending on the specific task and the success criteria. For today's task, her observation checklist includes each student's name, a list of anticipated strategies (Smith & Stein, 2011), the success criteria, and her planned questions.

During the next 40 minutes, Ms. McLellan confers with pairs while taking notes. When Ms. McLellan meets with students who are struggling, she connects them with a manipulative and asks focusing questions, such as "How could these Cuisenaire rods represent what we know?" "How will you know who has more?" There are some students who easily see and describe the equality. Ms. McLellan pushes them to consider multiple representations by asking additional questions: "How could you show they have the same number of matchbox cars using an equation?" "How could you use our mental math strategies to combine the numbers more efficiently?" She knows representing the problem with multiple representations supports the development of conceptual understanding (NCTM, 2014).

Based on her conferences and observations, Ms. McLellan selects and sequences five pairs to share:

1. Yah'Meen and James snapped together cubes that match the color of the matchbox cars. Then they lined up the stacks to compare. They drew and labeled their stacks.

2. Maliyah and Antonio lined up colored tiles to compare. They used graph paper to sketch their two rows. They made two separate equations that both summed to 20.

3. Kanice and Zimir used Cuisenaire rods to build each person's matchbox cars. Then they used a ten rod next to each set to show the sums are equal to 10. Their drawing matches their Cuisenaire rods, which also looks like a bar model.

4. Sinai and Raoul used the number balance to build each person's set and show equality by having the balance rest straight. Then they recorded an equation to match their number balance.

5. Lyric and Summer used doubles facts and sums of 10 to combine pairs of numbers.

Ms. McLellan knows that using a sequence of concrete/representational/abstract models for problem solving and making connections among the models is an effective scaffold for all students (Berry & Thunder, 2017). Her list of anticipated strategies also helps Ms. McLellan target the representations that will help her students meet the success criteria.

Teaching for Clarity at the Close

Ms. McLellan's students have cleaned up and are sitting with their partners on the front carpet. They are ready to share, discuss, question, and evaluate as a learning community. Each pair shares their model and equations. Ms. McLellan asks connecting questions as they share: How does this model show each person's total number of matchbox cars? How are these strategies similar? How does this model show that each person had the same number of cars? How does their equation match their sketch and their manipulatives?

Then, Ms. McLellan returns her students to the success criteria.

> As a team, we're going to practice this fourth success criterion. We're going to evaluate the quality of each pair's work. Let's look at the third success criterion: I can represent and describe equal values. How do you see Kanice and Zimir meeting this success criterion?

Teaching Takeaway

Providing closure to an instructional block promotes consolidation of mathematics learning, as well as enhances clarity of learning.

EFFECT SIZE FOR EVALUATION AND REFLECTION = 0.75

"They represented the values with Cuisenaire rods. Then they showed they were equal because they both equaled the ten rod," Ann says.

"Yeah, they could trade in the pink, yellow, and light-green rods for one orange rod. Then they could trade in the dark-green rod, a pink rod, and two white rods for one orange rod. That shows they both have the same number of cars: 10," explains Justice.

"Now, let's look at the first success criterion: I can use the equal sign to mean 'the same as.' I don't see an equation. How could we help them meet this success criterion based on their Cuisenaire work?" Ms. McLellan asks.

"We could write $2 + 5 + 3 = 10$ and $6 + 2 + 1 + 1 = 10$," suggests Tobias. Ms. McLellan records these equations.

The task, discourse, and teacher questions have made the students' operational thinking visible. Now, Ms. McLellan wants to move them to relational thinking: "How does the equal sign mean 'the same as' here?"

Quintus begins, "2 and 5 and 3 are the same as 10, just like 6 and 2 and 1 and 1 combined are the same as 10."

"I noticed Sinai and Raoul have one long equation: $6 + 6 + 4 + 4 = 5 + 7 + 3 + 5$. How are they using the equal sign to mean 'the same as'?" asks Ms. McLellan.

"Sinai and Raoul are saying the sum of 6 and 6 and 4 and 4 is the same as the sum of 5 and 7 and 3 and 5," continues Anissa.

"I wonder how we could combine the two equations Tobias made into one equation like Sinai and Raoul's. Turn and tell a neighbor how you would make one equation out of the two," directs Ms. McLellan. Partners talk and point. Ms. McLellan hears several students using Sinai and Raoul's example to guide their creation of a single equation. She also hears one pair wondering if they could include two equal signs in one equation. She wants to make sure this gets shared with the whole group.

Neil shares the equation, $2 + 5 + 3 = 6 + 2 + 1 + 1$, and then reads it using the phrase "is the same as."

Ms. McLellan asks, "What if I put the addends in a different order, like $3 + 2 + 5 = 1 + 6 + 1 + 2$? Would that still be true? Would that still represent the problem?"

Some students agree and some students disagree. "This is an important question we'll need to explore further," Ms. McLellan says. She records the question on a new anchor chart entitled, "Our Mathematical Questions," and inquires, "Who else has a burning or simmering mathematical question to ask?"

"James and I were wondering if you could put two equal signs in one equation," Mahammed shares.

"Say more about what you mean," responds Ms. McLellan.

"Like Kanice and Zimir's work, could you write 'equals 10' at the end?" Mahammed says.

"How would you read the equation then?"

"That sum and that sum are the same as 10," James answers pointing to each side of Neil's equation.

"Hmm, what do you think?" Ms. McLellan poses the question to her students and again there is agreement and disagreement. Rather than answer the question, she adds this question to the anchor chart and includes James and Mahammed's sample equation.

EFFECT SIZE FOR ELABORATIVE INTERROGATION = 0.42

"Could you flip it? Could you put Lyric's cars first and then Heidi's?" asks Anissa. After a brief debate, this question gets added to the anchor chart along with Anissa's example.

Ms. McLellan says, "This has been a really rich discussion about reading and representing values using the equal sign. You came up with so many questions for us to work toward answering!" She closes the whole-group discussion with many questions and ideas percolating. Ms. McLellan wants her students to know their questions and ideas are worth the time to investigate, and she will design future tasks around answering their questions. She also wants her students to know that perseverance is important as a mathematician and learner, so they do not finish tasks or answer all questions in one day.

Ms. McLellan transitions the class to self-evaluation.

Now, you're going to work one more time with your partner to evaluate your work using the success criteria. When you find evidence that you met the success criteria, get a green sticky note and put it on your work with a note explaining your reasoning. If you don't see evidence, you can make a revision with your partner right now and use a yellow sticky note to make a note. If you're not sure how to meet the success criteria, get a red sticky note and write your question or what you're not sure about. Finally, decide which partner will store the work in his or her math binder.

She continues to listen to and confer with pairs. She will use her observation checklist, the students' work and self-evaluations, as well as the anchor chart of questions to plan next steps. Her students are at the surface level of relational thinking, ready to dive deeper. Figure 3.4 shows how Ms. McLellan made her planning visible so that she could then provide an engaging and rigorous learning experience for her learners.

Ms. McLellan's Teaching for Clarity PLANNING GUIDE

ESTABLISHING PURPOSE

1 What are the key content standards I will focus on in this lesson?

Content Standards:

Nebraska Mathematical Standards

MA 1.2.1.a. Use the meaning of the equal sign to determine if equations are true and give examples of equations that are true (e.g., 4 = 4, 6 = 7 − 1, 6 + 3 = 3 + 6, and 7 + 2 = 5 + 4).

MA 1.2.2.a. Decompose numbers and use the commutative and associative properties of addition to develop addition and subtraction strategies including (making tens and counting on from the larger number) to add and subtract basic facts within 20 (e.g., decomposing to make 10, 7 + 5 = 7 + 3 + 2 = 10 + 2 = 12; using the commutative property to count on 2 + 6 = 6 + 2; and using the associative property to make 10, 5 + 3 + 7 = 5 + (3 + 7) = 5 + 10).

MA 1.2.3.b. Solve real-world problems that include addition of three whole numbers whose sum is less than or equal to 20 by using objects, drawings, and equations with a symbol to represent the unknown number in the problem.

Nebraska Mathematical Processes:

- *Solves mathematical problems.*
- *Communicates mathematical ideas effectively.*

2 What are the learning intentions (the goal and *why* of learning stated in student-friendly language) I will focus on in this lesson?

- *Content: I am learning to understand the meaning of the equal sign.*
- *Language: I am learning to understand the language and notation to describe equality.*
- *Social: I am learning to understand the quality of work we expect from ourselves and others.*

3 When will I introduce and reinforce the learning intention(s) so that students understand it, see the relevance, connect it to previous learning, and can clearly communicate it themselves?

- *Turn and tell*
- *Conference questions*
- *Evaluate shared work together*

SUCCESS CRITERIA

4 What evidence shows that students have mastered the learning intention(s)? What criteria will I use?

I can statements:

- *I can use the equal sign to mean "the same as."*
- *I can find and compare the values on each side of the equal sign.*
- *I can represent and describe equal values.*
- *I can evaluate the quality of my work.*

5 How will I check students' understanding (assess learning) during instruction and make accommodations?

Formative Assessment Strategies:

- *Conference/observation notes*
- *Student work*
- *Partner self-evaluation*

Differentiation Strategies:

- *Tiered tasks to differentiate the content by readiness*
- *Materials to differentiate the process and product by interest*

INSTRUCTION

6 What activities and tasks will move students forward in their learning?

- *Graffiti activity*
- *Numberless word problem*
- *Literacy comprehension strategies with think-aloud*
- *Sharing tools and strategies*

7 What resources (materials and sentence frames) are needed?

Graffiti posters

Anchor chart of literacy comprehension strategies

Anchor chart of conjectures/questions

Math binders

Tiered problems

Tiles

Cubes

Cuisenaire rods

Number balances

Number charts

Number lines

Graph paper

Colored pencils

Scissors

Glue

8 How will I organize and facilitate the learning? What questions will I ask? How will I initiate closure?

Instructional Strategies:

- *Graffiti*
- *Numberless word problem*
- *Literacy comprehension strategies*
- *Conferences*
- *Turn and talk*
- *Partner sticky note self-reflection*

Scaffolding Questions:

- *How could these Cuisenaire rods represent what we know?*
- *How will you know who has more?*

Extending Questions:

- *How could you show they have the same number of matchbox cars using an equation?*
- *How could you use our mental math strategies to combine the numbers more efficiently?*

Self-Reflection and Self-Evaluation Questions:

- *Green sticky note: met the success criteria*
- *Yellow sticky note: don't see evidence, need to make a revision*
- *Red sticky note: not sure how to meet the success criteria*

 This lesson plan is available for download at **resources.corwin.com/vlmathematics-k-2**.

Figure 3.4   Ms. McLellan's Conceptual Lesson on the Meaning of the Equal Sign

Ms. Busching and the Meaning of Addition

Hanging in the hallway are poems with photos and the opening line, "The important thing about me is. . ." Ms. Busching and her students have written poems about themselves. This work reflects Ms. Busching's core belief: Each student brings important, expert knowledge to school and her goal is to tap into their unique expertise for everyone to learn.

As her students begin second grade, Ms. Busching knows they are embarking on a new journey as mathematicians, one where they will shift from thinking about countable numbers to imagining the magnitude of very large numbers in the ever-expanding number system. This is their year-long focus. Although it is only the fourth day of school, Ms. Busching knows her students are ready to tackle the big ideas that will unite their year of mathematical work. Today, they will begin to answer two of the unit's essential questions: "What is addition?" and "How do we engage in the work of mathematicians?" Ms. Busching has answered these questions for herself: Addition is combining. The work of mathematicians is detailed in the eight Standards for Mathematical Practice and will begin today with two of them ("Make sense of problems and persevere in solving them" and "Model with mathematics").

Ms. Busching has created contextualized problems. She presents students with an anchor problem that all students will complete, as well as several extension problems from which students will choose one or more to complete (Thunder, 2014). The anchor problem is a join start unknown problem (Carpenter, Fennema, Franke, Levi, & Empson, 1999):

- *Anchor Problem:* Richard collects Pokémon balls. In June, he had some Pokémon balls. Over the summer, he bought 9 more. Now, he has 17 Pokémon balls. How many Pokémon balls did he have in June?

The extension problems are the more challenging addition and subtraction problem types, including separate change unknown and addend unknown problems (Carpenter et al., 1999):

- *Extension Problem 1:* Sonam opens a new box of 24 pieces of chalk. She shares some with Adric. She still has 12 to choose from. How many did she give Adric?

EFFECT SIZE FOR POSITIVE SELF-CONCEPT = 0.41

Teaching Takeaway

Using guiding or essential questions to frame the big ideas increases the motivation in learners.

EFFECT SIZE FOR ACHIEVING MOTIVATION AND APPROACH = 0.44

- *Extension Problem 2:* Jayla has 25 trolls. She likes to sort them by hair color. She has 8 with purple hair, 4 with pink hair, 7 with green hair, and some with orange hair. How many trolls have orange hair?

Ms. Busching begins her unit with the most challenging problem types of first grade and single-digit numbers that are solvable using strategies practiced in first grade. This allows her to formatively assess her students' retention of first grade standards while introducing them to the routines, structures, and expectations of second grade.

What Ms. Busching Wants Her Students to Learn

Ms. Busching examines all standards that help to answer the unit's essential questions. She also looks vertically to identify related first grade standards and how this year's work will support third grade's explorations. Today's lesson will address several mathematical content standards in order to answer the essential question "What is addition?"

MATHEMATICS CONTENT AND PRACTICE STANDARDS

2.OA.A.1. Use addition and subtraction within 100 to solve one- and two-step word problems involving situations of adding to, taking from, putting together, taking apart, and comparing, with unknowns in all positions, e.g., by using drawings and equations with a symbol for the unknown number to represent the problem.

2.NBT.B.9. Explain why addition and subtraction strategies work, using place value and the properties of operations

2.OA.B.2. Fluently add and subtract within 20 using mental strategies. By end of Grade 2, know from memory all sums of two one-digit numbers.

Ms. Busching is helping her learners develop the following Standards for Mathematical Practice:

- Make sense of problems and persevere in solving them.

- Model with mathematics.

Learning Intentions and Success Criteria

Ms. Busching believes her students learn best when they can answer the question "What are we learning and why?" Sharing the learning intentions and success criteria with students also enables them to show what they know, and Ms. Busching believes her students always know a lot.

Content Learning Intention: I am learning to understand the meaning of addition as combining.

Language Learning Intention: I am learning to understand the language of mathematical modeling.

Social Learning Intention: I am learning to understand how to listen and respond to my peers' ideas in ways that move us all forward as learners.

The success criteria explain to students how they will know when they have mastered the learning intentions:

- ☐ I can combine, separate, and find the difference in many contexts.
- ☐ I can explain the meaning and value of the unknown number in a context and representation.
- ☐ I can use mathematical models to represent addition and subtraction relationships.
- ☐ I can describe addition and subtraction situations using mathematical language and notation (addend, sum, difference, +, −).

By phrasing the success criteria as *I can* statements, Ms. Busching communicates to her students that she believes and expects them to meet the learning goals.

During this initial exploration into addition, Ms. Busching will share the essential questions while introducing the task. She does not want to give away answers to the essential questions, which are embedded in the learning intentions and success criteria. Instead, she will share the learning intentions and success criteria toward the end of working on the task, after students have engaged in discussion about their discoveries and used these discoveries to begin to answer the essential questions in their own words.

Activating Prior Knowledge

Ms. Busching begins math class where the mood is filled with excitement and fun: "We're going to play Go Fish!" Her students are hooked. Most students have played Go Fish before. They explain the basic rules and then Ms. Busching explains the twist. The cards have words naming mathematical representations or tools (*number line, number chart, bar model, table, equation, manipulatives,* or *diagram*) that match with images of those same representations or tools. Her students reorganize into pairs facing each other. They deal out three cards to each player and begin asking for matches.

Immediately, there is a chatter of descriptions and mathematical terms between each pair. After 3 minutes, a few pairs finish and Ms. Busching sounds her chime. She says, "Wherever you are, stop. Reveal the cards to your partner and talk through making the matches you didn't get to." Ms. Busching hears laughter, math talk, and exclamations like, "Oh yeah, we used open number lines last year."

"Are there any terms you want to talk more about or ask questions about?"

Lily raises her hand and asks, "What's a bar model?"

"Who can respond to Lily's question?" Ms. Busching returns the question back to the students. They are just learning the expectation that they ask *and* answer the questions in this classroom.

"We didn't know what a bar model was either, but we made a match with the last picture of rectangles with numbers inside," responds Tashi.

"It looks like a sketch of Cuisenaire rods," adds Luciana. Many students comment that they do not know what those are.

Ms. Busching summarizes, "It sounds like many people haven't used a bar model or Cuisenaire rods before. I'm glad we already know a lot and we have so much more to learn together." She makes note of this question. She will need to teach a mini-lesson on Cuisenaire rods and bar models, and she wants to watch to see if there are any student experts who already know and use these tools.

THE MATHEMATICAL TOOLBOX

Tool	manipulatives	diagram	bar model	number line	number chart	table	equation
Description							
Example							
When It Works Best							

Image Source: Lazarev/iStock.com.

 This lesson plan is available for download at **resources.corwin.com/vlmathematics-k-2**.

Figure 3.5

"This is your mathematical toolbox," Ms. Busching says as she passes out a chart to each student and offers the following explanation (Figure 3.5).

> One of our goals this year is to gather mathematical tools, learn how to use them, and then add them to our toolbox so we can use them whenever we need. Right now, your toolbox has seven tools from Go Fish. We will learn more about each of them and, gradually, we'll add more tools.

EFFECT SIZE FOR
EXPLICIT TEACHING
STRATEGIES = 0.57

We're going to take a moment so you and your partner can make some quick notes for yourself on your toolbox. There is space for you to include a description in your own words, an example, and a reminder of when it works best in problem solving. This is *your* toolbox, so you write what you know right now. It is okay to have a lot of blanks. We will add more to it later.

Ms. Busching gives students 3 minutes to talk, write, and sketch. She then says, "Today, we are starting our first unit of study in math. These are our four essential questions that we will work toward answering over the next few weeks. Let's read the questions and think about what they mean." Ms. Busching points to where the unit essential questions are displayed. She reads them aloud and then pauses to allow silence while everyone thinks.

Ms. Busching continues, "Pair up and talk about these questions. What are you thinking about?" After a minute of talk, she says, "Let's have two people share what they said or what their partner said."

Deshawn begins, "We did a lot of adding last year. I remember $5 + 5 = 10$."

Bryant adds, "Emma and I talked about the Go Fish words. Those are tools. Maybe mathematicians actually use those tools."

Ms. Busching says, "Today, and for the next few days, we are going to focus on just two of the essential questions: *What is addition? How do we engage in the work of mathematicians?*" As she speaks, she passes out the anchor problem. Students glue it into their mathematician's journals (Thunder & Demchak, 2012), which consist of legal-size paper stapled together with a fold 2 inches from the end.

In the large part of each journal page, students glue in their anchor and extension problems and record lists, tables, definitions, diagrams, and sketches that support their problem-solving process and evaluation of their solution. On the folded part, students record questions that arise and the answers, connections, reflections, and big ideas. Together, the two sections of the mathematician's journal require students to record their process and solution while also monitoring their thinking. Students organize and transform their work as a reference for sharing and future problem solving.

Ms. Busching continues on to describe the STAR (Search, Translate, Answer, Review) strategy (Gagnon & Maccini, 2001).

> I'm going to read the task and you can read along with me. We're going to use a strategy called STAR to help us understand the problem *before* we start work on it. The first step in the STAR strategy is *Search* for important information. When I search, I reread and look for the information I need to remember to help me solve the problem. They're like clues in a mystery.

EFFECT SIZE FOR UNDERLINING AND HIGHLIGHTING = 0.50

Ms. Busching models each step in her mathematician's journal and asks, "What might be important information? I'm going to use colored pencils and highlighters to keep track."

"Richard has 17 Pokémon balls."

"He bought nine."

"He didn't always have 17 Pokémon balls."

"How many did he used to have?"

"That's what we're figuring out, I think."

"We're figuring out how many balls Richard had in June."

"It says 'some.' He had some balls."

"Yeah, but how much is some?"

"It has to be less than 17 because after he bought more, he had 17 total."

Ms. Busching has highlighted, circled, and made notes of questions and phrases in her journal. She allows the students to talk, pose questions, answer each other's questions, express confusion, and seek clarity. She knows spending this time to make sure the problem is understood will pay off as students move on to selecting representations and strategies and to checking the reasonableness of solutions.

EFFECT SIZE FOR HELP SEEKING = 0.72

Ms. Busching says, "With your elbow partner, decide what is important information that you want to keep track of and then make some notes." She listens in on conversations and then moves to the second step.

"The next step of STAR is *Translate—Translate* the words into models, pictures, or symbols," she says. Ms. Busching will eventually create an anchor chart with the class, which will list the four steps of the STAR strategy for problem solving:

- *Search* the word problem for important information (not key words).

- *Translate* the words into models, pictures, or symbols.

- *Answer* the problem.

- *Review* your solution for reasonableness.

For now, she is modeling and allowing students time to practice, as shown in the following.

> In our mathematical toolbox, there are seven models. Some may be new and some may be familiar. I want you to choose a model that you might translate the words of this problem into and visualize how you would make the model. How will you represent Richard's changing Pokémon ball collection? Turn and tell your elbow partner what you are visualizing.

Again, Ms. Busching listens in on conversations and asks focusing questions.

> I heard a lot of great visualizing. First, I'm going to share my image. I can see one option is coloring in a number chart. I could color in to 17 yellow. That would be all the Pokémon balls Richard has now. Then I could color over nine of those boxes with blue. Those are the Pokémon balls Richard bought over the summer. The rest of the yellow boxes are the ones he started with. I heard Imani describing a diagram she would draw. Imani, what did you visualize?

Imani responds, "I saw an empty circle. That's the 'some' balls Richard has in June. I don't know how many balls to put in there." She draws a big circle in the air. "Then another circle has nine small circles in it. Those are the balls he bought." Imani air draws as she talks, and Ms. Busching draws a sketch. Imani says, "Somehow I want to draw a big circle around both and make that have 17 small circles in it. I already have 9 though. So I have to draw more in that empty circle." Ms. Busching labels the numbers 17 and 9.

> So we have *Searched* the problem for important information and visualized some ways to *Translate* the words into models, pictures, or symbols. The next two steps in STAR are *Answer* the problem and then *Review* your solution for reasonableness. There are lots of materials available from your mathematical toolbox. You can work alone or with a partner as you complete the anchor problem and move on to the extension problems. Remember to keep track of your strategies, solution, and thinking in your mathematician's journal. I will be conferring with you as you work. During our last 15 minutes, I will ask some pairs to share the tools from the mathematical toolbox that worked or didn't work for solving this problem, and we will reflect back on our learning intentions and success criteria.

EFFECT SIZE FOR
EVALUATION AND
REFLECTION = 0.75

EFFECT SIZE FOR
CONCENTRATION,
PERSISTENCE, AND
ENGAGEMENT
= 0.56

Scaffolding, Extending, and Assessing Student Thinking

The classroom becomes a buzz of activity as students rearrange to find suitable work spaces, desired materials, and partners of interest. Ms. Busching knows it is important for all students to see themselves as capable problem solvers and mathematicians. She uses rich tasks, classroom discourse, choice, and teacher questioning to develop her students' competency, identity, and agency (Thunder & Berry, 2016). Conferences serve as an additional opportunity for her to scaffold, extend, and formatively assess student thinking. By documenting her conferences and observations, Ms. Busching is able to use her notes and student work to plan next instructional steps as well as differentiate future tasks.

For today's task, Ms. Busching creates a conference/observation chart with two sections. The first section is focused on the third success criterion: "I can use mathematical models to represent addition and subtraction relationships." The seven models from the mathematical toolbox are listed, so she can note who is using which representation as well as who will share and in what sequence (Fennell et al., 2017). The second

Teaching Takeaway

We, as teachers, must document evidence of our impact on student learning.

Video 9
Using Guided Questions
to Clarify and Extend
Understanding

*https://resources.corwin.com/
vlmathematics-k-2*

section is focused on the other three success criteria. There is open space to note how each student is demonstrating the success criteria or misconceptions. Ms. Busching also includes the teacher questions she planned for quick reference (Figure 3.6).

Megan and Adrian have a pile of cubes that they repeatedly count and move. Ms. Busching joins them and asks, "What are you working on?"

"We're trying to act out Richard's collection with cubes. We're pretending the cubes are his Pokémon balls," explains Adrian.

"Show me how you act it out," Ms. Busching says.

"Well, we don't know how many he has to start, so we just made a big pile. Then he buys nine more during the summer. That's these." Megan pushes nine cubes into the big pile. "And now there should be 17 cubes. But there aren't. We keep counting them and there's too many and then not enough."

"I see you starting with some and then buying nine more. Now you're checking for 17 balls at the end of the story. You are using all the important information from this problem," Ms. Busching shares her noticing of their strategy. Then she interprets their understanding and decides how to respond to move them forward (Jacobs, Lamb, & Philipp, 2010). She says, "You need to adjust your pile of cubes to have 17. I wonder if there's a way to keep track of the nine balls so you know to keep those in the pile. What might be a way to know which balls are the newly purchased ones?"

"We could make them a different color," suggests Megan.

"Or we could draw a circle like Imani did and keep the nine balls in there," says Adrian.

"Which would you like to try: a different color or a circle?" asks Ms. Busching. Both students choose color. Megan counts out nine red cubes. Again they make an initial pile of cubes. They move the nine red cubes onto the pile. Then they count the big pile. They remove cubes that are not red and recount until they have 17 cubes total. Then they count the not-red cubes.

"Eight!" they both shout.

OBSERVATION/CONFERENCE CHART

Anchor Problem & Extension Problems
Observation/Conference Chart
Date _____

Questions:

- What tool from your toolbox could you use?
- How could these _____ represent what we know?
- How does this representation show the relationship?
- How is the unknown value represented?
- How could you represent your strategy using an equation?
- How could you use a strategy you know for mental math?
- How does this model help you clearly communicate your strategy and thinking?
- How does this model help you efficiently solve the problem?

Name	SC #3: I can use mathematical models to represent addition/subtraction relationships. C: Manipulatives R: Diagram, Bar Model, Number line A: Number chart, Table, Equation	SC #1: I can combine, separate, find the difference in many contexts. SC #2: I can explain the meaning and value of the unknown number in a context and representation. SC #3: I can describe addition and subtraction situations using mathematical language and notation (addend, sum, difference, +, -).	Derived Fact Strategies (sums of ten, doubles, near-doubles, make ten)

Figure 3.6

 This template is available for download at **resources.corwin.com/vlmathematics-k-2**.

Teaching Takeaway

Teachers must map out their line of questioning to support learners as they progress toward conceptual understanding. Questioning should be by design.

"You revised your strategy, which helped you get unstuck," Ms. Busching notes. "Now, how will you record your work in your mathematician's journal? Let's look at your mathematical toolbox for some ideas." The transfer from concrete to pictorial or abstract representations is often a challenge when developing conceptual understanding. She wants to stay and scaffold this process.

"Let's make an equation," says Megan.

Adrian agrees, and they record the following: $8 + 9 = 17$.

"How will you show what those numbers mean?" Ms. Busching asks.

"We could make the nine red with a color pencil and then label it," Adrian replies.

"And then we could label the other numbers so you know eight are the Pokémon balls he began with," Megan adds. Ms. Busching documents their conversation in her conference chart. Before she leaves, she asks, "What will you do next? Will you try to solve the problem a different way or work on an extension problem?" Megan wants to try Cuisenaire rods. She used them in first grade and Adrian has not used them before.

Before conferring with another pair, Ms. Busching observes the class as a whole. She notes that Jayla and Phoebe are tracing their Cuisenaire rods. Agustin and Gyaltsen seem stuck.

"What are you two working on?" Ms. Busching asks as she sits down with Agustin and Gyaltsen.

"I don't know. A number line," Agustin responds quietly.

"We're trying to make hops on a number line to show Richard's Pokémon balls, but we got stuck," Gyaltsen adds.

"What have you tried so far?" Ms. Busching is researching to find out more about their thinking.

"We didn't know where to start because we just know Richard has some. So we started on a spot and didn't label it. Then we made a jump of nine and landed on 17. But now we don't know what to do," Agustin points to their paper.

"Why did you jump nine?" Ms. Busching asks.

"Because that's how many more balls he bought."

"And how did you know to land on 17?"

"Because we know that's how many he has in the end."

"What are you trying to figure out now?"

"How many Pokémon balls he had to start with."

"Where would his starting amount be on the number line?"

Both Agustin and Gyaltsen point to the spot on the number line where the nine-jump intersects.

"You've figured out how to show Richard's purchase and you know the point on the number line that represents how many he started with. What do we know about the number that is at this point?" Ms. Busching summarizes their reasoning and asks a probing question.

"It's less than 17."

"It's nine hops away from 17."

"Oh, we could count backwards: 16, 15, 14, 13, 12, 11, 10, 9, 8," Agustin keeps track of how many numbers he has said using his fingers. "It's eight!" Agustin writes eight on the number line.

"How could you check that?" Ms. Busching asks.

"That would mean eight and nine more equals 17. I know eight and eight is 16. Nine is one more so that makes 17. Yes!" Gyaltsen reasons aloud.

"You used your number line two ways to find the unknown value. You counted backwards and you used a near-doubles fact. I wonder how you can record your thinking," Ms. Busching says. She describes their process and solution to support their metacognition and agency. Then she makes notes in her chart, including a note to have them connect their number line to an equation.

Again, Ms. Busching surveys her class and makes observation notes. Zoe asks if she can use a calculator. Ms. Busching asks her how it would help and then shows her where they are. She makes a note about this interaction and joins another pair for a conference.

Video 10
Feedback Without Taking Over the Thinking

https://resources.corwin.com/ vlmathematics-k-2

By the end of work time, Ms. Busching has observational or conference notes on every student. She also has selected and sequenced four students who will share based on the representations they used (Smith & Stein, 2011):

1. Megan and Adrian will share their manipulatives and equation.

2. Jayla and Phoebe will share their Cuisenaire rods and tracing to lead to a bar model.

3. Gyaltsen and Agustin will share their number line.

4. Zoe and Bryant will share their use of the calculator.

Teaching for Clarity at the Close

As each of the four pairs shares their representations with the whole class, Ms. Busching creates an anchor chart that mirrors the information of the mathematical toolbox. For each example, she asks students to describe an equation that matches their representation. She also asks focusing questions to highlight the connections among the representations, the usefulness of the representations, and the relationships among the values:

**Teaching
Takeaway**

Using the learning intentions and success criteria to guide closure allows learners to make meaning of the day's content and processes.

- Where do you see the number of _____ represented?
- Where do you see unknown value represented?
- How are the quantities changing?
- How does this model represent the relationship between the quantities?
- How does this model help you clearly communicate your strategy and thinking?
- How does this model help you efficiently solve the problem?
- What is similar among the models? What is different?

Her questions align with the essential questions and learning intentions to develop students' conceptual understanding of addition.

Ms. Busching notices her students' bringing their prior knowledge of direct modeling with manipulatives and pictures, counting on and back, and derived fact strategies (Carpenter et al., 1999) to bear on these problem types. They are engaged in surface-level learning related to addition. She says, "I hear you describing the many ways you put together parts to create a whole. Many of you were thinking about how many more to complete a set or how to combine sets. Talk with your partner about how you would answer each of the essential questions for today based on our work."

The students have started to answer the essential questions. Now, they are ready to connect their informal language to the formal school language of the operations and mathematical notation in a meaningful way (Thunder, 2011). Ms. Busching says, "Mathematicians like to be efficient in their problem solving and flexible in their thinking. Many of you commented on how the number you were solving for could be represented in a different place in each story and equation." Ms. Busching returns to the anchor chart and uses the language of the story contexts to describe various equations where the solution is sometimes an addend and sometimes a sum. She instructs, "With your partner, return to your representations and make sure you have an equation for each. Label the story's solution within each equation." Pairs work and then share.

Ms. Busching shares the learning intentions and success criteria for today's work. She says, "Each day, we will have learning intentions or goals for the day and success criteria or ways to evaluate your work to know if you met the goals completely or partially. Today, we will evaluate our work as a class." Ms. Busching reads each learning intention and its related success criteria. Then she asks groups of four to discuss whether they completely or partially met the success criteria and says, "Also discuss evidence you can cite to defend your evaluation." This is the first time this year that her students are using learning intentions and success criteria to orient their work. Ms. Busching knows she has to teach her students what these are and how they can guide their work.

After discussing each success criterion in their small group, the whole class shares their ideas. Ms. Busching returns to her mathematician's journal and the anchor chart. She models noting their evidence using colored pencils and highlighters. She also models using the flap of the mathematician's journal to keep track of mistakes, questions, and big

Video 11
Building Metacognition

https://resources.corwin.com/ vlmathematics-k-2

Teaching Takeaway

Having learners answer the essential questions for the day provides evidence of their learning, as well as offers them an opportunity to consolidate their learning.

EFFECT SIZE FOR DIRECT/ DELIBERATE INSTRUCTION = 0.60

EFFECT SIZE FOR
SELF-REGULATION
STRATEGIES = 0.52

ideas she wants to remember. She gives her students 2 minutes to reflect on their work and record on their mathematician's journal flap.

Tomorrow, they will begin by adding a new tool to their mathematical toolbox: the calculator. From their class evaluation and her observation chart, Ms. Busching knows her students need explicit instruction on how to use many mathematical models to solve these more challenging problem types. She also has an initial list of students who are fluently using derived fact strategies and those who need time for deliberate practice. Figure 3.7 shows how Ms. Busching made her planning visible so that she could then provide an engaging and rigorous learning experience for her learners.

Ms. Busching's Teaching for Clarity PLANNING GUIDE

ESTABLISHING PURPOSE

1 What are the key content standards I will focus on in this lesson?

Content Standards:

2.OA.A.1. Use addition and subtraction within 100 to solve one- and two-step word problems involving situations of adding to, taking from, putting together, taking apart, and comparing, with unknowns in all positions, e.g., by using drawings and equations with a symbol for the unknown number to represent the problem.

2.NBT.B.9. Explain why addition and subtraction strategies work, using place value and the properties of operations

2.OA.B.2. Fluently add and subtract within 20 using mental strategies. By end of Grade 2, know from memory all sums of two one-digit numbers.

Standards for Mathematical Practice:

- Make sense of problems and persevere in solving them.
- Model with mathematics.

2 What are the learning intentions (the goal and *why* of learning stated in student-friendly language) I will focus on in this lesson?

- Content: I am learning to understand the meaning of addition as combining.
- Language: I am learning to understand the language of mathematical modeling.
- Social: I am learning to understand how to listen and respond to my peers' ideas in ways that move us all forward as learners.

3   When will I introduce and reinforce the learning intention(s) so that students understand it, see the relevance, connect it to previous learning, and can clearly communicate it themselves?

- Essential questions
- Small group discussion
- Evaluate shared work together

SUCCESS CRITERIA

4   What evidence shows that students have mastered the learning intention(s)? What criteria will I use?

I can statements:

- I can combine, separate, and find the difference in many contexts.
- I can explain the meaning and value of the unknown number in a context and representation.
- I can use mathematical models to represent addition and subtraction relationships.
- I can describe addition and subtraction situations using mathematical language and notation (addend, sum, difference, +, -).

5   How will I check students' understanding (assess learning) during instruction and make accommodations?

Formative Assessment Strategies:

- Conference/observation checklist
- Student work and reflection in mathematician's journals
- Mathematical toolbox

Differentiation Strategies:

- Differentiate the content by situational interest: anchor problem and extension problems
- Differentiate the process and product by situational interest: choice of materials and partners or alone

INSTRUCTION

6 What activities and tasks will move students forward in their learning?

- Go Fish
- Mathematical toolbox
- Anchor problem and extension problems
- Create anchor chart of mathematical tools

7 What resources (materials and sentence frames) are needed?

Anchor chart of mathematical tools
Mathematical toolbox
Go Fish cards
Mathematician's journal: students and model
Anchor problems and extension problems
Tiles
Cubes
Cuisenaire rods
Number charts
Number lines and whiteboard markers
Graph paper
Colored pencils
Scissors
Glue
Highlighters
Colored pencils

8   How will I organize and facilitate the learning? What questions will I ask? How will I initiate closure?

Instructional Strategies:

- Go Fish
- Graphic organizer
- STAR
- Visualizing and modeling
- Conferences and teacher questioning
- Sharing
- Modeling self-evaluation and self-reflection

Scaffolding Questions:

- What tool from your toolbox could you use?
- How could these ___ represent what we know?
- How does this representation show the relationship among the numbers?
- How is the unknown value represented?

Extending Questions:

- How could you represent your strategy using an equation?
- How could you use a strategy you know for mental math to solve this problem more efficiently?
- How does this model help you clearly communicate your strategy and thinking?
- How does this model help you efficiently solve the problem?

Connecting Questions:

- Where do you see the number of _____ represented?
- Where do you see unknown value represented?
- How are the quantities changing?
- How does this model represent the relationship between the quantities?
- What is similar among the models? What is different?

Self-Reflection and Self-Evaluation Questions:

- Mathematician's journal reflection

 This lesson plan is available for download at **resources.corwin.com/vlmathematics-k-2**.

Figure 3.7   Ms. Busching's Conceptual Lesson on the Meaning of Addition

Reflection

These three examples from Mr. Southall, Ms. McLellan, and Ms. Busching exemplify teaching mathematics for conceptual understanding. As in the previous chapter, these three teachers selected a different approach or combination of approaches from the other two classrooms.

Using what you have read in this chapter, reflect on the following questions:

1. In your own words, describe what teaching for conceptual understanding looks like in your mathematics classroom.

2. How does the Teaching for Clarity Planning Guide support your intentions in teaching for conceptual understanding?

3. Compare and contrast the approaches to teaching taken by the classroom teachers featured in this chapter.

4. Consider the following statement: *Conceptual understanding occurs at the surface, deep, and transfer phases of learning.* Do you agree or disagree with the statement? Why or why not? How is this statement reflected in this chapter?

5. How did the classroom teachers featured in this chapter adjust the difficulty and/or complexity of the mathematics tasks to meet the needs of all learners?

TEACHING FOR PROCEDURAL KNOWLEDGE AND FLUENCY

4

CHAPTER 4 SUCCESS CRITERIA:

(1) I can describe what teaching for procedural knowledge in the mathematics classroom looks like.

(2) I can apply the Teaching for Clarity Planning Guide to teaching procedural knowledge.

(3) I can compare and contrast different approaches to teaching for procedural knowledge with those of teaching for conceptual understanding and application.

(4) I can give examples of how to differentiate mathematics tasks designed for procedural knowledge.

Procedural knowledge: is the ability to select, use, and transfer mathematics procedures in problem solving. With procedural knowledge, learners know when one procedure is more appropriate than another one for a particular problem.

EFFECT SIZE FOR VOCABULARY INSTRUCTION = 0.62

Teaching Takeaway

A word wall helps make learners' progress in vocabulary learning visible.

EFFECT SIZE FOR COGNITIVE TASK ANALYSIS = 1.29

In mathematics, you have to be able to solve problems and reason quantitatively. The successful teaching and learning of mathematics may involve the execution of procedures and quantitative reasoning that yield an expression, value, or set of values. Acquiring and consolidating **procedural knowledge**—which is the ability to select, use, and transfer mathematics procedures in problem solving—is a necessary aspect of mathematics if learners are to have the appropriate tools for taking on the next challenge in their learning progression. As we make our final visit to our three featured teachers, we want to take a look at how each teacher created learning experiences that allowed students to learn the necessary procedural skills and progress toward fluency with those skills. Also, you'll notice the adjustments each teacher made to the learning experience so that learners at the surface, deep, and transfer phases of learning could all engage in the mathematics task. And as before, you'll see how Mr. Southall, Ms. McLellan, and Ms. Busching were able to differentiate the rigor of the mathematics tasks.

Mr. Southall and Multiple Representations

Mr. Southall and his class are in the midst of a deep dive into problem solving through pattern seeking. They have solved contextualized problems where repeating, growing, and shrinking patterns are the key to finding solutions. They have made connections to real-life experiences through Three-Act Tasks (Lomax et al., 2017) and to storytelling through mathematical literature. The language of the classroom has shifted as students' academic vocabulary for talking and writing about patterns has steadily grown with explicit vocabulary instruction and a lot of opportunity to talk.

On the walls, there are anchor charts illustrating ways to represent patterns, shape names, repeating pattern cores, changing pattern rules, and examples/nonexamples of patterns. These charts track the classroom community's growing expertise and serve as problem-solving resources. There is also a word wall with vocabulary, images, related words, and examples/nonexamples.

Mr. Southall wants his students to use their deep conceptual understanding of the unit big idea (*Mathematicians look for patterns to problem solve*) to develop procedural knowledge related to translating, comparing, and categorizing patterns. He believes his students must build their procedural knowledge from conceptual understanding (NCTM, 2014) so they can explain why a procedure works, evaluate whether a procedure will always work, and develop procedures that will transfer to new situations. In today's lesson, the big practice idea is *Mathematicians use representations*. The big content ideas are as follows:

- The same pattern can be represented in many ways, including numbers and shapes.

- A pattern's core, unit, or rule can be described with symbols.

His students will select three tasks from a choice board to complete (Figure 4.1). Each column of tasks emphasizes particular aspects of the practice and content big ideas.

The first column's tasks ("What's the Core?") engage students in deliberate practice analyzing and naming the core of repeating patterns. The second column's tasks ("Translating Patterns") engage students in representing the same pattern in multiple ways using different materials. The third column's tasks ("What's the Rule?") engage students in analyzing and naming the rule that predictably changes a growing or shrinking pattern.

Each column includes tasks and materials that mathematize or make the connection between patterns in familiar materials and contexts and new formal pattern language and notation: songs and books, noodles, buttons, and calendars. Students will choose one task from each column to create three in a row across or diagonally. This strategy provides students with choice while also ensuring that they engage in tasks that align with the lesson's big ideas (Thunder, 2014).

What Mr. Southall Wants His Students to Learn

When we last peeked into Mr. Southall's classroom, his students were engaged in surface-level learning. They have moved along the continuum and are currently digging deeply into the language, strategies, notation, and models related to problem solving through pattern seeking. Orientation, location, color, size, shape, and many more attributes are all important features to attend to when comparing and

---

Teaching Takeaway

Developing a learning progression within an instructional block supports learners as they activate prior learning, assimilate that prior learning with new learning, and then consolidate the learning at the end of the instructional block.

Teaching Takeaway

Providing learners with carefully planned choices helps support time on task.

EFFECT SIZE FOR TIME ON TASK = 0.49

TIC-TAC-TOE BOARD

_____'s Tic-Tac-Toe Board

Color 3 in a row or diagonal.

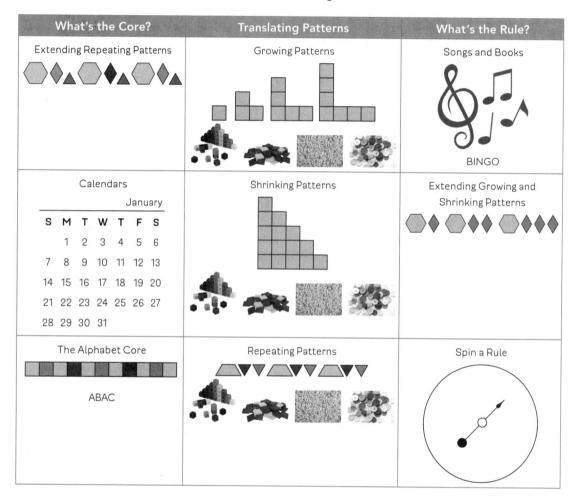

Pattern image sources under Growing, Shrinking, and Repeating pattern examples (left to right): EAI® Education Katie Kubes™. EAI Education / www.eaieducation.com; Hands-On Math Centers: Color Tile Student Set of 40. EAI Education / www.eaieducation.com; ruzanna/iStock.com; leelakajonkij/iStock.com

Figure 4.1

online resources ⇗ This tic-tac-toe board is available for download at **resources.corwin.com/vlmathematics-k-2**.

categorizing patterns. There are two Virginia Standards of Learning that align with the big content ideas of the lesson and unpack the procedural knowledge and fluency needed to analyze patterns.

Video 12

Choosing the Right Task for Procedural Knowledge

https://resources.corwin.com/vlmathematics-k-2

VIRGINIA MATHEMATICS STANDARDS OF LEARNING

K.13. The student will identify, describe, extend, create, and transfer repeating patterns.

K.10. The student will (a) identify and describe plane figures (circle, triangle, square, and rectangle); (b) compare the size (smaller, larger) and shape of plane figures (circle, triangle, square, and rectangle); and (c) describe the location of one object relative to another (above, below, next to) and identify representations of plane figures (circle, triangle, square, and rectangle) regardless of their positions and orientations in space.

Mr. Southall is helping his learners develop the following Standards for Mathematical Practice:

- Look for and express regularity in repeated reasoning.

- Use appropriate tools strategically.

- Reason abstractly and quantitatively.

Learning Intentions and Success Criteria

While unit planning, Mr. Southall identified several places along students' learning paths where the learning intentions signaled significant procedural knowledge.

Content Learning Intention: I am learning that the same pattern can be represented in many ways, including numbers and shapes.

Language Learning Intention: I am learning the mathematical symbols that describe a pattern's core or unit.

Social Learning Intention: I am learning to talk and listen about our mathematical ideas.

By identifying these critical learning points prior to teaching the unit, Mr. Southall is able to plan exit tasks (Fennell et al., 2017) that check for mastery of critical procedural knowledge. He then analyzes student work on the exit tasks and adjusts his instruction to target his students' specific needs while they are in the deep learning phase of the unit.

To make these learning intentions accessible and achievable by his students, Mr. Southall creates the following success criteria:

> ☐ I can represent the same pattern in multiple ways, including numbers and shapes.
>
> ☐ I can describe a repeating pattern's core and a changing pattern's rule using symbols.
>
> ☐ I can compare and categorize patterns and explain my reasoning.
>
> ☐ I can respond to someone else's ideas with questions, noticings, and connections.

Mr. Southall will use the think-aloud strategy (Trocki et al., 2014/2015) to model the technical mathematical language and notation necessary to meet the language learning intention. He plans to explicitly connect the whole-group activity and each of the choice board tasks to the success criteria so that students can see exactly when and how they will be working toward their learning goals. He wants his to students to see what mastery of the critical procedural knowledge looks like from the start of their work.

Activating Prior Knowledge

Mr. Southall counts down; at zero, the class has gathered in a circle to begin their work as mathematicians. He says, "We're going to play 'Which One Doesn't Belong?' I'm going to show you the cores or rules of four patterns. Use everything you know about patterns to decide which core or rule doesn't belong. Remember, you can use the word wall and anchor charts. After some quiet think time, you can use your fellow mathematicians" (Figure 4.2).

WHICH PATTERN DOESN'T BELONG?

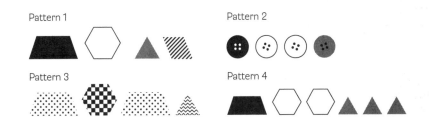

Pattern 1

Pattern 2

Pattern 3

Pattern 4

Figure 4.2

There is a brief period of hush as students look and think. Gradually, students start putting their thumbs up at chest level. Mr. Southall says, "Turn knee-to-knee, eye-to-eye with a person sitting next to you and discuss which pattern doesn't belong and why." All around the circle, pairs form and excited voices share their ideas. Then it is time to share with whole group.

"Pattern 3 doesn't belong because it has designs not just white, black, gray," Nayquon begins.

Mr. Southall takes this opportunity to point out an important misconception about patterns that they have previously discussed:

> Nayquon is remembering our discussion about the difference between a pattern and a design. The dots and zigzags— those are designs. But a design is not always a mathematical pattern because it's not always a predictable sequence. When something doesn't have a design, it is a solid color. These are solid colors.

Mr. Southall points to the white, black, and gray shapes.

"I think Pattern 2 is the one that doesn't fit. It's circles instead of pattern blocks," Kalden suggests.

"Pattern 1 doesn't belong. It has four parts to its core. The others just have three," Equasha says.

"I think Pattern 4 doesn't belong. It looks like a growing pattern. The others are repeating cores," Alisha proposes.

"Why does Pattern 4 look like a growing pattern?" Mr. Southall probes.

"It goes one trapezoid, two hexagons, three triangles. Then I think it's four next and then five," responds Alisha.

"Pattern 1 doesn't fit because it only has one of each color. The others have one or two or three," says Rodrigo.

Mr. Southall offers further explanation.

> Let's dig a little deeper into your ideas. One of our goals for today is to learn how the same pattern can be represented using lots of different materials. We can see four patterns represented with different colors and shapes. You also identified the types of patterns. Another way to compare and categorize patterns is by using mathematical symbols to name a repeating pattern's core and a changing pattern's rule. This way you don't have to show a lot of the pattern to analyze it. You only have to show the core or rule. We can use numbers or letters to do this.

He uses a think-aloud to model labeling the letters and symbols, as follows:

EFFECT SIZE
FOR DIRECT/
DELIBERATE
INSTRUCTION
= 0.60

> Pattern 1 becomes ABCD or 1234, Pattern 2 becomes ABBC or 1223, Pattern 3 becomes ABAC or 1213, and Pattern 4 becomes ABBCCC or 122333.

Mr. Southall asks students to turn knee-to-knee, eye-to-eye with a partner to talk about how he used letters and numbers to rename each pattern. From the partner talk, Xavier suggests that Pattern 4 could also just be labeled as 123, and the class agrees.

Next, Mr. Southall displays the tic-tac-toe choice board. He thinks aloud again as he reads each task's title and image, points to where the corresponding materials and task cards are located, and then labels each column with one of the success criteria cards written in words and images.

This middle column is called "Translating Patterns." I see growing patterns, shrinking patterns, and repeating patterns. I can tell by the picture and words. I also see for each type of pattern, there are lots of different materials to practice translating the pattern into different representations. I could use cubes, tiles, noodles, or buttons. I wonder if there will be other materials too. On our anchor chart named "Ways to Represent Patterns," I also see pattern blocks, paper shapes, numbers, and letters. Success criteria 1 matches this column, "Translating Patterns." When I work on one of these translating patterns tasks, I will practice representing the same pattern in multiple ways, including numbers and shapes.

Similarly, Mr. Southall thinks aloud for each column and success criterion and tells students what to expect during sharing time. Today, their content share will help add to three of their anchor charts: ways to represent patterns, repeating pattern cores, and changing pattern rules.

He says, "Think about which row or diagonal of tasks you want to complete. Color in three boxes." Mr. Southall draws a horizontal line (—) and two diagonal lines (\ and /) to model the options and continues, "When you've chosen your three tasks, decide where you will start. Remember to support your classmates as you work by sharing things you notice, asking questions, and making connections to their work." As some students begin their first task, Mr. Southall checks in with others and provides prompts to help them make a plan. Once everyone has started with a task, Mr. Southall begins his monitoring work (Van de Walle et al., 2018).

Scaffolding, Extending, and Assessing Student Thinking

Mr. Southall values each phase of his lessons for the unique opportunities they present to build a learning community, facilitate peers learning from each other, monitor progress, foster independence and perseverance, and provide targeted instruction that meets individual students' needs. In this problem-solving phase, he alternates between conferring, observing, and meeting with needs-based strategy groups.

Teaching Takeaway

Modeling think-alouds is a way to support assessment-capable visible learners as they develop meta-cognitive strategies and self-questioning.

EFFECT SIZE FOR HELP SEEKING = 0.72

EFFECT SIZE FOR SMALL GROUP LEARNING = 0.47

EFFECT SIZE
FOR SETTING
STANDARDS FOR
SELF-JUDGMENT
= 0.62

Teaching Takeaway

Formative evaluation provides evidence with which we can make decisions about where to go next in teaching and learning.

He has prepared two charts. One has the success criteria organized as a checklist with each student's name and a space to record the student's chosen tasks. Mr. Southall plans to select students who find new ways to represent patterns, repeating cores, and changing pattern rules to share with the whole group.

The second chart lists Mr. Southall's three needs-based strategy groups and the mini-lesson plans he prepared for each. Based on previous conferences, observations, and student work, he plans to meet for 5 to 10 minutes each with three groups of two to five students. One group is practicing counting strategies to find what comes next when counting one more and one less. One group is practicing naming two-dimensional shapes regardless of their orientation in a pattern. Another group is using location words to describe patterns. The mini-lessons within the needs-based strategy groups rely on direct instruction to target critical learning intentions that students have not yet met.

Teaching for Clarity at the Close

The kindergarteners sit in a circle holding their math folders with work from their tic-tac-toe choice boards. Mr. Southall begins the sharing portion of class as follows:

> Today, we're going to begin with a partner share based on our success criteria. Turn knee-to-knee, eye-to-eye with a partner. Now, each of you needs to find evidence of working toward the first success criterion: "I can represent the same pattern in multiple ways, including numbers and shapes." Look through your work from today. When you share it with your partner, you will take turns. One person will share and then the listener will respond with something he or she notices, wonders, or connects with. Then switch.

Mr. Southall repeats this process to facilitate the partner share for the first three success criteria. Through this share, the students all practice the fourth success criterion, which he will assess during the whole group share next.

> Now, we're going to share whole group. Think back to
> the work your partner shared with you. Raise your hand
> if your partner found a new way to represent a pattern, a
> new repeating pattern core, or a new changing pattern rule.
> Remember, you are sharing your partner's work, not yours.

Sometimes, Mr. Southall has students share their partner's ideas to ensure they are actively listening and to emphasize the importance of learning from each other.

"Valerie found a new way to represent a repeating pattern. She used days of the week and months of the year," Adar shares. "They're repeating patterns."

"The days of the week core is 1234567. The months of the year core is ABCDEFGHIJKL. I was going to represent both cores with numbers but 10, 11, and 12 look confusing," Valerie explains.

As Mr. Southall records this representation and the two cores on the corresponding anchor charts, he asks, "Did anyone else discover something new while working with the calendars?"

"Tareek represented the seasons. He used weather symbols and words to show seasons repeat," Meredyth responds.

"I used snow for winter, lightning for spring, sun for summer, and rain for fall. It's ABCDABCDABCD," Tareek adds.

Mr. Southall records both the weather symbols and seasons as ways to represent a pattern.

"Ollie made a new changing pattern rule. But we can't decide if it's growing or shrinking. The rule is add two, take away one," Faduma says.

"What did you two think about as you were trying to decide?" Mr. Southall probes.

"Well, adding two would make it a growing pattern, but taking away one makes it a shrinking pattern," answers Ollie.

"Show us your representation of the pattern," Mr. Southall says.

Ollie has a stair stack of cubes and a paper where she recorded numbers to label each stack: 0, 1, 2, 3, 4, 5. She acts out the rule to extend the pattern.

"How are the stacks of cubes changing?" Mr. Southall asks the class. He emphasizes visual descriptions first to make sure all students have access to the problem.

"It's getting higher like stairs. Up, up, up."

"Each step is one more cube."

"Even though she takes some away, it's still getting taller."

The class decides the pattern is growing, and Mr. Southall records the new rule on the anchor chart.

He transitions the class to the exit task and passes it out (Figure 4.3).

> During our share, I saw and heard you representing patterns in many different ways, naming cores and rules, and using lots of mathematical representations and words. Now, we're going to do one more task, but you will do this one by yourself. Usually we are talking and working together because that is when our best learning takes place. For this task, I want to learn about how just your brain is thinking about our work.

EFFECT SIZE FOR
FEEDBACK = 0.70

Mr. Southall displays an enlarged version and reads the task aloud. He highlights the *R* for repeating pattern and *G* for growing pattern. He models writing in the known information through the sixth term and repeats the following: "On the left side, show how the pattern continues if this is the core of a repeating pattern. On the right side, show how the pattern continues if this is a growing pattern and the rule is add one."

His students rearrange themselves. Some students lay on their stomachs to work, others lean against the wall. Mr. Southall circulates the classroom to reread the task, answer questions, and observe processes. If students finish early, he asks them to see how far they can continue each pattern.

When most students are finished, Mr. Southall brings their attention to the giant bulls-eye.

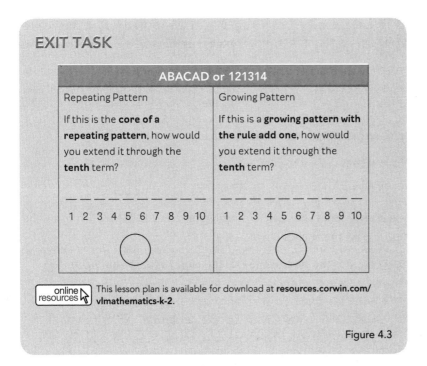

EXIT TASK

ABACAD or 121314	
Repeating Pattern	Growing Pattern
If this is the **core of a repeating pattern**, how would you extend it through the **tenth** term?	If this is a **growing pattern with the rule add one**, how would you extend it through the **tenth** term?
— — — — — — — — — — 1 2 3 4 5 6 7 8 9 10	— — — — — — — — — — 1 2 3 4 5 6 7 8 9 10

online resources: This lesson plan is available for download at **resources.corwin.com/ vlmathematics-k-2**.

Figure 4.3

Remember the green circle with the tooth-smiley face means "I've got it!" The yellow ring with the smiley face is "I need a little more time. I'm just starting to get it." The red ring with the straight face is "I'm stuck. I don't understand." You're going to make the face that matches how you feel about extending each pattern. This will help me know who I need to meet with so we can all continue learning new things about using patterns to problem solve.

Again, Mr. Southall circulates the classroom and checks in with students as they reflect and self-evaluate. Finally, he collects exit tasks and has students return their tic-tac-toe choice board work to their math folders. He will analyze this exit task to determine his next needs-based strategy groups, appropriately providing challenging new tasks to extend thinking and appropriately timed deliberate practice to solidify thinking. Figure 4.4 shows how Mr. Southall made his planning visible so that he could then provide an engaging and rigorous learning experience for his learners.

Mr. Southall's Teaching for Clarity PLANNING GUIDE

ESTABLISHING PURPOSE

1 What are the key content standards I will focus on in this lesson?

Content Standards:

Virginia Mathematics Standards of Learning

K.13. The student will identify, describe, extend, create, and transfer repeating patterns.

K.10. The student will (a) identify and describe plane figures (circle, triangle, square, and rectangle); (b) compare the size (smaller, larger) and shape of plane figures (circle, triangle, square, and rectangle); and (c) describe the location of one object relative to another (above, below, next to) and identify representations of plane figures (circle, triangle, square, and rectangle) regardless of their positions and orientations in space.

Standards for Mathematical Practice:

- Look for and express regularity in repeated reasoning.
- Use appropriate tools strategically.
- Reason abstractly and quantitatively.

2 What are the learning intentions (the goal and *why* of learning stated in student-friendly language) I will focus on in this lesson?

- Content: I am learning that the same pattern can be represented in many ways, including numbers and shapes.
- Language: I am learning the mathematical symbols that describe a pattern's core or unit.
- Social: I am learning to talk and listen about our mathematical ideas.

3 When will I introduce and reinforce the learning intention(s) so that students understand it, see the relevance, connect it to previous learning, and can clearly communicate it themselves?

Think-aloud connecting success criteria to choice board

Conference questions

Partner share based on success criteria

Exit task self-evaluation

SUCCESS CRITERIA

4 What evidence shows that students have mastered the learning intention(s)? What criteria will I use?

I can statements:

- I can represent the same pattern in multiple ways, including numbers and shapes.
- I can describe a repeating pattern's core and a changing pattern's rule using symbols.
- I can compare and categorize patterns and explain my reasoning.
- I can respond to someone else's ideas with questions, noticings, and connections.

5 How will I check students' understanding (assess learning) during instruction and make accommodations?

Formative Assessment Strategies:

- Conference/observation notes

- Student work
- Exit task with self-evaluation

Differentiation Strategies:

- Differentiate the process and product by situational interest: choice board

INSTRUCTION

6   What activities and tasks will move students forward in their learning?

"Which One Doesn't Belong?"

Think-aloud

Tic-tac-toe choice board

Needs-based strategy groups

Partner sharing

Anchor charts

Exit tasks with self-evaluation

7   What resources (materials and sentence frames) are needed?

Word wall words

Anchor chart of representations, repeating pattern cores, changing pattern rules, and examples/nonexamples of patterns

"Which One Doesn't Belong?" images

Math folders

Tic-tac-toe choice boards and task cards

Tiles

Cubes

Paper tiles

Paper shapes

Pattern blocks

Buttons

Noodles

Keys

Counting bears, dinosaurs, insects

Pattern song books

Mathematical literature with patterns

Pattern task cards

Alphabet dice

Rule spinner

Calendars

Number charts

Number lines

Markers

Scissors

Glue

8 How will I organize and facilitate the learning? What questions will I ask? How will I initiate closure?

Instructional Strategies:

- "Which One Doesn't Belong?"
- Think-aloud
- Tic-tac-toe choice board
- Needs-based strategy groups
- Exit tasks with self-evaluation

- Partner sharing of success criteria
- Anchor charts
- Talk knee-to-knee, eye-to-eye

Scaffolding Questions:

- What do you see happening? How are the ____ changing?
- How could you use words to describe and point to the pattern?
- What would you predict comes next? Why?
- How will you record your thinking on paper?
- What kind of pattern is this?
- What is the core of the repeating pattern?
- What is the rule for changing the growing pattern?
- How could you represent the same pattern using ____?

Extending Questions:

- How are these representations similar? Different?
- How would you write a description of the core using letters? Using numbers?
- How would you write a description of the rule for changing the growing pattern using numbers? Using letters?
- What if I changed this, how would that change the pattern?

Self-Reflection and Self-Evaluation:

- The green circle in the middle with the tooth-smiley face means "I've got it!"
- The yellow middle ring with the smiley face is "I need a little more time. I'm just starting to get it".
- The red outer ring with the straight face is "I'm stuck. I don't understand".

online resources   This lesson plan is available for download at **resources.corwin.com/vlmathematics-k-2**.

Figure 4.4   Mr. Southall's Procedural Knowledge Lesson on Multiple Representations

Ms. McLellan and Equality Conjectures

Ms. McLellan's class is deeply examining what equality means in a variety of contexts. A combination of teacher- and student-initiated questions have sparked investigations into the associative, commutative, and additive identity properties and the order of the operations addition and subtraction. Some students have made the connection that pattern blocks could represent equality, such as six green triangles is the same as one yellow hexagon. This connection has led to an inquiry into decomposing and composing two-dimensional shapes. Ms. McLellan posed a challenge for students to find a rule for a card game called Double Compare. The rule must explain a strategy for comparing without combining the card values.

EFFECT SIZE FOR QUESTIONING = 0.48

While students continue pursuing these contexts, today they will also learn new procedural knowledge built on their conceptual understanding and will deepen their problem-solving skills. The big idea is that *Relationships between values can be expressed in many different, correct ways.* Ms. McLellan organizes her students' problem-solving time into centers (Figure 4.5). She has a series of discrete tasks at the same readiness level that provide students with the opportunity to meet the same learning intentions based on the big idea (Thunder & Demchak, 2017).

EFFECT SIZE FOR SMALL GROUP LEARNING = 0.47

At the center on true-or-false statements (Carpenter, Franke, & Levi, 2003), students use number balances, Cuisenaire rods, weights and balance scales, bar models, number lines, and equations to prove whether a mathematical statement is true or false. For example, $10 - 2 = 8 + 3$ and $9 = 4 + 0 + 5$. Ms. McLellan strategically creates statements that will address the misconceptions of operational thinking while adjusting the complexity of the equations to explore mathematical properties.

At the center on open sentences (Carpenter et al., 2003), students use the same materials to solve for missing values in equations, where the missing values are represented by boxes, question marks, and letters. For example, $9 + 9 + d = 10 + 10$. Students must prove their solutions are true. Ms. McLellan also uses this as an opportunity to move her students forward from surface to deep to transfer levels of understanding related to previously studied addition and subtraction strategies. She adjusts the complexity of the equations by including some with two missing values or some equations in which the missing value could have multiple correct answers.

Teaching Takeaway

When using centers in mathematics teaching and learning, we still must have clear learning intentions, success criteria, and formative evaluation of learners at each center.

RELATIONAL THINKING CENTERS

Name: _____

Check off as you complete each center.

☐ True-or-False Statements

☐ Open Sentences

☐ Shape Puzzles

☐ Double Compare

Stoplight Self-Evaluation	Success Criteria	Evidence
○○○	I can read and write mathematical symbols [=, +, -, ()] to show equality.	
○○○	I can read equations left to right and right to left.	
○○○	I can decide if an equation is true and justify my decision.	
○○○	I can explain the meaning of equations with words and models.	

Figure 4.5

> EFFECT SIZE FOR PROBLEM-SOLVING TEACHING = 0.68

At the center on shape puzzles, students use pattern blocks, two-dimensional paper shapes, scissors, and glue to decompose and compose shapes. They record equalities using mathematical notation. For example, 5 ▲ = 1 ◼ + 1 ▲. Ms. McLellan knows it is important for her students to develop fluent spatial structuring and spatial sense in contexts that support number sense (National Research Council, 2009). She also knows that developing meaningful procedural knowledge occurs when students can experiment in multiple contexts with multiple representations. This task prompts students to move from concrete shapes to pictorial representations to increasingly abstract equations with numbers and letters and to make connections among these representations (Berry & Thunder, 2017).

At the center on Double Compare, students continue to decipher a rule for comparing two addends without combining their values first. In the game, two students each flip two, one-digit numeral cards. Whoever has the greatest sum wins all four cards. For example, if Player A flips a 5 card and an 8 card and Player B flips a 4 card and a 3 card, is there a way to determine who has the greatest sum without comparing sums (14 > 7)? Ms. McLellan uses this card game as an opportunity to put students' relational thinking strategies for mental math into words. The emphasis on strategic thinking within a game provides a high-interest context for deliberate practice (Thunder & Demchak, 2017).

EFFECT SIZE
FOR STRATEGY
MONITORING
= 0.58

Ms. McLellan will introduce the learning intentions and success criteria after activating students' prior knowledge. The success criteria are included in the centers checklist as a way to hold individual students accountable for self-monitoring and self-evaluating.

What Ms. McLellan Wants Her Students to Learn

The unifying standard of the relational thinking unit is MA 1.2.1.a. Each center provides students with opportunities to develop and practice procedures related to this standard as well as three additional content standards:

NEBRASKA MATHEMATICS STANDARDS

MA 1.2.1.a. Use the meaning of the equal sign to determine if equations are true and give examples of equations that are true (e.g., 4 = 4, 6 = 7 − 1, 6 + 3 = 3 + 6, and 7 + 2 = 5 + 4).

MA 1.2.1.d. Determine the unknown whole number in an addition or subtraction equation (e.g., 7 + ? = 13).

(Continued)

(Continued)

MA 1.1.1.f. Compare two two-digit numbers by using symbols <, =, and > and justify the comparison based on the number of tens and ones.

MA 1.2.2.a. Decompose numbers and use the commutative and associative properties of addition to develop addition and subtraction strategies including (making 10's and counting on from the larger number) to add and subtract basic facts within 20 (e.g., decomposing to make 10, 7 + 5 = 7 + 3 + 2 = 10 + 2 = 12; using the commutative property to count on 2 + 6 = 6 + 2; and using the associative property to make 10, 5 + 3 + 7 = 5 + (3 + 7) = 5 + 10).

MA 1.3.1.c. Use two-dimensional shapes (e.g., rectangles, squares, trapezoids, triangles, half-circles, and quartercircles) to compose and describe new shapes.

Ms. McLellan is helping her learners develop the following Nebraska Mathematical Processes:

- Models and represents mathematical problems.

- Makes mathematical connections.

Teaching Takeaway

Balanced mathematics instruction requires us to have clarity about what our learners must know, understand, and be able to do.

Ms. McLellan unpacks the standards carefully to make sure she is addressing each component. She also keeps the end in mind: first graders will transfer their knowledge again toward the end of this unit to connect relational thinking with measurement.

Learning Intentions and Success Criteria

Ms. McLellan creates learning intentions that reflect her students' movement from surface to deep learning:

Content Learning Intention: I am learning to understand the many ways mathematical relationships can be expressed and defended.

Language Learning Intention: I am learning to understand the mathematical ways to read, write, and talk about math symbols.

Social Learning Intention: I am learning to understand the decisions we make and how they help us grow as individuals and a community of learners.

Ms. McLellan will begin her lesson by introducing the centers. Two are familiar and two are new. She plans to emphasize the learning intentions and success criteria that unite the centers:

Video 13
Setting the Stage for Procedural Learning

https://resources.corwin.com/vlmathematics-k-2

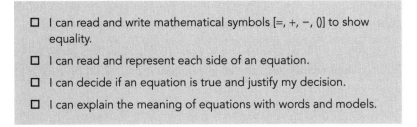

☐ I can read and write mathematical symbols [=, +, −, ()] to show equality.

☐ I can read and represent each side of an equation.

☐ I can decide if an equation is true and justify my decision.

☐ I can explain the meaning of equations with words and models.

As they work, students will gather evidence of mastering each success criterion. This allows students to work at their own pace and to begin with tasks that interest them while also holding them all accountable to the same learning intentions.

Activating Prior Knowledge

"You can make 10 out of nine and six," Zimir says. Ms. McLellan's students are gathered around the carpet for a math talk on building a mental number line. Ms. McLellan uses the problem 6 + 9 to start the conversation. "Making 10" is a strategy that all of her students are practicing.

"How would you visualize making 10 on a number line?" Ms. McLellan focuses the students on this particular tool.

"I would start at nine. Then hop one more to 10. Then hop five more to 15," Zimir continues. Ms. McLellan sketches the open number line as Zimir describes it.

"How does that show nine and six is the same as 15?" asks Ms. McLellan. She wants students to hear Zimir's reasoning and her questions help make each step transparent.

"Well, I just decomposed the six into one and five. I started at nine. I made one hop and then five more hops, so that's six hops total and I landed on 15," Zimir points as he explains.

Next Ms. McLellan writes

$$6 + 9 = (5 + 1) + 9 = 5 + (1 + 9) = 5 + 10 = 15$$

She then says, "Is this statement true or false? Turn and talk to your neighbor." Ms. McLellan listens to some pairs talk and sees some pointing to the math talk number line as a reference.

"Who thinks this statement is true?" she asks. Almost every hand is raised. She continues, "Then, let's start with the people who think it's false."

"Yah'Meen and I thought it might be false because the parentheses moved. Without any parentheses, we think it's true. So I guess we're not sure," explains Harmony.

"Who would like to respond to Harmony and Yah'Meen's thinking?" Ms. McLellan asks. They are practicing their responses to each other and their analysis of decision-making steps.

"We noticed that too, but parentheses can move. They show which numbers to combine first," Neil responds.

"We made the connection to the number line from Zimir's thinking. He decomposed the six into five and one. He made 10 first. Then he added five more. It's the same strategy, just on a number line instead," connects Raoul.

"Turn and tell your neighbor what the parentheses mean and the connection Raoul just made," Ms. McLellan says. She uses this strategy of "press and release" (Almarode & Miller, 2013) to allow students time to make sense of new knowledge in their own words.

Ms. McLellan says, "There are many parts to this equation. The little parts connected by equal signs are expressions. Let's see if we can find each part or expression on the number line. Where do you see 9 + 6?" She continues scaffolding students' connection of the abstract representation of the equality with the number line. She uses different colored pencils to show each expression.

During your work today, you can visualize a number line to help you combine, separate, and find the difference between values. You can also sketch the number line using colored pencils. Remember to make your number line values proportional. That means you show how much a number is worth by how close or far you place it to other numbers.

Her students are warmed up. They are building mental number lines, using strategy and relational language, and remembering how to connect open number lines with equations.

Ms. McLellan passes out the centers checklist and self-evaluation.

> Today, we are examining ways mathematical relationships can be expressed and defended. We're working to read, write, and talk about mathematical symbols with meaning. We're also thinking a lot about our decisions, including how we use symbols and how we justify equations. Your success criteria are at the bottom of your checklist. You'll gather evidence of the success criteria from the centers you work at. Turn and tell your neighbor what we are working on today and how we'll know we've got it.

Ms. McLellan listens in on a few pairs and then continues.

> Let's check in with our thinking for this problem. Have we met the success criteria? You might think to yourself, "Yes, I can read and write mathematical symbols to show equality here." I used the equal sign, parentheses, and the addition sign. I would color the green light on the stoplight and record this equation as evidence. We worked together to explain the equation with a number line model and words. I would color green again on the stoplight. We read and represented each part of the equation on our open number line. That's another green stoplight.

> Okay, the last success criterion is deciding if the equation is true and justifying our reasoning. We decided this equation is true, but how can we justify our reasoning? Let's look at our anchor chart on levels of justification (Carpenter et al., 2003). We've moved past *Appeal to Authority*—no one is going to say because Zimir told me so, right? Our model is a form of *Justification by Example*. We proved this example with a number line that matches it. I wonder if we can reach the highest level of justification: *Generalizable Argument*. We would have to use properties to help us. Hmm. What property allows us to move parentheses so we combine two values but then change our mind and combine a different two first?

EFFECT SIZE FOR IMAGERY = 0.45

EFFECT SIZE FOR SETTING STANDARDS FOR SELF-JUDGMENT = 0.62

"Associative property," Kanice responds, pointing to the anchor chart of properties they created during previous lessons.

Ms. McLellan finishes her model self-evaluation and reminds students of expectations for their problem-solving time.

> You may work alone, with a partner, or a team, but you are each recording your own self-evaluation. Consider carefully who would make a good collaborator for you to work with. You may choose which center to go to and for how long. I will give you warnings when we are halfway through our problem-solving time so you can make sure you have evidence of half of the success criteria.

Teaching Takeaway

Flexible grouping, not ability grouping.

Ms. McLellan has intentionally chosen not to create groups or partners in advance today. Class work has focused on making decisions as learners and reflecting on those decisions. She wants to give students an opportunity to practice making decisions about who to work with similar to the way they practice deciding where to work and what materials to use.

EFFECT SIZE FOR DELIBERATE PRACTICE = 0.79

EFFECT SIZE FOR SPACED VERSUS MASS PRACTICE = 0.60

Spaced practice: is practice that occurs over time rather than in a single setting or practice session.

Scaffolding, Extending, and Assessing Student Thinking

Ms. McLellan knows her students are at varying levels of surface, deep, and transfer learning and need deliberate practice with immediate, specific feedback. She also knows some students need additional time to explore a concept, learn notation, and practice academic language, while others are interested in pursuing concepts that are beyond the standards yet still significant to their relational thinking. Meeting with flexible, needs-based strategy groups throughout the week allows Ms. McLellan the opportunity to provide this deliberate **spaced practice** in small groups for short periods of time while continuing to move the whole class forward.

Based on conference notes and student work analyses, Ms. McLellan identified small groups of students with similar, targeted needs related to the unit's conceptual understandings and procedural knowledge. One group needs to revisit turn-around facts and the commutative property.

Another group needs to practice reading and modeling equations that begin with the total sum or difference, such as 9 = 10 − 1. A third group of students has been asking about making long equations with multiple addition and subtraction signs; for example, they know they can solve 9 + 6 − 10 by adding first and then subtracting, but can they combine and separate in any order?

Ms. McLellan is not positioning herself at one center for the whole lesson. Between each of her needs-based strategy groups, Ms. McLellan circulates the classroom and confers with pairs. She values their engagement in productive struggle as problem solvers because she knows this is when they are learning. She carefully chooses when to model academic language to describe mathematical notation, to ask focusing questions, and to refer students to anchor charts. Ms. McLellan encourages partners to think aloud while sketching in order to make their thinking visible to their peers. She knows peers' language, reasoning, and representations are often more powerful for students' sense making than when the teacher does the majority of the talking and thinking.

Ms. McLellan has planned focusing questions that reflect the learning intentions of the lesson:

- How can you use properties to prove this statement is true or false?

- Why does this value complete this equation?

- What other values are possible?

- How could you model this relationship?

- How could you record this relationship more efficiently?

She has questions written on her conference note chart for quick reference. Today, her chart is set up as a checklist to quickly note which students have demonstrated the targeted procedural knowledge of the lesson: modeling relationships using specific tools (number balance, weights and scales, Cuisenaire rods, bar models, number lines, pattern blocks representations, and equations) and justifying their solutions using the properties (generalizable arguments).

EFFECT SIZE FOR RECORD KEEPING = 0.52

EFFECT SIZE FOR RECIPROCAL TEACHING = 0.74

Video 14
Supporting Procedural Learning and Checking for Understanding

https://resources.corwin.com/vlmathematics-k-2

Teaching for Clarity at the Close

After Ms. McLellan gives a 2-minute warning, her students begin to gather at the carpet with their math binders and checklists. Based on her conferences, Ms. McLellan has selected four groups of students to share who paired their models in ways that emphasize the connections among concrete, representational, and abstract representations (Berry & Thunder, 2017).

Anissa and Ann share first. They used weights on a balance scale to determine if the statement, $7 + 6 = 1 + 6 + 6 + 1$, is true or false. Then they checked their work with a number balance. They have two justifications by example as their proof. Ms. McLellan asks connecting questions to highlight the similarities between the two tools and the parallel between a balanced scale and equality.

DeAndre shares next. He built the open sentence, $7 + 5 = 10 + \boxed{}$, using Cuisenaire rods. He solved for the missing value by placing a rod at the end of the 10 rod that equaled the length of the seven and five rods. Then he drew a bar model to represent his Cuisenaire rods. DeAndre also created a generalizable argument: "I can break 5 into $3 + 2$. I know $7 + 3 = 10$. I used the associative property." Ms. McLellan asks connecting questions to compare the concrete representation of the Cuisenaire rods with the pictorial representation of the bar model and the abstract representation of DeAndre's written justification. Students notice that the making 10 strategy is paired with the associative property again.

Maliyah and James moved from building equalities with pattern blocks to drawing their equalities to creating equations. They used sketches of the shapes at first and then began using letters. For example, Maliyah built four rhombi and four triangles, while James built two trapezoids and one hexagon. They traded and rearranged their builds and then recorded the equation:

$$4 \text{ Rh} + 4 \text{ Tri} = 3 \text{ Rh} + 6 \text{ Tri} = 2 \text{ Trap} + 1 \text{ H} = 4 \text{ Trap.}$$

They explained how they could keep trading to find all the possible combinations to make two hexagons.

Heidi and Justice share last. They propose a new rule for the Double Compare game: If each person has one numeral card that is the same,

EFFECT SIZE FOR REHEARSAL AND MEMORIZATION = 0.73

then compare the different cards. The person with the greater unique card has the greater total. They recorded their rule as follows:

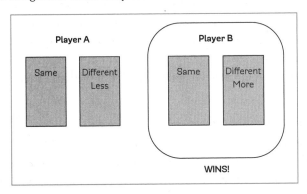

Ms. McLellan engages the class in justifying by example or checking with sample numbers. Then they work as a team to write a generalizable argument or rule that will always work:

$$S + L < S + M \text{ because } L < M.$$

Ms. McLellan is excited at the depth of the whole-class discussion.

> I can tell you really dug into the tasks that motivated you to persevere, pose questions, and seek answers to your questions. I see and hear you thinking relationally and teaching each other through sharing your representations, questions, and connections. We've done a lot of growing as a community of learners. Now we're going to take time for you to check in with yourself to see how your thinking and knowledge has grown and changed today. Look back at your centers checklist and think about each success criterion. Which stoplight color fits where you are right now: red (I am stuck or confused), yellow (I'm still working. I need to revise.), or green (I've mastered it!)? Look back through your work to find evidence of each.

As students look at their work in their math binders, Ms. McLellan confers with students and continues to make notes in her checklist. After 5 minutes, students return their work to their math binders and give their neighbor a high-five. Ms. McLellan notes an increasing number of students moving along the continuum from surface to deep to transfer learning. Figure 4.6 shows how Ms. McLellan made her planning visible so that she could then provide an engaging and rigorous learning experience for her learners.

EFFECT SIZE FOR
EVALUATION AND
REFLECTION = 0.75

Ms. McLellan's Teaching for Clarity PLANNING GUIDE

ESTABLISHING PURPOSE

1 What are the key content standards I will focus on in this lesson?

Content Standards:

Nebraska Mathematical Standards

MA 1.2.1.a. Use the meaning of the equal sign to determine if equations are true and give examples of equations that are true (e.g., 4 = 4, 6 = 7 – 1, 6 + 3 = 3 + 6, and 7 + 2 = 5 + 4).

MA 1.2.1.d. Determine the unknown whole number in an addition or subtraction equation (e.g., 7 + ? = 13).

MA 1.1.1.f. Compare two two-digit numbers by using symbols <, =, and > and justify the comparison based on the number of tens and ones.

MA 1.2.2.a. Decompose numbers and use the commutative and associative properties of addition to develop addition and subtraction strategies including (making 10's and counting on from the larger number) to add and subtract basic facts within 20 (e.g., decomposing to make 10, 7 + 5 = 7 + 3 + 2 = 10 + 2 = 12; using the commutative property to count on 2 + 6 = 6 + 2; and using the associative property to make 10, 5 + 3 + 7 = 5 + (3 + 7) = 5 + 10).

MA 1.3.1.c. Use two-dimensional shapes (e.g., rectangles, squares, trapezoids, triangles, half-circles, and quartercircles) to compose and describe new shapes.

Nebraska Mathematical Processes:

- *Models and represents mathematical problems.*
- *Makes mathematical connections.*

2 What are the learning intentions (the goal and *why* of learning stated in student-friendly language) I will focus on in this lesson?

- *Content: I am learning to understand the many ways mathematical relationships can be expressed and defended.*

- *Language: I am learning to understand the mathematical ways to read, write, and talk about math symbols.*
- *Social: I am learning to understand the decisions we make and how they help us grow as individuals and a community of learners.*

3 When will I introduce and reinforce the learning intention(s) so that students understand it, see the relevance, connect it to previous learning, and can clearly communicate it themselves?

- *Turn and tell*
- *Conference questions*
- *Centers checklist with self-evaluation*

SUCCESS CRITERIA

4 What evidence shows that students have mastered the learning intention(s)? What criteria will I use?

I can statements:

- *I can read and write mathematical symbols [=, +, -, ()] to show equality.*
- *I can read and represent each side of an equation.*
- *I can decide if an equation is true and justify my decision.*
- *I can explain the meaning of equations with words and models.*

5 How will I check students' understanding (assess learning) during instruction and make accommodations?

Formative Assessment Strategies:
- *Conference/observation checklist*
- *Student work*
- *Centers checklist self-evaluation*

Differentiation Strategies:
- *Choice of centers to differentiate the content by interest*
- *Materials to differentiate the process and product by interest*

INSTRUCTION

6 What activities and tasks will move students forward in their learning?

- *Math talk*
- *Modeling*
- *Conferences*
- *Needs-based strategy groups*
- *Sharing tools and representations*

7 What resources (materials and sentence frames) are needed?

Anchor chart of properties

Anchor chart of levels of justification

Math binders

Centers checklist

True-or-false statements

Open sentences

Playing cards

Cuisenaire rods

Number balances

Weights and scales

Pattern blocks

Two-dimensional paper shapes

Number lines

Graph paper

Colored pencils

Scissors

Glue

8 How will I organize and facilitate the learning? What questions will I ask? How will I initiate closure?

Instructional Strategies:
- *Math talk*
- *Modeling*
- *Conferences*
- *Needs-based strategy groups*
- *Turn and tell*
- *Centers checklist self-reflection*

Scaffolding Questions:
- *Why does this value complete this equation?*
- *What other values are possible?*
- *How could you model this relationship?*

Extending Questions:

- *How can you use properties to prove this statement is true or false?*
- *How could you record this relationship more efficiently?*

Self-Reflection and Self-Evaluation Questions:

- *Green stoplight: I've mastered it!*
- *Yellow stoplight: I'm still working. I need to revise.*
- *Red stoplight: I am stuck or confused.*

online resources This lesson plan is available for download at **resources.corwin.com/vlmathematics-K-2**.

Figure 4.6 Ms. McLellan's Procedural Knowledge Lesson on Equality Conjectures

Ms. Busching and Modeling Subtraction

> Teaching mathematics in the Visible Learning classroom is not just about evidence-based practices but using evidence-based practices at the right time.

> EFFECT SIZE FOR HELP SEEKING = 0.72

Ms. Busching's students are deeply engaged in answering the essential questions of their addition and subtraction unit: What is addition? What is subtraction? How are they related? and How do we engage in the work of mathematicians? Over the last couple of weeks, they solved 12 types of addition and subtraction problems, including join (add to), separate (take from), part-part-whole (pull together/take apart), and compare problems (Carpenter et al., 1999; NRC, 2009). This work developed their conceptual understanding of the meanings of addition and subtraction.

The class has added to their anchor chart of mathematical tools and shown how each is useful for thinking flexibly about addition and subtraction. Students self-selected to sign up as experts of different mathematical tools on the anchor chart. When a student has a question about how to use a specific tool, the student checks the expert list and then meets with the peer expert. During her conferences, Ms. Busching also encourages students to sign up as experts based on ongoing assessment. In this way, she is creating a classroom community where every student's expertise is valued.

Through a series of number talks and problem-solving tasks, the students have learned and practiced new mental math strategies for addition within 100: doubles/near doubles, making tens, making landmark numbers, breaking each number into its place value, compensation, and adding up in chunks (Parrish, 2014). These strategies are gathered on an anchor chart. Students' next step in developing procedural knowledge and fluency is to apply these strategies to subtraction problems. Ms. Busching knows that procedural fluency is built upon conceptual understanding (NCTM, 2014). Her students will need to use the meanings and inverse relationship of the operations to transfer and revise the addition strategies to subtract.

EFFECT SIZE FOR STRONG CLASSROOM COHESION = 0.44

Ms. Busching's students are at different levels of procedural knowledge for addition strategies. She knows that her students will not all reach mastery at the same time nor through the same experiences. Ms. Busching carefully plans today's work to allow students to work on their basic fact fluency within 20, their conceptual understanding of addition and subtraction, and their procedural knowledge of subtraction strategies. Her students will have a list of tasks to complete. The must-do task aligns with the lesson's learning intentions and provides targeted opportunities for students to demonstrate the success criteria. The may-do tasks provide optional, additional opportunities for students to deliberately practice areas of need related to the unit's essential questions (Thunder & Demchak, 2017).

The must-do task asks students to use the meanings of the operations to transfer and revise addition strategies into efficient and accurate subtraction strategies (Figure 4.7).

Some may-do tasks allow time for students to deliberately practice their basic fact fluency within 20 by playing games (Hidden Parts, Make 100, Magic Square, and Capture the Flags on a number chart). One may-do task engages students in extending their conceptual understanding of addition by figuring out rules for adding even and odd numbers. Other may-do tasks engage students in bolstering their conceptual understanding of the inverse relationship between addition and subtraction by solving additional contextualized problems, including the more challenging language of compare problems. Through this mixture of must-do and may-do tasks, Ms. Busching will meet her students where they are in their growth toward mastery of the unit and the lesson's learning intentions.

ADDING TO SUBTRACT

How can I use what I know about addition strategies to solve 65 – 29?

Mathematicians value using what they know to figure out what they don't know. Instead of always creating new strategies, they often apply known strategies to new operations and make revisions.

We need to know which of our six mental math strategies for addition can work as mental math strategies for subtraction:

- Doubles/near doubles
- Making tens
- Making landmark numbers
- Breaking each number into its place value
- Compensation
- Adding up in chunks

A mental math strategy works if it is accurate (Will you always get the right answer using the strategy?) and efficient (Is this a quick strategy that is easy to keep track of?).

You may need to use equations or other models to reason about and revise the strategy.

Decide which addition strategies will work for subtraction. You may work alone or with classmates.

Figure 4.7

 This lesson plan is available for download at **resources.corwin.com/vlmathematics-k-2**.

What Ms. Busching Wants Her Students to Learn

Although her students will work on may-do tasks that address additional standards from throughout the unit, the must-do task targets three standards for second grade:

MATHEMATICS CONTENT AND PRACTICE STANDARDS

2.NBT.B.9. Explain why addition and subtraction strategies work, using place value and the properties of operations.

2.NBT.B.5. Fluently add and subtract within 100 using strategies based on place value, properties of operations, and/or the relationship between addition and subtraction.

2.MD.B.6. Represent whole numbers as lengths from 0 on a number line diagram with equally spaced points corresponding to the numbers 0, 1, 2, …, and represent whole-number sums and differences within 100 on a number line diagram.

Ms. Busching is helping her learners develop the following Standards for Mathematical Practice:

- Reason abstractly and quantitatively.

- Use appropriate tools strategically.

Learning Intentions and Success Criteria

Ms. Busching organizes each of her units around a central big idea and then groups and sequences related big ideas within the unit. Currently, her students have moved from surface-level learning to digging deeply into the procedures, strategies, and models related to addition and subtraction within 100.

Her learning intentions and success criteria reflect this movement. Students' are expected to make more connections among ideas, use more mathematical language and notation, and serve as resources to each other:

Content Learning Intention: I am learning to understand the inverse relationship of addition and subtraction.

Language Learning Intention: I am learning to understand how the language of inverse operations can be used to explain the meaning of addition and subtraction models.

Social Learning Intention: I am learning to understand the importance of learning from each other and valuing each person's expertise.

Procedural knowledge is not rote rehearsal. Procedural knowledge includes relationships between processes.

Ms. Busching will begin her lesson by sharing the day's tasks. Each activity provides students with the opportunity to practice and make sense of the success criteria:

☐ I can describe representations, strategies, and contexts as both addition and subtraction situations.

☐ I can explain how an addition strategy can be adjusted and applied to subtraction.

☐ I can teach and learn efficient mathematical models to represent addition and subtraction strategies.

☐ I can explain the inverse relationship between addition and subtraction.

Activating Prior Knowledge

One equation is written in the corner of the whiteboard: $54 + 10 = 64$. The expression $54 + 30$ is written in the middle of the board. The room is silent as students raise their thumbs. Everyone agrees on the same solution, 84. "Who will defend 84?" Ms. Busching asks.

"I used the problem before and kept counting on from 54 by tens: 54, 64, 74, 84," Cory explains.

"What is another way to confirm Cory's solution?" Ms. Busching asks. The students know what to expect in this routine, called a number talk (Parrish, 2014). They know they are practicing mental math strategies because this form of procedural fluency is one of their year-long goals.

"I know five and three is eight, so 50 and 30 is 80. You just need four more to make 84," Emma describes.

"Think about how you can use the two previous problems to help you fluently solve $54 + 36$." Ms. Busching records the next problem in the number string. She allows wait time until the majority of students have raised their thumbs.

Ms. Busching gathers solutions to $54 + 36$ and records them on the board: 80 and 90. "Who will defend one of the solutions?"

"I will defend 80. I used Emma's strategy: $50 + 30$ is 80 and $4 + 6$ is 10. Wait. Then $80 + 10 = 90$. It's not 80," Richard thinks aloud. He says, "I would like respectfully disagree with myself."

"What are you realizing?" Ms. Busching asks. She knows that mistakes can be just as powerful to learn from as correct strategies.

"I think I just forgot about the 10 when I was holding the numbers in my head. I knew I needed a zero in the ones place and just stopped there," Richard answers.

Ms. Busching says, "I'm so glad you shared your realization. That's a really important mistake for us to think about. I know I've made that mistake before. Has anyone else?" Students shake their heads yes as Ms. Busching makes sharing and celebrating learning from mistakes a norm. "Let's go back and record Richard's strategy," she says. As Richard retells his strategy accurately, Ms. Busching records the equations:

$$50 + 30 = 80$$
$$4 + 6 = 10$$
$$80 + 10 = 90$$

She says, "Keeping all three steps in your head can be a challenge! Thank you for sharing your thinking, Richard. Richard's mistake and realization helped us find one way to defend 90. Who has another strategy?"

David says, "I will defend 90. I visualized a number line. I used Cory's strategy first but I just counted on by 30: 54, 84. And then I added six more to land on 90." Ms. Busching sketches David's open number line.

"Use the previous problems to solve this final sum." Ms. Busching erases the work and leaves the list of previous problems in the corner:

$$54 + 10 = 64$$
$$54 + 30 = 84$$
$$54 + 36 = 90$$

She writes the final problem: 54 + 39. Again, she waits for students to raise their thumbs. Some students are showing a thumb and an index finger to indicate they have solved the problem in two different ways. As always, she begins by recording all answers: 93 and 94.

Sonam volunteers to defend 93: "I just used the work we already did. I know 39 is three more than 36, so I just have to add three more to 90."

"I visualized David's number line. David got us to 90 and then I made another hop of three to 93," explains Adric.

The teacher says, "Compare this mental math strategy for addition to our anchor chart. What strategy did we use to find the sum of 54 and 39? Turn and talk to a partner." Six strategies are displayed on an anchor chart with examples and strategy names (Parrish, 2014). Naming the strategies with common language enables the students to talk and make decisions about the strategies.

"Deshawn and I think it's adding up in chunks. We wanted to solve 54 + 39, so we added up chunks of 39 to 54," Lily says.

"We thought it's making landmark numbers because we made 90," shares Sammy.

EFFECT SIZE FOR CLASSROOM DISCUSSION = 0.82

"I disagree. If we were making landmark numbers, we would have gone to 60 first and then added on the rest," replies Bryant.

"We made a landmark number but we also added up chunks," reflects Sammy.

Ms. Busching says, "I agree, Sammy. We often use landmark numbers in each of the strategies because they're so friendly for mental math. But sometimes we use landmark numbers in combination with another strategy." She concludes the number talk and transitions to introducing today's task:

> Your must-do task today will be to analyze each of the mental math addition strategies and decide which ones can be used for subtraction and how. Let's try one out together. How could we use adding up in chunks to help us solve 65 − 29? Turn and talk with a partner.

Many students are talking to their partners in their heritage language. This is an important first step in making sense of academic language (Hansen & Thunder, 2014), and Ms. Busching's students know they can always talk in their heritage language to help them make sense of new vocabulary, academic sentence structures, and problem contexts. Ms. Busching takes suggestions and writes the ideas in words.

"You could subtract down in chunks. You know, take away part after part until you've taken away all 29."

"You could start at 29 and add up in chunks to get to 65 and then figure out how much you added."

"These are great starts for using a mental math addition strategy and revising it to work as a subtraction strategy," Ms. Busching says. Next, she introduces the must-do task. She passes the task out and reads it aloud as students glue it into their mathematician's journal. She says, "Talk with a partner. How are you making sense of your must-do task today? What will you do? What will your product be?" After talking, students ask clarifying questions and their peers respond. Students make notes and highlight in their journals.

Ms. Busching continues, "We are answering the following essential question: How are addition and subtraction related? Now read the learning intentions and success criteria. Where do you see opportunities in the must-do task to show what you know?"

Students talk in pairs about the learning intentions and success criteria. Several students share that they are not sure what the phrase "inverse relationship" means. Others respond by pointing out the answers to the other essential questions. Luciana says, "When you subtract, you do the opposite of adding—you take something away." Ms. Busching asks them to be on the lookout for more examples and ways to explain this big idea as they work.

> For today's must-do task, I have assigned partners. You will work together to engage in rough-draft talk and rough-draft writing. Rough-draft talk and rough-draft writing means you are brainstorming, testing out ideas, making mistakes, making conjectures, and experimenting with numbers (Jansen et al., 2016). Nothing is final. Nothing gets erased. Solving 65 − 29 may give you enough information to evaluate the strategy or you may need to create additional problems. Remember to make notes about what works and doesn't work on the flap of your journal. After working today, we will share our progress.

EFFECT SIZE
FOR MASTERY
LEARNING = 0.57
AND FEEDBACK
= 0.70

Video 15
Differentiating Procedural Learning

https://resources.corwin.com/ vlmathematics-k-2

Since rough-draft talk and metacognition are emphases of today's lesson, Ms. Busching has purposefully paired students who speak the same heritage language. She hopes this will allow them the time and space to rough-draft talk in their heritage language before sharing with the whole class. The pairs have also listed themselves as experts of different strategies, so they bring different strengths to their collaboration.

Finally, Ms. Busching reminds students of the may-do task list posted on the whiteboard: Hidden Parts, Make 100, Magic Square, and Capture the Flags on a 100 Chart, Adding Odd and Even Numbers, and the newly added option—More Addition and Subtraction Situations. Partners find each other, gather their math binders, and move to work areas. Some students remain to ask Ms. Busching questions and then begin their work.

Scaffolding, Extending, and Assessing Student Thinking

As students work, Ms. Busching has three monitoring tasks. She will confer with pairs to hear their rough-draft talk about the must-do task. She will check in with students who move on to may-do tasks to hear their decision-making processes for selecting the task and what they are learning from it. In each conference, she will ask questions to scaffold and extend students' thinking. She will also have specific students complete a Show Me formative assessment (Fennell et al., 2017) to check their understanding of previous learning intentions. Each of these monitoring tasks enables Ms. Busching to document her students' progress at varying levels of surface, deep, and transfer learning.

EFFECT SIZE FOR RECORD KEEPING = 0.52

Ms. Busching has two observation charts in hand as she circulates the classroom (Figure 4.8). One chart has a space to record the task each student is working on and evidence of the success criteria.

The second chart has three variations of the Show Me task and the list of students Ms. Busching will meet with for each variation. The Show Me task is as follows: *Show me how you would mentally solve: _____.* The variations are addition strings that check for targeted basic fact strategies: making 10s, near doubles, and a combination. This formative assessment will allow Ms. Busching to assess students' progress toward

OBSERVATION/CONFERENCE CHART

Dates: _____

Essential Questions: What is addition? What is subtraction? How are they related? How do we engage in the work of mathematicians?

Agustin Task:	Adrian Task:	Adric Task:	Bryant Task:	Cory Task:	D'angelo Task:
David Task:	Deshawn Task:	Emma Task:	Gyaltsen Task:	Hailey Task:	Imani Task:
Jayla Task:	Lily Task:	Luciana Task:	Mateo Task:	Megan Task:	Mia Task:
Phoebe Task:	Richard Task:	Sammy Task:	Sonam Task:	Tashi Task:	Zoe Task:

Success Criteria	Questions
1. I can describe representations, strategies, and contexts as both addition and subtraction situations.	• How did you revise the addition strategy for subtraction? Why?
2. I can explain how an addition strategy can be adjusted and applied to subtraction.	• How is this strategy similar to the addition version?
3. I can teach and learn efficient mathematical models to represent addition and subtraction strategies.	• What would be a story for 65 – 29? How is this story represented in your work? What does the answer mean?
4. I can explain the inverse relationship between addition and subtraction.	• Will this strategy always work? Why or why not?
	• For what numbers would this strategy be inefficient?
	• How does this representation show why the strategy works?

Overall Patterns:

Figure 4.8

meeting the end-of-year goal: Fluently add and subtract within 20 using mental strategies.

Ms. Busching alternates between conferring with students and meeting with small groups for the Show Me tasks. This way, she has a clear, documented picture of what her students worked on independently as well as where her students are along the path toward mastery. She will use this documentation as well as students' progress share and student work to plan tomorrow's math routines, mini-lesson, must-do and may-do tasks, and sharing.

Teaching for Clarity at the Close

As work time ends, Ms. Busching notes two patterns in her observation chart: only one pair of students moved on to may-do tasks and two students need additional practice using open number lines to represent a contextualized comparing problem. Tomorrow, she will meet with these two students in a needs-based strategy group to model and practice using number lines.

EFFECT SIZE FOR RESPONSE TO INTERVENTION = 1.29

On different days, the closing share has various focuses. Sometimes students share the content of their work, the craft or representations they choose, their processes or strategies, or their progress toward the learning intentions or a personal learning goal (Thunder & Demchak, 2012). Ms. Busching recognizes that tomorrow will be a continuation of today's work. The upcoming progress share (Figure 4.9) will be important for students as they record what they have completed and what they will do next.

Ms. Busching says,

> Today, we will bring our work to a close with a progress share. Everyone will share with a partner, a different partner than you worked with today. You will each share three reflections:
>
> - What did you work on?
> - How did this help you work toward the learning intentions and demonstrate the success criteria?
> - What does this mean you need to work on tomorrow?
>
> You will each have 3 minutes to talk. Decide who will be Partner A and who will be Partner B. Partner A, raise your hand. You go first.

Ms. Busching records the three reflection questions on the whiteboard and then listens in on her students' conversations. She makes additional notes in her observation chart. She gives a 30-second warning to wrap up and then announces Partner B's turn. She sees students

A PROGRESS SHARE PROTOCOL

Everyone shares with a partner, a different partner than you worked with today.

You will each share three reflections: .

- What did you work on?

- How did this help you work toward the learning intentions and demonstrate the success criteria?

- What does this mean you need to work on tomorrow?

You will each have 3 minutes to talk. Decide who will be Partner A and who will be Partner B. Partner A begins.

Figure 4.9

looking back and forth between their work and the learning intentions and success criteria.

EFFECT SIZE FOR SUMMARIZATION = 0.79

Ms. Busching says, "At the beginning of class, there was some uncertainty and conjectures about the phrase 'inverse relationship' in the learning intentions and success criteria. Based on your work today, what do you think this means?" Pairs join other pairs to have a small group discussion. Then they share ideas with the whole group. Students make connections like "They're opposite operations," "You can think addition when you subtract," and "It reminds me of finding the missing part to make a whole. Sometimes I count up and sometimes I count back." Ms. Busching knows her students are beginning to make sense of this academic language through the problem-solving tasks and classroom discourse.

Next, Ms. Busching passes out a reflection paper with three sections. The first section is a box with the sentence starter "Today I worked on." The second section is a table with each of the success criteria listed and a dot. Students color the dot green (got it), yellow (partially got it), or red (stuck/confused) and make a note with evidence of meeting or working toward the success criteria. The third section is another box with the sentence starter "Tomorrow I will."

She says, "We will take 3 minutes to record reflections. When you evaluate your work on the success criteria, remember how we have evaluated ourselves using colored pencils, highlighters and evidence in our journals. This self-evaluation is just like that but it will be on a separate page." Ms. Busching observes, takes notes, and confers with students who have questions.

Ms. Busching wants to allow students to finish at varying times. As students turn in their self-evaluation and plan, they are invited to silently consider a problem posed through another typical math routine: "Which One Doesn't Belong?"

25	21
19	24

This task is both open middled and open ended, meaning there are multiple strategies for solving and multiple correct answers.

When all students have submitted their exit tasks and self-evaluations, Ms. Busching has students talk in triads about their solutions and reasoning. After 2 minutes, she invites responses.

Imani says, "Twenty-five doesn't belong because it is a landmark number. The others are all one away from being a landmark number."

Mia sees it differently and says, "Nineteen doesn't belong because it only has one full group of 10. The other numbers have two 10s."

Agustin relies on doubles, "Twenty-four doesn't belong because it's even. You can split 24 in half because $12 + 12 = 24$. The other numbers are all odd."

Phoebe is quick to add, "I want to add on to what Agustin said about 24 not belonging. Twenty-four doesn't belong because it's a double: $12 + 12 = 24$. The other numbers are all near-double facts." She completed Show Me tasks today to demonstrate she could use doubles facts to fluently problem solve beyond 20.

Ms. Busching congratulates the class on their perseverance, use of mathematical language, and respectful debate. She and her students can see and hear their growth toward mastery of critical procedural knowledge within their unit on addition and subtraction. Although the students are at different levels of surface, deep, and transfer thinking, they have each taken significant steps forward in their learning today. Figure 4.10 shows how Ms. Busching made her planning visible so that she could then provide an engaging and rigorous learning experience for her learners.

Ms. Busching's Teaching for Clarity PLANNING GUIDE

ESTABLISHING PURPOSE

1

What are the key content standards I will focus on in this lesson?

Content Standards:

2.NBT.B.9. Explain why addition and subtraction strategies work, using place value and the properties of operations.

2.NBT.B.5. Fluently add and subtract within 100 using strategies based on place value, properties of operations, and/or the relationship between addition and subtraction.

2.MD.B.6. Represent whole numbers as lengths from 0 on a number line diagram with equally spaced points corresponding to the numbers 0, 1, 2, ..., and represent whole-number sums and differences within 100 on a number line diagram.

Standards for Mathematical Practice:

- Reason abstractly and quantitatively.
- Use appropriate tools strategically.

2

What are the learning intentions (the goal and *why* of learning stated in student-friendly language) I will focus on in this lesson?

- Content: I am learning to understand the inverse relationship of addition and subtraction.
- Language: I am learning to understand how the language of inverse operations can be used to explain the meaning of addition and subtraction models.
- Social: I am learning to understand the importance of learning from each other and valuing each person's expertise.

3 When will I introduce and reinforce the learning intention(s) so that students understand it, see the relevance, connect it to previous learning, and can clearly communicate it themselves?

- Essential questions
- Turn and talk
- Reflection plan and self-evaluation

SUCCESS CRITERIA

4 What evidence shows that students have mastered the learning intention(s)? What criteria will I use?

I can statements:

- I can describe representations, strategies, and contexts as both addition and subtraction situations.
- I can explain how an addition strategy can be adjusted and applied to subtraction.
- I can teach and learn efficient mathematical models to represent addition and subtraction strategies.
- I can explain the inverse relationship between addition and subtraction.

5 How will I check students' understanding (assess learning) during instruction and make accommodations?

Formative Assessment Strategies:

- Conference/observation checklist
- Student work and reflection in the mathematician's journal
- Show Me tasks
- Reflection plan and self-evaluation

Differentiation Strategies:

- Differentiate the content by situational interest: must do and may do
- Differentiate the process and product by situational interest: choice of materials and partners or alone

INSTRUCTION

6 What activities and tasks will move students forward in their learning?

- Number talk: adding up in chunks
- Must-do task: Adding to Subtract
- May-do tasks: Hidden Parts, Make 100, Magic Square, Capture the Flags on a 100 Chart, Adding Odd and Even Numbers, and More Addition and Subtraction Situations
- "Which One Doesn't Belong?"

7 What resources (materials and sentence frames) are needed?

Number talk

Anchor chart of addition strategies

Mathematician's journal

Must-do and may-do tasks

Reflection plan and self-evaluation

Base-ten blocks

Cuisenaire rods

Number charts

Number lines and whiteboard markers

Graph paper

Highlighters

Colored pencils

---

8 How will I organize and facilitate the learning? What questions will I ask? How will I initiate closure?

Instructional Strategies:

- Number talk
- Anchor chart
- Must-do and may-do tasks
- Show Me tasks

Scaffolding Questions:

- How did you revise the addition strategy for subtraction? Why?
- How is this strategy similar to the addition version?

Extending Questions:

- What would be a story for 65 - 29? How is this story represented in your work? What does the answer mean?
- Will this strategy always work? Why or why not?
- For what numbers would this strategy be inefficient?
- How does this representation show why the strategy works?

Connecting Questions:

- What did you work on?
- How did this help you work toward the learning intentions and demonstrate the success criteria?

- What does this mean you need to work on tomorrow?
- What does "inverse relationship" mean to you now?

Self-Reflection and Self-Evaluation:
- Mathematician's journal
- Self-reflection and plan

 This lesson plan is available for download at **resources.corwin.com/vlmathematics-k-2**.

Figure 4.10   Ms. Busching's Procedural Knowledge Lesson on Modeling Subtraction

Reflection

Our final visit to these three classrooms focused on the development of procedural knowledge and fluency. Using what you have read in this chapter, reflect on the following questions:

1. In your own words, describe what teaching for procedural knowledge looks like in your mathematics classroom.

2. How does the Teaching for Clarity Planning Guide support your intentionality in teaching for procedural knowledge?

3. Compare and contrast the approaches to teaching taken by the classroom teachers featured in this chapter.

4. Consider the following statement: *Procedural knowledge is more than "drill and kill."* Do you agree or disagree with the statement? Why or why not? How is this statement reflected in this chapter?

5. How did the classroom teachers featured in this chapter adjust the difficulty and/or complexity of the mathematics tasks to meet the needs of all learners?

KNOWING YOUR IMPACT: EVALUATING FOR MASTERY 5

CHAPTER 5 SUCCESS CRITERIA:

(1) I can describe what mastery learning is in my classroom.

(2) I can compare and contrast checks for understanding with the evaluation of mastery.

(3) I can explain how to evaluate mastery in my own classroom using tasks and tests.

(4) I can identify characteristics of challenging mathematics tasks.

(5) I can explain the role of feedback in supporting students' journey to mastery.

Let us end right where we began—Ms. Paulson's kindergarten classroom. Ms. Paulson established clear learning intentions and success criteria, and she designed a challenging mathematics task that allowed learners to see themselves as their own teachers. Just like Mr. Southall, Ms. McLellan, and Ms. Busching, Ms. Paulson created many opportunities for learners to make their thinking visible through her checks for understanding. Formative evaluation and feedback are critical components to teaching mathematics in the Visible Learning classroom.

EFFECT SIZE
FOR PROVIDING
FORMATIVE
EVALUATION = 0.48
AND FEEDBACK
= 0.70

However, this chapter focuses on determining students' learning over the long haul. In other words, how do teachers assess for mastery? And in doing so, how do teachers and learners make evidence-informed decisions about when to move forward in the learning progression? Knowing our impact on student learning in mathematics involves more than just formative evaluation of learning. Knowing our impact also involves recognizing student mastery in their mathematics learning.

What Is Mastery Learning?

Mastery learning
is the expectation
that learners will
grasp specific
conceptual
understanding,
procedural
knowledge, and
the application of
specific concepts
and thinking skills.

Mastery learning is the expectation that learners will grasp specific conceptual understanding, procedural knowledge, and the application of specific concepts and thinking skills. This requires that teachers establish clarity about the learning in mathematics classrooms and then organize a series of logical experiences, noticing which students do and don't learn along the way. When students experience lesson clarity, they progress toward mastery. The claim underlying mastery learning is that all children can learn when provided with clear explanations of what it means to "master" the material being taught. Although mastery learning does not speak to the time learners need to reach mastery, all students continuously receive evaluative feedback on their performance. Learners know where they are at in their learning, where they are going, and what they can do to bridge the gap.

EFFECT SIZE
FOR MASTERY
LEARNING = 0.57

EFFECT SIZE FOR
TEACHER CLARITY
= 0.75

In true mastery learning, students do not progress to the next unit until they have mastered the previous one. But "moving on" could mean that learners move forward in the learning progression or that they are provided additional learning experiences at the surface, deep, or transfer level to address gaps in their learning if they are not yet able to demonstrate mastery. Ms. Paulson notes,

To check to see if my students "get it" and are "ready to move on," I map out what this looks like for my kindergarteners—from those who are at a high level of readiness all the way to those who are in need of the most support. How I work with each student, from small group to whole group and even to centers, depends on the specific things my learners can do and those items that they cannot do yet.

Mastery learning is an essential part of building assessment-capable visible learners in the mathematics classroom. If learners are to know where they are going next in their learning, select the right learning tools to support the next steps (e.g., manipulatives, problem-solving approaches, and/or meta-cognitive strategies), and know what feedback to seek about their own learning, they must have opportunities to assess their own mastery with mathematics content. This, of course, comes after learners have engaged in multiple mathematics tasks replete with checks for understanding that allow teachers and students to adjust learning in the moment. Once that has occurred, it is time to determine students' level of mastery in the mathematics learning. So how do we determine what mastery looks like for specific content in the mathematics classroom?

Using Learning Intentions to Define *Mastery Learning*

Learning intentions provide the framework for defining mastery in learning, developing the assessments used to determine student mastery, and gathering the information necessary to plan learning experiences for students. Ms. Paulson, Mr. Southall, Ms. McLellan, and Ms. Busching had to answer the question "What do my students need to learn?" The answer to this question represents mastery for the specific content in each of their classrooms. In the above example from Ms. Paulson's classroom, the learning intention stated I *am learning about part-whole relationships with numbers*. Therefore, to demonstrate mastery, her learners must be able to recognize, describe, and investigate part-whole relationships. For this specific standard, her learners only need to demonstrate mastery for numbers up to 10 (Virginia Department of Education, 2016).

Assessments of mastery require both the teacher and the learners to focus on the essential learning for a particular unit or series of lessons.

Teaching Takeaway

Effective feedback is an essential feature of the Visible Learning mathematics classroom.

Teaching Takeaway

Features of mastery learning include the following:

1. Clear learning expectations
2. Feedback that is specific, constructive, and timely
3. Sufficient time, attention, and support to ensure learning

Teachers must unpack the language of the specific standard to have a clear sense of the conceptual understanding, procedural knowledge, and applications expected in the mastery of the standard. Let us look at the following specific content standard associated with Ms. Paulson's lesson in Chapter 1. How would she assess for mastery?

> The student will (a) recognize and describe with fluency part-whole relationships for numbers up to 5; and (b) investigate and describe part-whole relationships for numbers up to 10.

As you can see, this is not very helpful in developing and implementing an assessment of mastery learning. For example, to what depth are students expected to investigate, what does the description of these relationships involve (i.e., written, verbal, visual, or some combination of the three), and what must they recognize? Looking closer at the curriculum documents that accompany this specific standard, Ms. Paulson is able to narrow in on tasks that will allow students to demonstrate mastery. Learners are only focusing on pictographs and bar graphs. To effectively evaluate for mastery, teachers must specifically define what the learner will know, understand, and be able to do. Ms. Paulson and her collaborative planning team defined *mastery* as follows:

> Given a number story, I can represent numbers many different ways to solve the problem and explain the process for completing the task.

In addition, Ms. Paulson and her colleagues have developed the following number stories or problem cards from which learners can select and solve. The front of each card includes a written description of a story or problem, and the back of the card is a visual representation of the story or problem. Some examples are as follows:

- Ally had 5 pencils. Ben gave her 4 more pencils. How many pencils does Ally have altogether?

- Ally had 3 pencils. Ben gave her some more pencils. Now Ally has 7 pencils. How many did Ben give her?

- Ally had some pencils. Ben gave her 6 more. Now Ally has 8 pencils. How many pencils did Ally have to start with?

- Kailey had 10 cookies. She gave 6 cookies to Joe. How many cookies does Kailey have now?

- Kailey had 10 cookies. She gave some to Joe. She has 4 cookies left. How many cookies did Kailey give to Joe?

- Kailey had some cookies. She gave 6 to Joe. Now she has 4 cookies left. How many cookies did Kailey start with?

- Tia has 3 red markers and 2 blue markers. How many markers does she have?

- Tia has 10 markers. Four of the markers are red, and the rest are blue. How many blue markers does Tia have?

- Tia has a pack of red and blue markers. She has 8 markers in all. How many markers could be red? How many could be blue? (adapted from Virginia Department of Education, 2016)

In addition, Ms. Paulson and her colleagues have specifically identified vocabulary that represents key concepts within this standard that learners must use fluently in their work: *part, whole, compose, decompose,* and *solution.*

In Figure 5.1, Mr. Southall, Ms. McLellan, and Ms. Busching also define mastery for their particular standard(s) or learning intention.

Establishing the Expected Level of Mastery

From the preestablished levels of mastery, which is based on the standard(s), teachers can identify measurable indicators that students are or are not at the level of mastery. These indicators should focus on what students are doing rather than what they are not doing. This helps identify current performance levels and is suggestive of the types of experiences students need to have to progress in their learning. In other words, what does progress toward mastery look like in this specific standard? Learners progress toward mastery at different rates, and teachers should map out that progress so that both the teacher and the learners can make an informed decision about where they are in their learning.

Ms. Paulson and her colleagues identified the incremental steps along the pathway to achieving mastery for the functional relationship standard using the SOLO Taxonomy (see Figure 1.5 in Chapter 1). If students

EXAMPLES OF MASTERY FOR SPECIFIC CONTENT STANDARDS

	Mathematics Content Standard	What Mastery Looks Like
Mr. Southall	**From Chapter 3:** The student will identify, describe, extend, create, and transfer repeating patterns. The student will (a) count forward orally by ones from 0 to 100; (b) count backward orally by ones when given any number between 1 and 10; (c) identify the number after, without counting, when given any number between 0 and 100 and identify the number before, without counting, when given any number between 1 and 10; and (d) count forward by tens to determine the total number of objects to 100.	Given multiple choices of manipulatives (e.g., color cubes, tiles, squares, pattern blocks, snap cubes, and counters), learners must create their own pattern in their mathematics journals, identify the type of pattern and its core or rule, and then see how many different ways they can represent the same pattern.
Ms. McLellan	**From Chapter 4:** Use the meaning of the equal sign to determine if equations are true and give examples of equations that are true (e.g., $4 = 4$, $6 = 7 - 1$, $6 + 3 = 3 + 6$, and $7 + 2 = 5 + 4$). Determine the unknown whole number in an addition or subtraction equation (e.g., $7 + ? = 13$). Compare two two-digit numbers by using symbols $<$, $=$, and $>$ and justify the comparison based on the number of tens and ones. Decompose numbers and use the commutative and associative properties of addition to develop addition and subtraction strategies including (making 10's and counting on from the larger number) to add and subtract basic facts within 20 (e.g., decomposing to make 10, $7 + 5 = 7 + 3 + 2 = 10 + 2 = 12$; using the commutative property to count on $2 + 6 = 6 + 2$; and using the associative property to make 10, $5 + 3 + 7 = 5 + (3 + 7) = 5 + 10$). Use two-dimensional shapes (e.g., rectangles, squares, trapezoids, triangles, half-circles, and quartercircles) to compose and describe new shapes.	Given an authentic scenario (e.g., number stories), learners must model the scenario using an equal sign and/or greater than and less than symbols, find an unknown value, and interpret the mathematical results in the context of the scenario.
Ms. Busching	**From Chapter 2:** Add and subtract within 1,000, using concrete models or drawings and strategies based on place value, properties of operations, and/or the relationship between addition and subtraction; relate the strategy to a written method. Understand that in adding or subtracting three-digit numbers, one adds or subtracts hundreds and hundreds, tens and tens, ones and ones; and sometimes it is necessary to compose or decompose tens or hundreds.	Given an authentic scenario (e.g., word problems), learners must model the scenario using addition and subtraction strategies, find a solution, and interpret the mathematical results in the context of the scenario.

Mathematics Content Standard	What Mastery Looks Like
Mentally add 10 or 100 to a given number 100–900, and mentally subtract 10 or 100 from a given number 100–900. Explain why addition and subtraction strategies work, using place value and the properties of operations.	

Figure 5.1

perceive or actually are far from meeting the highest level of proficiency, making the progression visible allows them to answer the questions "Where am I going, how am I going, and where to go next?" These are essential in developing assessment-capable visible learners. Together, Ms. Paulson and her colleagues developed the progression in shown in Figure 5.2.

When we revisit the classrooms of Mr. Southall, Ms. McLellan, and Ms. Busching, we see that they provide similar levels of clarity about what mastery looks like as their learners progress through the big ideas around the content standards (see Figure 5.3). Teachers know their students best and therefore can use evaluation of student learning—within a set of learning intentions—to designate their students' levels of proficiency on the pathway to mastery. That said, there is no prescribed number of these levels.

Collecting Evidence of Progress Toward Mastery

To determine progress and to support the grades given to students, teachers must be able to clearly answer the question "What evidence suggests that the learners have mastered the learning or are moving toward mastery?" The evidence used to determine mastery is typically more formal than the evidence used to check for understanding. For example, an exit ticket could easily be used to determine which students mastered a given learning intention on a given day. But that may not be sufficient evidence for determining mastery of a standard or set of standards. Checks for understanding gather and provide *evidence of a*

Teaching Takeaway

In addition to knowing what we want our students to learn, we have to know what evidence will demonstrate that they have learned it.

EXAMPLE OF PROGRESS TOWARD MASTERY FOR A SPECIFIC CONTENT STANDARD

Unit: Number and Number Sense						
Content Standard The student will (a) recognize and describe with fluency part-whole relationships for numbers up to 5; and (b) investigate and describe part-whole relationships for numbers up to 10.	**Learning Intention:** I am learning about part-whole relationships with numbers.					**Vocabulary** part, whole, compose, decompose, solution
	How will I know when I have it? The following mastery levels will let you know how you are progressing toward this learning goal.					**Prior Knowledge** counting
	Level 4	*Level 3*	*Level 2*	*Level 1*	*Level 0*	
	I was able to represent numbers in a variety of configurations and in a variety of ways to solve the problem and explain the process for completing the task.	I was able to represent numbers in a variety of configurations and in a variety of ways to solve the problem. However, I struggled to explain the process for completing the task.	I was able to represent numbers in a limited number of ways to solve only specific types of problems. I struggled to explain the process for completing the task.	I was able to represent numbers one way and solve only a specific type of problem. I could not explain the process for completing the task.	I am not able to represent numbers in a variety of configurations and in a variety of ways to solve the problem. I could not explain the process for completing the task.	

Source: **Adapted from** Ashley Norris, Mathematics Teacher, Columbia County Public Schools, Georgia

Figure 5.2

 This lesson plan is available for download at **resources.corwin.com/vlmathematics-k-2**.

Video 16
Assessing Student Progress and Planning Next Steps

https://resources.corwin.com/vlmathematics-k-2

learner's progress toward a learning intention, whereas an evaluation of mastery provides *evidence that a student has demonstrated mastery* of a standard or set of standards.

The difference between checks for understanding and evaluating for mastery lies in the focus of the task, as well as the use of the evidence. In a check for understanding, teachers and students are gathering evidence about learning around specific learning intentions and success criteria (see Figure 5.4).

Mr. Southall, Ms. McLellan, and Ms. Busching had multiple checks for understanding throughout their lessons. In each of their classrooms,

EXAMPLES OF LEVELS OF PROFICIENCY FOR SPECIFIC CONTENT STANDARDS

	Mathematics Content Standard	Levels of Proficiency—Progress Toward Mastery
Mr. Southall	**From Chapter 3:** The student will identify, describe, extend, create, and transfer repeating patterns. The student will (a) count forward orally by ones from 0 to 100; (b) count backward orally by ones when given any number between 1 and 10; (c) identify the number after, without counting, when given any number between 0 and 100 and identify the number before, without counting, when given any number between 1 and 10; and (d) count forward by tens to determine the total number of objects to 100.	**Level 1:** Shows minimal attempt on the problem (guess and check); has no clear problem-solving approach; provides no reasoning with the answer; or provides no answer. **Level 2:** Shows signs of coherent problem solving; gives minimal evidence to support the answer; fails to address some of the constraints of the problem; occasionally makes sense of quantities in relationships in the problem; has trouble generalizing or using the mathematical results. **Level 3:** Response shows the main elements of solving the problem and an organized approach to solving the problem; there are errors, but of a kind that the student could well fix, with more time for checking and revision and some limited help; makes sense of quantities and their relationships in the specific situation; response uses assumptions, definitions, and previously established results. **Level 4:** Shows understanding and use of stated assumptions, definitions, and previously established results in construction arguments; makes conjectures and builds a logical progression of statements; routinely interprets mathematical results in the context of the situation and reflects on whether the results make sense; communication is precise, using definitions clearly.
Ms. McLellan	**From Chapter 4:** Use the meaning of the equal sign to determine if equations are true and give examples of equations that are true (e.g., $4 = 4$, $6 = 7 - 1$, $6 + 3 = 3 + 6$, and $7 + 2 = 5 + 4$). Determine the unknown whole number in an addition or subtraction equation (e.g., $7 + ? = 13$). Compare two two-digit numbers by using symbols $<$, $=$, and $>$ and justify the comparison based on the number of tens and ones.	**Level 1:** Shows minimal attempt on the problem (guess and check); has no clear problem-solving approach; provides no reasoning with the answer; or provides no answer. **Level 2:** Shows signs of coherent problem solving; gives minimal evidence to support the answer; fails to address some of the constraints of the problem; occasionally makes sense of quantities in relationships in the problem; has trouble generalizing or using the mathematical results. **Level 3:** Response shows the main elements of solving the problem and an organized approach to solving the problem; there are errors, but of a kind that the student could well fix, with more time for checking and revision and some limited help; makes sense of quantities and their relationships in the

(Continued)

(Continued)

	Mathematics Content Standard	Levels of Proficiency—Progress Toward Mastery
	Decompose numbers and use the commutative and associative properties of addition to develop addition and subtraction strategies including (making 10's and counting on from the larger number) to add and subtract basic facts within 20 (e.g., decomposing to make 10, $7 + 5 = 7 + 3 + 2 = 10 + 2 = 12$; using the commutative property to count on $2 + 6 = 6 + 2$; and using the associative property to make 10, $5 + 3 + 7 = 5 + (3 + 7) = 5 + 10$). Use two-dimensional shapes (e.g., rectangles, squares, trapezoids, triangles, half-circles, and quartercircles) to compose and describe new shapes.	specific situation; response uses assumptions, definitions, and previously established results. **Level 4:** Shows understanding and use of stated assumptions, definitions, and previously established results in construction arguments; makes conjectures and builds a logical progression of statements; routinely interprets mathematical results in the context of the situation and reflects on whether the results make sense; communication is precise, using definitions clearly.
Ms. Busching	**From Chapter 2:** Add and subtract within 1,000, using concrete models or drawings and strategies based on place value, properties of operations, and/or the relationship between addition and subtraction; relate the strategy to a written method. Understand that in adding or subtracting three-digit numbers, one adds or subtracts hundreds and hundreds, tens and tens, ones and ones; and sometimes it is necessary to compose or decompose tens or hundreds. Mentally add 10 or 100 to a given number 100–900, and mentally subtract 10 or 100 from a given number 100–900. Explain why addition and subtraction strategies work, using place value and the properties of operations.	**Level 1:** No solution is provided, or the solution has no relationship to the task; solution addresses none of the mathematical components presented in the task; inappropriate concepts are applied and/or procedures are used. **Level 2:** Solution is not complete, indicating that parts of the problem are not understood; solution addresses some, but not all, of the mathematical components presented in the task. **Level 3:** Solution shows that the student has a broad understanding of the problem and the major concepts necessary for its solution; solution addresses all of the components presented in the task. **Level 4:** Solution shows a deep understanding of the problem, including the ability to identify the appropriate mathematical concepts and the information necessary for its solution; solution completely addresses all mathematical components presented in the task; solution puts to use the underlying mathematical concepts upon which the task is designed.

Figure 5.3

RELATIONSHIP BETWEEN LEARNING INTENTIONS AND CHECKS FOR UNDERSTANDING

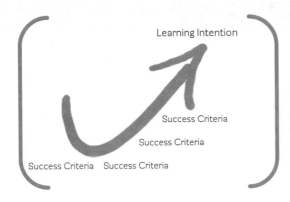

Learning Intention

Success Criteria

Success Criteria

Success Criteria   Success Criteria

Checks for
Understanding
gather and provide *evidence
of learners' progress* toward
a learning intention using the
success criteria as guides for
this progression.

Figure 5.4

learners engaged in checks for understanding that targeted the specific learning intentions and success criteria for the lesson.

Although we can use formative assessments collected over time to evaluate mastery—evidence over time—our classrooms require single tasks that evaluate mastery (e.g., performance-based learning tasks and well-designed standardized tests). These tasks evaluate student mastery by focusing on the standard(s), asking learners to assimilate all of the learning into *a challenging mathematics task* (sometimes called a *rich mathematical task*) (Hattie et al., 2017). Again, evaluating student mastery brings together multiple concepts, procedures, and applications into a single task rather than rich tasks that target specific success criteria within a standard or standards. These tasks can include, but are not limited to, performance-based learning tasks and well-designed standardized tests (see Figure 5.5).

Figure 5.6 includes a checklist useful in creating assessment of mastery. As Ms. Paulson says,

> After we map out how we are going to make sure our kindergartens have "got it," we each take time to ensure

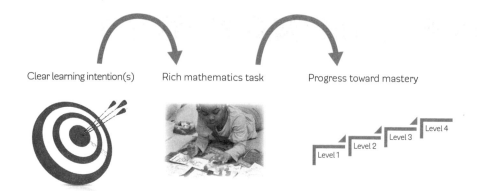

Clear learning intention(s)   Rich mathematics task   Progress toward mastery

Level 1 · Level 2 · Level 3 · Level 4

Source: Samarskaya/iStock.com

Figure 5.5

that the assessment will tell us what we want and need to know about our learners. In other words, we often discuss what learners might do with this task and how we can provide enough guidance to keep them on track, but not so much guidance that we no longer know if they have mastered the learning. After all, this is the evidence or proof that suggests students are mastering content or when students need more learning.

A poorly designed task washes out the benefit of determining learner mastery. For example, a group of teachers were looking to see if learners could compare the properties of two functions represented multiple ways. The teachers developed a sorting and matching task, but that did not provide them with the evidence needed to make a decision about student proficiency. We are not saying that a sorting or matching task never works; however, a sorting task at this time, for this content will not provide the evidence needed to make a decision

CHECKLIST FOR CREATING OR SELECTING TASKS THAT ASSESS MASTERY

All Items

❑ Is this the most appropriate type of item to use for the intended learning outcomes?

❑ Does each item or task require students to demonstrate the performance described in the specific learning outcome it measures (relevance)?

❑ Does each item present a clear and definite task to be performed (clarity)?

❑ Is each item or task presented in simple, readable language and free from excessive verbiage (conciseness)?

❑ Does each item provide an appropriate challenge (ideal difficulty)?

❑ Does each item have an answer that would be agreed upon by experts (correctness)?

❑ Is there a clear basis for awarding partial credit on items or tasks with multiple points (scoring rubric)?

❑ Is each item or task free from technical errors and irrelevant clues (technical soundness)?

❑ Is each test item free from cultural bias?

❑ Have the items been set aside for a time before reviewing them (or being reviewed by a colleague)?

Performance Items

❑ Does the item focus on learning outcomes that require complex cognitive skills and student performances?

❑ Does the task represent both the content, skills, processes, and practices that are central to learning outcomes?

❑ Does the item minimize dependence on skills that are irrelevant to the intended purpose of the assessment task?

❑ Does the task provide the necessary scaffolding for students to be able to understand the task and achieve the task?

❑ Do the directions clearly describe the task?

❑ Are students aware of the basis (expectations) on which their performances will be evaluated in terms of scoring rubrics?

Source: Adapted from Linn, R. L., & Gronlund, N. E. (2000). *Measurement and assessment in teaching* (8th ed.). Upper Saddle River, NJ: Merrill Prentice Hall. Used with permission.

Figure 5.6

online resources ↖ This checklist is available for download at **resources.corwin.com/vlmathematics-k-2**.

about student proficiency. Furthermore, if the task is not engaging and relevant to our students, their level of persistence will likely skew the evidence as well. Whether the evaluation of mastery provides evidence to the teacher and student about the current level of mastery is in the nature of the task itself. In other words, poorly designed tasks yield poor evidence and poor decisions about where to go next.

In order to develop an effective evaluation that provides opportunities for learners to demonstrate mastery while at the same time provides evidence for feedback or next steps, teachers should consider the ways students can make their mathematics thinking visible. What separates a challenging, rich mathematics task from a rote exercise is the nature of the cognitive engagement required to complete the task. In mathematics exercises, learners repeat terms, concepts, ideas, procedures, or processes and apply those in novel situations.

Let us look back to the set of mastery tasks developed by Ms. Paulson and her team. How learners approach these tasks and the thinking these tasks generate provide valuable information to both the teacher and the learners, allowing learners to gain an understanding of where they are in their learning progression, identify where they need to go next in their learning, and what learning tools are needed to support this next step. What do we mean by *challenging, rich mathematics tasks*? There are many definitions:

- Accessible to all learners ("low floor, high ceiling")
- Real-life task or application
- Multiple approaches and representations
- Collaboration and discussion
- Engagement, curiosity, and creativity
- Making connections within and/or across topics and domains, vertically and horizontally
- Opportunities for extension (adapted from Boaler, 2015, 2016; Wolf, 2015)

These tasks are far different from forced-choice items that may only assess the guesswork of mathematics learners. Bringing the previous definitions to life, Antonetti and Garver (2015) reported on data from classroom walk-throughs that focused on eight features that differentiated mathematics tasks from mere rote exercises. Observers measured consistent and sustained engagement when three or more of the features were present. The eight characteristics of challenging mathematics tasks are as follows:

1. **Personal response:** Do students have the opportunity to bring their own personal experiences with mathematics to the task? Examples include any task that invites learners to bring their own background, interests, or expertise to the task. This might be an activity that provides learners with the option to create their own analogies or metaphors, allows them to select how they will share their responses to a question (e.g., writing, drawing, speaking, etc.), or lets them select the context in which a concept is explored (e.g., selection of a specific book or create their own problem). These examples have one thing in common: They allow learners to personalize their responses to meet their background, interests, or expertise. As we evaluate mastery, insight into how learners are making meaning of the conceptual understanding, procedural knowledge, and the application of concepts and thinking skills is important.

2. **Clear and modeled expectations:** Do learners have a clear understanding of what they are supposed to do in this mathematics task? This characteristic refers us to clear learning intentions, success criteria, learning progressions, exemplars, models, worked examples, and rubrics. We will take an additional look at the role of rubrics later in this chapter. Do your learners know what success looks like in this task, or are they blindly hoping to hit the end target that you have in mind for them?

3. **Sense of audience:** Do learners have a sense that this mathematics work matters to someone other than the teacher and the gradebook? Tasks that have a sense of audience mean something to individuals beyond the teacher, which provides authenticity. Sense of audience can be established by cooperative learning or group work in which individual members have specific roles, as in a jigsaw. Other examples include community-based projects or service projects that use mathematics and contribute to the local, school, or classroom community (e.g., analyzing data from a local stream).

> What separates a challenging, rich mathematics task from a rote exercise is the nature of the cognitive engagement required to complete the task.

4. **Social interaction:** Do learners have opportunities to socially interact with their peers? Providing learners with opportunities to talk about mathematics and interact with their peers supports their meaning making and development of conceptual understanding as well as the application of concepts and thinking skills. In addition, teachers and learners get to hear other students' mathematics thinking.

5. **Emotional safety:** Do learners feel safe in asking questions or making mistakes? Even though this task seeks to evaluate the level of mastery in mathematics content, learners must still believe that they will learn from mistakes and that errors are welcomed even at this stage of their learning. To be blunt, if learners feel threatened in your mathematics classroom, they will not engage in any mathematics task.

6. **Choice:** Do learners have choices in how they access the mathematics task? As learners engage with procedures, concepts, or their application, we should offer choices of whom they work with, what materials and manipulatives are available, and what mathematics learning strategies they can use to accomplish the task. In addition, we should offer them multiple ways to show us what they know about the mathematics content.

7. **Novelty:** Does the task require learners to approach the mathematics from a unique perspective? Examples of this characteristic include engaging scenarios, discrepant events, scientific phenomena demonstrations, or games and puzzles.

8. **Authenticity:** Does the task represent an authentic learning experience, or is the experience sterile and unrealistic (e.g., a worksheet, problem-solving scenario)? We can offer learners a scenario around community and school events, have them address STEM tasks that model simple machines and require measurements, or manipulate weather data and interpret trends in weather. (adapted from Schlechty, 2011)

To evaluate the level of mastery in mathematics learning, teachers must design and implement tasks that provide opportunities for learners to truly demonstrate what they know, how they know it, and why they know it.

Ensuring Tasks Evaluate Mastery

Ms. Paulson is preparing to evaluate students' mastery in understanding part-whole relationships and how to visually represent those relationships. Throughout the week, she has used checks for understanding to gather and provide evidence of her learners' progress in the following tasks related to recognizing, describing, and investigating part-whole relationships:

- Composing and decomposing numbers up to 10
- Using five-frames, ten-frames, beads, tiles, toothpicks, dot cards, and beaded number frames to represent parts of numbers
- Identifying and describing pictures of part-whole relationships
- Describing part-whole relationships to peers
- Comparing and contrasting different ways of representing part-whole relationships

She aligned her checks for understanding with the success criteria and specific learning intentions for each lesson. Ms. Paulson's checks for understanding allow her to evaluate her students' progress and adjust their learning experiences, but they do not allow her to determine mastery of the content. Mastery assessments are used more summatively, whereas checks for understanding are used more formatively. But know that assessments are neither formative nor summative by nature; it's all in the use of the tool. And as you will see, the mastery assessments are often used to guide future learning experiences for students. Thus, they are tools that include multiple learning intentions, are typically administered at the unit level, can be used as evidence of longer-term learning, and are often used as the basis for grades. Having said that, if we really believe in mastery, grades would be updated throughout the year as students demonstrate competency of previous content. Thus, the grades for a unit taught in October might be updated when students demonstrate deeper understanding in December. For more information on competency-based or standards-based grading, see Guskey (2014). To design or select a task or possibly a cohesive set of tasks for evaluating mastery, teachers should do the following:

1. Return to the learning intentions and success criteria associated with content for which we are evaluating mastery. What is it that students were supposed to learn?

2. Create or select a challenging mathematics task (or a set of tasks) that requires learners to demonstrate their proficiency for each specific learning intention and success criterion. In other words, can students do what each of the learning intentions says they should be able to do?

3. Identify criteria for mastery and levels of progress toward mastery.

Ensuring Tests Evaluate Mastery

Tasks are great, but there will always be mathematics tests. Tests are not only common in the mathematics classroom, but they can also be an effective means for determining the mastery of learners. The intention and design of any test determines the usefulness of the evidence generated about learner mastery. Whether multiple choice or open ended, tests must provide the necessary evidence about student learning so that both the teacher and the learners can make a clear evaluation of their understanding with the specific mathematics content. In designing mathematics tests, we must take into account several aspects of that test if we are to achieve high-quality evaluation of student learning.

The first aspect of a well-designed test is that the test items align with the expectations of the standard and associated learning intentions and success criteria.

Whether in our own classroom or in the classrooms of the teachers featured in this book, a test designed to evaluate learner mastery must contain questions or items that are consistent with the teaching and learning in that classroom. If the focus in Ms. McLellan's first grade classroom is on explaining the meaning of the equal sign, representing and describing equal values, and determining the unknown whole number, then an end-of-unit or standard test cannot contain items that solely focus on conceptual understanding or application to provide a clear evaluation of student mastery (e.g., explaining the meaning of the equal sign). Likewise, if the focus in Ms. McLellan's class is on the conceptual understanding of the equal sign and comparing values on each side of the equal sign, a test for mastery cannot contain items that only focus on determining the unknown whole number. Therefore, the first aspect of a well-designed test is that the test items align with the expectations of the standard and associated learning intentions and success criteria.

Test items should provide learners with the opportunity to demonstrate different levels of mastery. In addition to having test items that align with the expectations of the standard, a well-designed test will have questions that fall in the progression toward the standard.

In addition, the test might ask learners to explain how each approach allows them to support their solution. Including the components that build up to the standard will allow Ms. Busching, for example, to determine how much learners have mastered if they have not fully mastered the standard.

As we reflect on our days as elementary mathematics students, we can likely recall instances in which we missed questions on a test because we were not clear on what the questions were asking us to do. When we received feedback on the test, we may have responded to that feedback with, "Oh, that's what you wanted on number 15?" Using consistent language on a test is vital in evaluating the learning of mathematics compared to semantics. As students engage in mathematics learning, we must ensure that the language we expect them to master is the language we use in the learning experiences. For example, if Ms. Busching plans to include questions on her test that use the terms *combining*, *separating*, and *comparing*, then these concepts should be introduced during the learning experiences. Likewise, if she is going to use *associative property*, *commutative property*, or other terms for adding and subtracting larger numbers, learners need experiences with that vocabulary or terminology. Using consistent language applies to the cognitive aspects of the questions as well. We must ensure learners know what we mean by *analyze*, *explain*, or *support your answer.*

Figure 5.7 provides additional guidelines for developing well-designed tests. These checklists help to ensure that our tests provide clear evidence about our learners' mastery in mathematics.

If our ultimate goal is for students to see themselves as their own mathematics teacher, we have to devote time to helping them prepare for assessments. Simply telling our learners to "pay attention" or "practice" is not enough to support them in their journey to becoming assessment-capable visible learners in mathematics. As you can see, we have come full circle in this book. Ensuring that learners have clarity about the learning intentions, success criteria, and their progress toward those items will then help them prepare for this evaluation of mastery. Providing learners with opportunities to connect the learning intentions and success

Teaching Takeaway

There should be items on the test that build up to the standard or mastery level.

Teaching Takeaway

Students should be familiar with the language of the test.

CHECKLISTS FOR CREATING TESTS THAT ASSESS MASTERY

Short-Answer Items

❑ Can the items be answered with a number, symbol, word, or brief phrase?

❑ Has textbook language been avoided?

❑ Have the items been stated so that only one response is correct?

❑ Are the answer blanks equal in length (for fill-in responses)?

❑ Are the answer blanks (preferably one per item) at the end of the items, preferably after a question?

❑ Are the items free of clues (such as *a* or *an*)?

❑ Has the degree of precision been indicated for numerical answers?

❑ Have the units been indicated when numerical answers are expressed in units?

Binary (True–False) and Multiple-Binary Items

❑ Can each statement be clearly judged true or false with only one concept per statement?

❑ Have specific determiners (e.g., *usually, always*) been avoided?

❑ Have trivial statements been avoided?

❑ Have negative statements (especially double negatives) been avoided?

❑ Does a superficial analysis suggest a wrong answer?

❑ Are opinion statements attributed to some source?

❑ Are the true and false items approximately equal in length?

❑ Is there approximately an equal number of true and false items?

❑ Has a detectable pattern of answers (e.g., *T, F, T, F*) been avoided?

Matching Items

❑ Is the material for the two lists homogeneous?

❑ Is the list of responses longer or shorter than the list of premises?

❑ Are the responses brief and on the right-hand side?

❑ Have the responses been placed in alphabetical or numerical order?

❑ Do the directions indicate the basis for matching?

❑ Do the directions indicate how many times each response may be used?

❑ Are all of the matching items on the same page?

Multiple-Choice Items
❑ Does each item stem present a meaningful problem?
❑ Is there too much information in the stem?
❑ Are the item stems free of irrelevant material?
❑ Are the item stems stated in positive terms (if possible)?
❑ If used, has negative wording been given special emphasis (e.g., capitalized)?
❑ Are the distractors brief and free of unnecessary words?
❑ Are the distractors similar in length and form to the answer?
❑ Is there only one correct or clearly best answer?
❑ Are the distractors based on specific misconceptions?
❑ Are the items free of clues that point to the answer?
❑ Are the distractors and answer presented in sensible (e.g., alphabetical, numerical) order?
❑ Has *all of the above* been avoided and *none of the above* used judiciously?
❑ If a stimulus is used, is it necessary for answering the item?
❑ If a stimulus is used, does it require use of skills sought to be assessed?

Source: Adapted from Linn, R. L., & Gronlund, N. E. (2000). *Measurement and assessment in teaching* (8th ed.). Upper Saddle River, NJ: Merrill Prentice Hall. Used with permission.

Figure 5.7

online resources These checklists are available for download at **resources.corwin.com/vlmathematics-k-2**.

criteria to the type of question they will likely see on an assessment encourages them to take ownership of their mathematics learning.

Feedback for Mastery

With the learning intention clear, a definition of *success* established, and a challenging mathematics assessment of mastery developed and implemented, the next key item is feedback. The nature of the feedback on learners' performance is an essential and necessary component in the Visible Learning mathematics classroom. Depending on the level

Teaching Takeaway

We must help our learners understand what it means to prepare to show what they know.

of proficiency demonstrated by the learner, specific, constructive, and timely feedback supports learners as they—together with the teacher—evaluate where they are going, how they are going, and where they are going next (see Hattie & Timperley, 2007).

Task Feedback

For learners at the earliest level of mastery, **task feedback** develops student understanding of specific procedures, concepts, and applications. This type of feedback is corrective, precise, and focused on the accuracy of the learners' responses to the mastery task. For example, Ms. Paulson may provide written or verbal feedback that says, "Take a look at your parts. They do not combine to make 7." She may indicate to a learner that a specific question is wrong and needs revisiting before moving on in the learning. On the other hand, she may point out, "You have correctly decomposed that number and represented the process with counters. Now move on to another number."

Learners rely on task feedback to add additional structure to their conceptual understanding, procedural knowledge, and application of concepts and thinking skills. This may include examples and non-examples, additional learning on procedural steps, and contexts of the task. Ms. Paulson may sit down with a learner who has continued to miss a specific type of problem and provide additional deliberate instruction and examples. She may even provide two examples and ask the learner to compare and contrast them to clarify understanding. Each learner's successful assimilation of feedback, and thus use of the feedback to decide where to go next, rests solely on whether each learner understands what the feedback means and how he or she can use it to move forward with mathematics learning. Effective feedback (Figure 5.8) and effective use of that feedback supports this initial learning.

Process Feedback

As learners begin to develop proficiency with specific content, ideas, and terms, the feedback should increasingly shift to process feedback. **Process feedback** is critical as learners explore the *why* and the *how* of specific mathematics content. In their initial assessment of mastery, learners received and assimilated task feedback into their work to develop a

Task feedback addresses how well the task has been performed—correct or incorrect.

Depending on the level of proficiency demonstrated by the learner, specific, constructive, and timely feedback supports learners as they—together with the teacher—evaluate where they are going, how they are going, and where they are going next.

Process feedback focuses on the strategies needed to perform the task.

ELEMENTS OF EFFECTIVE FEEDBACK

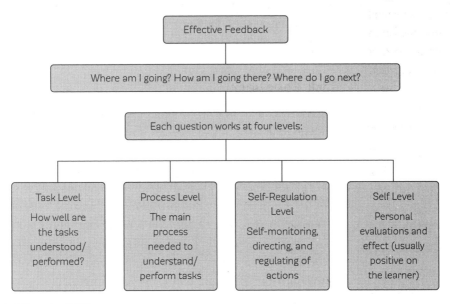

Source: Hattie & Timperley (2007).

Figure 5.8

deeper understanding of procedures, concepts, and applications. To move learners beyond what is simply right or wrong, example or non-example, they must receive and incorporate feedback that focuses on the processes or strategies associated with accomplishing the specific task. Returning to Ms. Paulson's classroom, she may not indicate whether a particular response is correct or incorrect, but she might simply ask, "Why do you believe that this is the best way to represent the number? Why did you make that choice? How could you check your work?"

Whether from the teacher or peers, learners should receive feedback on their thinking, not just the accuracy of their response. For example, teachers might engage students in further dialogue about the use of specific strategies to solve a particular problem. Again, this feedback can come from the teacher or their peers. For example, Figure 5.9 shows an example of peer-assisted reflection (PAR) (Almarode, Fisher, Assof, Hattie, & Frey, 2019). In this scenario, learners complete their task—along with

Teaching Takeaway

Feedback should answer three questions for the learner: Where am I going? How am I going? Where am I going next?

Success Criteria

[ ] I can make sense of the magnitude of large numbers by noticing, wondering, and representing their values.

[ ] I can decompose and compose quantities to efficiently add and subtract.

[ ] I can apply the commutative and associative properties to addition of large numbers.

[ ] I can transfer and revise efficient strategies for addition and subtraction of large numbers.

The Challenging Mathematics Task

What do you wonder?

What do you notice?

Life Spans	
Animal	Maximum Life Span (in years)
Koi	226
Giant Tortoise	225
Bowhead Whale	210
Red Sea Urchin	200
Tuatara	150
Lobster	140
Box Turtle	123
Human	122
Crocodile	100
Carp	100
Cockatoo	92
Tarantula	49
Dog	29

1. Create your own addition and subtraction problems using these data. Consider all the unknown values and actions possible in problems.

2. Test strategies you know from the anchor charts to solve the problems you create.

3. Research and share new data to include and ask questions about.

Reviewed by: _____

Rate your peer's mastery of the success criterion (this is the *last* thing you do):

[ ] I can make sense of the magnitude of large numbers by noticing, wondering, and representing their values.

0—DO NOT check that box	1—ALMOST check that box	2—CHECK that box
Many mathematical errors and/ or incomplete or unclear annotations	Few mathematical errors and/ or somewhat incomplete or unclear annotations	No mathematical errors and/or perfectly complete and clear annotations

[ ] I can decompose and compose quantities to efficiently add and subtract.

0—DO NOT check that box	1—ALMOST check that box	2—CHECK that box

[ ] I can apply the commutative and associative properties to addition of large numbers.

0—DO NOT check that box	1—ALMOST check that box	2—CHECK that box

[ ] I can transfer and revise efficient strategies for addition and subtraction of large numbers.

0—DO NOT check that box	1—ALMOST check that box	2—CHECK that box

DRAFT SOLUTION

ANNOTATIONS (author's and peer's)

REVISED SOLUTION

ANNOTATIONS (author's only)

Figure 5.9

 This peer-assisted reflection task is available for download at **resources.corwin.com/vlmathematics-k-2**.

EFFECT SIZE FOR ASSESSMENT-CAPABLE VISIBLE LEARNERS = 1.33

Video 17
Developing Conceptual Learning in a Buddy Lesson

https://resources.corwin.com/vlmathematics-k-2

their mathematics story that explains the process for completing the task (not just *what* they did, by *why* they did it)—that is ready to be reviewed by a peer. The peer feedback is offered in two phases. First, peers provide each other written feedback in the form of annotations and a rating toward mastery of each success criterion during a silent review phase. Second, peers discuss the written feedback they provided and ask any clarifying questions they might have about that feedback. The final step for students is to revise their draft solution into a final submission and include a reflection of how their thinking changed throughout this process. Let's look at how Ms. Busching might use PAR when helping her learners give and receive feedback on the transfer of strategies for adding and subtracting small numbers and large numbers.

The PAR cycle gives students the opportunity to compare and contrast: T*his is what I used to be able to do; this is what I can do now. This is how I used to think about this problem; this is how I think about it now. This is what I used to know; this is what I know now.* In addition to these before-and-after snapshots, the feedback and annotation components of PARs can collect much of the connective tissue that bridged students from where they were to where they are. In other words, not only does growth as an outcome become blatant to students, but students become aware of their own growth process as well.

Process feedback supports making connections, use of multiple strategies, self-explanation, self-monitoring, self-questioning, and critical thinking. For example, Ms. Paulson may ask the learner what strategies he or she used in making the decisions about specific numbers and problems and ask if the strategy worked well or if a different strategy may be more efficient. Rather than focusing solely on the correct answer regarding the relationship between an independent and a dependent variable, a teacher may ask a student, "What is your explanation for your answer?" The focus of process feedback is on the relationships between ideas, students' strategies for evaluating the reasonableness of an answer or solution, explicitly learning from mistakes, and helping the learner identify different strategies for addressing a task.

Like task feedback, process feedback should be specific and constructive and should support learners' pathways toward self-regulation feedback. That is, the feedback should deepen thinking, reasoning, explanations, and connections. Does the teacher prompt learners through strategic questioning related to the learning process? What appears to be wrong, and why? What approach or strategies did the learner use or apply to the task? What is an explanation for the answer, response, or solution? What are the relationships with other parts of the task?

Self-Regulation Feedback

Self-regulation feedback is the learner knowing what to do when she or he approaches a new and different problem, is stuck, or has to apply concepts and thinking in a new way. Learners who have reached a deep level of conceptual understanding and are armed with multiple strategies are equipped to self-regulate as they transfer their learning to more rigorous tasks. Highly proficient learners benefit from self-regulation feedback, although this is not the only type of feedback that is important to these learners. For example, when teachers detect a misconception or notice a gap in foundational or background learning, learners benefit from both task and process feedback in these situations. However, a majority of the feedback at this part of the learning process should be self-regulation through meta-cognition. The teacher's role in the feedback at this level is to ask questions to prompt further meta-cognition.

Eventually, learners practice meta-cognition independently through self-verbalization, self-questioning, and self-reflection. Ms. Paulson recalls a student working diligently on the first part of the mastery task at the beginning of this chapter. Midway through the task, the learner stopped and began to erase his work, stating, "This answer does not make sense with the number story, and I don't think this is right. It must be wrong. I need to start again." Learners take personal ownership of their learning, which provides increased motivation and understanding. This has been and continues to be a well-documented finding in education research (e.g., National Research Council, 2000). The ability to think about your own thinking promotes learners' self-awareness, problem solving around the learning task, and understanding of what they need to do to complete the task.

Self-regulation feedback involves the learner self-monitoring his or her own progress toward a specific goal.

EFFECT SIZE FOR SELF-VERBALIZATION AND SELF-QUESTIONING = 0.55 AND EVALUATION AND REFLECTION = 0.75

The ability to think about your own thinking promotes learners' self-awareness, problem solving around the learning task, and understanding of what they need to do to complete the task.

To reiterate, assessment-capable visible learners know what to do when they get stuck, when a new challenge arises, and when their teacher may not be available to help. This is self-regulation feedback.

Conclusion

Over the course of this book, we set out to portray the teaching of mathematics in the Visible Learning classroom. This brought together three elements of mathematics learning (conceptual understanding, procedural knowledge, and the application of concepts and thinking skills) with three phases of learning: surface, deep, and transfer.

Visible mathematics learning is an attainable goal when mathematics teachers *see* learning through the eyes of their students and students *see* themselves as their own mathematics teachers. Together, this type of learning environment develops assessment-capable visible learners. These learners can do the following:

1. Know their current level of mathematics learning

2. Know where they are going next in meeting their current mathematics learning goals and are confident to take on the challenge

3. Select the most appropriate tools, problem-solving approaches, and skills to guide their learning

4. Seek feedback and recognize errors are opportunities to enhance their mathematics learning

5. Monitor their progress and adjust their mathematics learning

6. Recognize their learning and support their peers in their own mathematics learning journey

Teaching mathematics in the Visible Learning classroom demands as much from the teacher as from the learner. We have to create a learning environment that promotes clarity in learning, provides challenging mathematics tasks, checks for understanding, and enables a clear evaluation of mastery. We must know our impact on learning! Yes, there will be days that are better than others. Learning will be stronger with some content than other content. On the most successful days, celebrate the learning that your students do. On days when there is a less-than-desirable impact on student learning, stay focused on the main thing. We keep the main thing *the main thing* by recalibrating our mindframes about teaching and learning in the mathematics classroom. We can do this by asking ourselves these recalibrating questions:

1. What do I want my students to learn?

2. What evidence will convince me that they have learned it?

3. How will I check learners' understanding and progress?

4. What tasks will get my students to mastery?

5. How will I adjust the rigor of the tasks to meet the needs of all learners?

6. What resources do I need?

7. How will I manage the learning?

The classrooms of Mr. Southall, Ms. McLellan, Ms. Busching, and Ms. Paulson do just that daily (Figures 5.10 through 5.12 on the next page).

MR. SOUTHALL'S VISIBLE LEARNING IN THE MATHEMATICS CLASSROOM

Conceptual Understanding: the ways patterns repeat, grow, and shrink—the mathematical behavior of patterns.

Procedural Knowledge: representing patterns multiple ways; repeating the core and finding the rules of a pattern.

Application: decomposing and composing numbers using benchmarks of fives and tens.

Figure 5.10

MS. MCLELLAN'S VISIBLE LEARNING IN THE MATHEMATICS CLASSROOM

Conceptual Understanding: the meaning of the equal sign.

Procedural Knowledge: how to represent mathematical relationships—how to express and defend those relationships.

Application: how known values help in determining the unknown values and the reasonableness of values.

Figure 5.11

MS. BUSCHING'S VISIBLE LEARNING IN THE MATHEMATICS CLASSROOM

Conceptual Understanding: the meaning of addition as the combining of numbers

Procedural Knowledge: inverse relationship of addition and subtraction.

Application: how strategies for adding and subtracting small numbers can be transferred and revised to add and subtract large numbers.

Figure 5.12

Final Reflection

Summarizing the content in this book, reflect on the following questions:

1. Using a specific standard or standards for an upcoming unit, describe what mastery would look like for that content.

2. How will you check for understanding as your learners progress toward mastery? How will these checks be different from your evaluation of their mastery of the standard or standards?

3. How do you plan to evaluate mastery of this particular content—task, test, or both?

4. Reflect on a recent mathematics task in your classroom. Using the definition and characteristics from this chapter, does it "qualify" as a challenging mathematics task?

5. Explain the role of feedback in supporting your learners' journey to mastery.

Appendix A

Effect Sizes

The Visible Learning research synthesizes findings from **1,800** meta-analyses of **80,000** studies involving **300** million students, into what works best in education.

STUDENT		ES
Prior knowledge and background		
Field independence	◐	0.68
Non-standard dialect use	○	−0.29
Piagetian programs	●	1.28
Prior ability	●	0.94
Prior achievement	◐	0.55
Relating creativity to achievement	◐	0.40
Relations of high school to university achievement	◐	0.60
Relations of high school achievement to career performance	●	0.38
Assessment-capable visible learners	●	1.33
Working memory strength	◐	0.57
Beliefs, attitudes, and dispositions		
Attitude to content domains	●	0.35
Concentration/persistence/engagement	◐	0.56
Grit/incremental vs. entity thinking	●	0.25
Mindfulness	●	0.29
Morning vs. evening	◔	0.12
Perceived task value	◐	0.46
Positive ethnic self-identity	◔	0.12
Positive self-concept	◐	0.41
Self-efficacy	●	0.92
Stereotype threat	○	−0.33
Student personality attributes	●	0.26
Motivational approach, orientation		
Achieving motivation and approach	◐	0.44
Boredom	○	−0.49
Deep motivation and approach	◐	0.69
Depression	○	−0.36
Lack of stress	◔	0.17
Mastery goals	◔	0.06
Motivation	◐	0.42
Performance goals	○	−0.01
Reducing anxiety	◐	0.42
Surface motivation and approach	○	−0.11
Physical influences		
ADHD	○	−0.90
ADHD – treatment with drugs	●	0.32
Breastfeeding	◔	0.04
Deafness	○	−0.61
Exercise/relaxation	●	0.26
Gender on achievement	◔	0.08
Lack of illness	●	0.26
Lack of sleep	○	−0.05
Full compared to pre-term/low birth weight	◐	0.57
Relative age within a class	◐	0.45

CURRICULA		ES
Reading, writing, and the arts		
Comprehensive instructional programs for teachers	●	0.72
Comprehension programs	◐	0.47
Drama/arts programs	●	0.38
Exposure to reading	◐	0.43
Music programs	●	0.37
Phonics instruction	●	0.70
Repeated reading programs	●	0.75
Second/third chance programs	◐	0.53
Sentence combining programs	◔	0.15
Spelling programs	◐	0.58
Visual-perception programs	◐	0.55
Vocabulary programs	◐	0.62
Whole language approach	◔	0.06
Writing programs	◐	0.45
Math and sciences		
Manipulative materials on math	●	0.30
Mathematics programs	◐	0.59
Science programs	◐	0.48
Use of calculators	●	0.27
Other curricula programs		
Bilingual programs	●	0.36
Career interventions	●	0.38
Chess instruction	●	0.34
Conceptual change programs	●	0.99
Creativity programs	◐	0.62
Diversity courses	◔	0.09
Extra-curricula programs	●	0.20
Integrated curricula programs	◐	0.47
Juvenile delinquent programs	◔	0.12
Motivation/character programs	●	0.34
Outdoor/adventure programs	◐	0.43
Perceptual-motor programs	◔	0.08
Play programs	◐	0.50
Social skills programs	●	0.39
Tactile stimulation programs	◐	0.58

Access the complete and most recent versions of the influence chart at: https://www.visiblelearningplus.com/content/research-john-hattie

HOME		ES
Family structure		
Adopted vs. non-adopted care	●	0.25
Engaged vs. disengaged fathers	●	0.20
Intact (two-parent) families	●	0.23
Other family structure	◔	0.16
Home environment		
Corporal punishment in the home	○	−0.33
Early years' interventions	◉	0.44
Home visiting	●	0.29
Moving between schools	○	−0.34
Parental autonomy support	◔	0.15
Parental involvement	◉	0.50
Parental military deployment	○	−0.16
Positive family/home dynamics	◉	0.52
Television	○	−0.18
Family resources		
Family on welfare/state aid	○	−0.12
Non-immigrant background	◔	0.01
Parental employment	◔	0.03
Socio-economic status	◉	0.52

SCHOOL		ES
Leadership		
Collective teacher efficacy	◉	1.57
Principals/school leaders	●	0.32
School climate	●	0.32
School resourcing		
External accountability systems	●	0.31
Finances	●	0.21
Types of school		
Charter schools	◔	0.09
Religious schools	●	0.24
Single-sex schools	◔	0.08
Summer school	●	0.23
Summer vacation effect	○	−0.02
School compositional effects		
College halls of residence	◔	0.05
Desegregation	●	0.28
Diverse student body	◔	0.10
Middle schools' interventions	◔	0.08
Out-of-school curricula experiences	●	0.26
School choice programs	◔	0.12
School size (600-900 students at secondary)	◉	0.43
Other school factors		
Counseling effects	●	0.35
Generalized school effects	◉	0.48
Modifying school calendars/timetables	◔	0.09
Pre-school programs	●	0.28
Suspension/expelling students	○	−0.20

CLASSROOM		ES
Classroom composition effects		
Detracking	◔	0.09
Mainstreaming/inclusion	●	0.27
Multi-grade/age classes	◔	0.04
Open vs. traditional classrooms	◔	0.01
Reducing class size	●	0.21
Retention (holding students back)	○	−0.32
Small group learning	◉	0.47
Tracking/streaming	◔	0.12
Within class grouping	◔	0.18
School curricula for gifted students		
Ability grouping for gifted students	●	0.30
Acceleration programs	◉	0.68
Enrichment programs	◉	0.53
Classroom influences		
Background music	◔	0.10
Behavioral intervention programs	◉	0.62
Classroom management	●	0.35
Cognitive behavioral programs	●	0.29
Decreasing disruptive behavior	●	0.34
Mentoring	◔	0.12
Positive peer influences	◉	0.53
Strong classroom cohesion	◉	0.44
Students feeling disliked	○	−0.19

TEACHER		ES
Teacher attributes		
Average teacher effects	●	0.32
Teacher clarity	●	0.75
Teacher credibility	●	0.90
Teacher estimates of achievement	●	1.29
Teacher expectations	◉	0.43
Teacher personality attributes	◉	0.23
Teacher performance pay	◔	0.05
Teacher verbal ability	●	0.22
Teacher-student interactions		
Student rating of quality of teaching	◉	0.50
Teachers not labeling students	◉	0.61
Teacher-student relationships	◉	0.52
Teacher education		
Initial teacher training programs	◔	0.12
Micro-teaching/video review of lessons	◉	0.88
Professional development programs	◉	0.41
Teacher subject matter knowledge	◔	0.11

Key for rating

◉	Potential to considerably accelerate student achievement
◉	Potential to accelerate student achievement
●	Likely to have positive impact on student achievement
◔	Likely to have small positive impact on student achievement
○	Likely to have a negative impact on student achievement
ES	Effect size calculated using Cohen's *d*

visible learning^plus™

corwin.com/visiblelearning

Access the complete and most recent versions of the influence chart at: https://www.visiblelearningplus.com/content/research-john-hattie

The Visible Learning research synthesizes findings from **1,800** meta-analyses of **80,000** studies involving **300** million students, into what works best in education.

TEACHING: Focus on student learning strategies		ES
Strategies emphasizing student meta-cognitive/self-regulated learning		
Elaboration and organization	●	0.75
Elaborative interrogation	○	0.42
Evaluation and reflection	●	0.75
Meta-cognitive strategies	○	0.60
Help seeking	●	0.72
Self-regulation strategies	○	0.52
Self-verbalization and self-questioning	○	0.55
Strategy monitoring	○	0.58
Transfer strategies	●	0.86
Student-focused interventions		
Aptitude/treatment interactions	◌	0.19
Individualized instruction	●	0.23
Matching style of learning	●	0.31
Student-centered teaching	●	0.36
Student control over learning	○	0.02
Strategies emphasizing student perspectives in learning		
Peer tutoring	○	0.53
Volunteer tutors	●	0.26
Learning strategies		
Deliberate practice	●	0.79
Effort	●	0.77
Imagery	○	0.45
Interleaved practice	●	0.21
Mnemonics	●	0.76
Note taking	◌	0.50
Outlining and transforming	○	0.66
Practice testing	○	0.54
Record keeping	○	0.52
Rehearsal and memorization	●	0.73
Spaced vs. mass practice	○	0.60
Strategy to integrate with prior knowledge	●	0.93
Study skills	○	0.46
Summarization	●	0.79
Teaching test taking and coaching	●	0.30
Time on task	○	0.49
Underlining and highlighting	○	0.50

TEACHING: Focus on teaching/instructional strategies		ES
Strategies emphasizing learning intentions		
Appropriately challenging goals	○	0.59
Behavioral organizers	○	0.42
Clear goal intentions	○	0.48
Cognitive task analysis	●	1.29
Concept mapping	○	0.64
Goal commitment	○	0.40
Learning goals vs. no goals	○	0.68
Learning hierarchies-based approach	◌	0.19
Planning and prediction	●	0.76
Setting standards for self-judgement	○	0.62
Strategies emphasizing success criteria		
Mastery learning	○	0.57
Worked examples	●	0.37
Strategies emphasizing feedback		
Classroom discussion	●	0.82
Different types of testing	◌	0.12
Feedback	●	0.70
Providing formative evaluation	○	0.48
Questioning	○	0.48
Response to intervention	●	1.29
Teaching/instructional strategies		
Adjunct aids	●	0.32
Collaborative learning	●	0.34
Competitive vs. individualistic learning	●	0.24
Cooperative learning	○	0.40
Cooperative vs. competitive learning	○	0.53
Cooperative vs. individualistic learning	○	0.55
Direct/deliberate instruction	○	0.60
Discovery-based teaching	●	0.21
Explicit teaching strategies	○	0.57
Humor	◌	0.04
Inductive teaching	○	0.44
Inquiry-based teaching	○	0.40
Jigsaw method	●	1.20
Philosophy in schools	○	0.43
Problem-based learning	●	0.26
Problem-solving teaching	○	0.68
Reciprocal teaching	●	0.74
Scaffolding	●	0.82
Teaching communication skills and strategies	○	0.43

Access the complete and most recent versions of the influence chart at: https://www.visiblelearningplus.com/content/research-john-hattie

TEACHING: Focus on implementation method		ES
Implementations using technologies		
Clickers	●	0.22
Gaming/simulations	●	0.35
Information communications technology (ICT)	◐	0.47
Intelligent tutoring systems	◐	0.48
Interactive video methods	◐	0.54
Mobile phones	●	0.37
One-on-one laptops	◌	0.16
Online and digital tools	●	0.29
Programmed instruction	●	0.23
Technology in distance education	◌	0.01
Technology in mathematics	●	0.33
Technology in other subjects	◐	0.55
Technology in reading/literacy	●	0.29
Technology in science	●	0.23
Technology in small groups	●	0.21
Technology in writing	◐	0.42
Technology with college students	◐	0.42
Technology with elementary students	◐	0.44
Technology with high school students	●	0.30
Technology with learning needs students	◐	0.57
Use of PowerPoint	●	0.26
Visual/audio-visual methods	●	0.22
Web-based learning	◌	0.18
Implementations using out-of-school learning		
After-school programs	◐	0.40
Distance education	◌	0.13
Home-school programs	◌	0.16
Homework	●	0.29
Service learning	◐	0.58
Implementations that emphasize school-wide teaching strategies		
Co- or team teaching	◌	0.19
Interventions for students with learning needs	●	0.77
Student support programs – college	●	0.21
Teaching creative thinking	●	0.34
Whole-school improvement programs	●	0.28

Key for rating

◐ Potential to considerably accelerate student achievement

◐ Potential to accelerate student achievement

● Likely to have positive impact on student achievement

◌ Likely to have small positive impact on student achievement

○ Likely to have a negative impact on student achievement

ES Effect size calculated using Cohen's *d*

Appendix B

Teaching for Clarity Planning Guide

Teaching for Clarity PLANNING GUIDE

ESTABLISHING PURPOSE

1   **What are the key content standards I will focus on in this lesson?**

2   **What are the learning intentions (the goal and *why* of learning, stated in student-friendly language) I will focus on in this lesson?**

Content:

Language:

Social:

3 When will I introduce and reinforce the learning intention(s), so that students understand it, see the relevance, connect it to previous learning, and can clearly communicate it themselves?

SUCCESS CRITERIA

4 What evidence shows that students have mastered the learning intention(s)? What criteria will I use?

I can statements:

5 How will I check students' understanding (assess learning) during instruction and make accommodations?

INSTRUCTION

6 What activities and tasks will move students forward in their learning?

7 What resources (materials and sentence frames) are needed?

8   How will I organize and facilitate the learning? What questions will I ask? How will I initiate closure?

Appendix C

Learning Intentions and Success Criteria Template

Learning Intentions	Conceptual Understanding	Procedural Knowledge	Application of Concepts and Thinking Skills
Unistructural (one idea)			
Multistructural (many ideas)			
Relational (related ideas)			
Extended abstract (extending ideas)			

Success Criteria	Conceptual Understanding	Procedural Knowledge	Application of Concepts and Thinking Skills
Unistructural (one idea)			
Multistructural (many ideas)			
Relational (related ideas)			
Extended abstract (extending ideas)			

Appendix D

A Selection of International Mathematical Practice or Process Standards*

*Note that this is a nonexhaustive list of international mathematical practice/process standards as of June 2016. Because standards are often under review, you can look to your own state or country's individual documents to find the most up-to-date practice/process standards.

USA Common Core State Standards 8 Mathematical Practices[a]	USA Texas Essential Knowledge and Skills TEKS 7 Mathematical Practice Standards[b]	USA Virginia Mathematics 5 Standards of Learning[c]	International Baccalaureate 6 Assessment Objectives[d]	Hong Kong Key Learning Area 7 Generic Skills[e]	Singapore Mathematical Problem-Solving Processes[f]	Australian F-10 Mathematics Curriculum Key Ideas[g]
1. Make sense of problems and persevere in solving them.	A. Apply mathematics to problems arising in everyday life, society, and the workplace.	Mathematical problem solving	Knowledge and understanding	Collaboration skills	Reasoning, communications, and connections	Understanding
2. Reason abstractly and quantitatively.	B. Use a problem-solving model that incorporates analyzing given information, formulating a plan or strategy, determining a solution, justifying the solution, and evaluating the problem-solving process and the reasonableness of the solution.	Mathematical communication	Problem solving	Communication skills	Applications and modeling	Fluency
3. Construct viable arguments and critique the reasoning of others.		Mathematical reasoning	Communication and interpretation	Creativity	Thinking skills and heuristics	Problem solving
4. Use appropriate tools strategically.	C. Select tools, including real objects, manipulatives, paper and pencil, and technology as appropriate.	Mathematical connection	Technology	Critical-thinking skills		Reasoning
5. Attend to precision.		Mathematical representations	Reasoning	Information technology skills		
6. Look for and make use of structure.	D. Communicate mathematical ideas, reasoning, and their implications using multiple representations, including symbols, diagrams, graphs, and language as appropriate.		Inquiry approaches	Numeracy skills		
				Problem-solving skills		

(Continued)

(Continued)

USA Common Core State Standards 8 Mathematical Practices[a]	USA Texas Essential Knowledge and Skills TEKS 7 Mathematical Practice Standards[b]	USA Virginia Mathematics 5 Standards of Learning[c]	International Baccalaureate 6 Assessment Objectives[d]	Hong Kong Key Learning Area 7 Generic Skills[e]	Singapore Mathematical Problem-Solving Processes[f]	Australian F-10 Mathematics Curriculum Key Ideas[g]
7. Look for and express regularity in repeated reasoning.	E. Create and use representations to organize, record, and communicate mathematical ideas.					
8. Model with mathematics.	F. Analyze mathematical relationships to connect and communicate mathematical ideas.					
	G. Display, explain, and justify mathematical ideas and arguments using precise mathematical language in written or oral communication.					

[a] Retrieved June 22, 2016, from http://www.corestandards.org/Math/Practice/.

[b] Retrieved June 22, 2016, from http://ritter.tea.state.tx.us/rules/tac/chapter111/ch111a.html.

[c] Retrieved June 22, 2016, from http://www.doe.virginia.gov/testing/sol/standards_docs/mathematics/2009/stds_math.pdf.

[d] Retrieved June 22, 2016, from http://www.ibo.org/globalassets/publications/recognition/5_mathsl.pdf.

[e] Retrieved June 22, 2016, from http://www.edb.gov.hk/attachment/en/curriculum-development/kla/ma/curr/Math_CAGuide_e_2015.pdf.

[f] Retrieved June 22, 2016, from https://www.moe.gov.sg/docs/default-source/document/education/syllabuses/sciences/files/mathematics-syllabus-(primary-1-to-4).pdf.

[g] Retrieved June 22, 2016, from http://www.australiancurriculum.edu.au/mathematics/curriculum/f-10?layout=1.

Source: Standards for Mathematical Practice, CCSSO.

References

Almarode, J. T., Fisher, D., Assof, J., Hattie, J. A., & Frey, N. (2019). *Teaching mathematics in the Visible Learning classroom, grades 9–12*. Thousand Oaks, CA: Corwin.

Almarode, J. T., & Miller, A. M. (2013). *Captivate, activate, and invigorate the student brain in science and math, grades 6–12*. Thousand Oaks, CA: Corwin.

American Psychological Association, Coalition for Psychology in Schools and Education. (2015). *Top 20 principles from psychology for preK–12 teaching and learning*. Retrieved from http://www.apa.org/ed/schools/cpse/top-twenty-principles.pdf

Antonetti, J., & Garver, J. (2015). *17,000 classroom visits can't be wrong*. Alexandria, VA: Association for Supervision and Curriculum Development.

Berry, R. Q., III, & Thunder, K. (2017). Concrete, representational, and abstract: Building fluency from conceptual understanding. *Virginia Mathematics Teacher, 43*(2), 28–32.

Biggs, J. B., & Collis, K. F. (1982). *Evaluating the quality of learning: The SOLO taxonomy (structure of observed learning outcome)*. New York, NY: Academic Press.

Boaler, J. (2015). *What's math got to do with it? How teachers and parents can transform mathematics learning and inspire success* (Rev. ed.). New York, NY: Penguin.

Boaler, J. (2016). *Mathematical mindsets*. New York, NY: Jossey-Bass.

Bushart, B. (2014). *Numberless word problems*. Retrieved from https://bstockus.wordpress.com/numberless-word-problems/

Carpenter, T. P., Fennema, E., Franke, M. L., Levi, L., & Empson, S. B. (1999). *Children's mathematics: Cognitively guided instruction*. Reston, VA: National Council of Teachers of Mathematics.

Carpenter, T. P., Franke, M. L., & Levi, L. (2003). *Thinking mathematically: Integrating arithmetic and algebra in elementary school*. Portsmouth, NH: Heinemann.

Clements, D. H. (2004). Major themes and recommendations. In D. H. Clements, J. Sarama, & A. DiBiase (Eds.), *Engaging young children in mathematics: Standards for pre-school and kindergarten mathematics education* (pp. 7–72). Mahwah, NJ: Lawrence Erlbaum Associates, Inc.

Clements, D. H., & Sarama, J. (2007). Early childhood mathematics learning. In F. K. Lester, Jr. (Ed.), *Second handbook of research on mathematics teaching and learning* (pp. 461–555). New York, NY: Information Age.

Clements, D. H., & Sarama, J. (2014). *Learning and teaching early math: The learning trajectories approach* (2nd ed.). New York, NY: Routledge.

Curriculum Services Canada. (2011). *Bansho (board writing)* (Special ed. 17). Ontario, Canada: Author.

Denton, P. (2013). *The power of our words: Teacher language that helps children learn* (2nd ed.). Turner Falls, MA: Center for Responsive Schools, Inc.

Fennell, F. S., Kobett, B. M., & Wray, J. A. (2017). *The formative 5: Everyday assessment techniques for every math classroom.* Thousand Oaks, CA: Corwin.

Frey, N., Hattie, J., & Fisher, D. (2018). *Developing assessment-capable visible learners.* Thousand Oaks, CA: Corwin.

Gagnon, J. C., & Maccini, P. (2001). Preparing students with disabilities for algebra. *Teaching Exceptional Children, 34*(1), 8–15.

Guskey, T. R. (2014). *On your mark: Challenging the conventions of grading and reporting.* Bloomington, IN: Solution Tree.

Hansen, J., & Thunder, K. (2014). Spanish, mathematics, and English: The languages of success in a grade 8 class. *Voices From the Middle, 21*(3), 18–23.

Hattie, J. (2009). *Visible learning: A synthesis of over 800 meta-analyses relating to achievement.* New York, NY: Routledge.

Hattie, J., Fisher, D., Frey, N., Gojak, L. M., Moore, S. D., & Mellman, W. (2017). *Visible learning for mathematics: What works best to optimize student learning.* Thousand Oaks, CA: Corwin.

Hattie, J., & Timperley, H. (2007). The power of feedback. *Review of Educational Research, 77*(1), 81–112.

Hattie, J., & Zierer, K. (2018). *10 mindframes for visible learning: Teaching for success.* New York, NY: Routledge.

Hook, P., & Mills, J. (2011). *SOLO taxonomy: A guide for schools. Book 1.* Laughton, United Kingdom: Essential Resources.

Jacobs, V. R., Lamb, L. L. C., & Philipp, R. A. (2010). Professional noticing of children's mathematical thinking. *Journal for Research in Mathematics Education, 41*(2), 169–202.

Kobett, B. M., Miles, R. H., & William, L. A. (2018). *The mathematics lesson-planning handbook, Grades K–2: Your blueprint for building cohesive lessons.* Thousand Oaks, CA: Corwin.

Kuehnert, E. R. A., Eddy, C. M., Miller, D., Pratt, S. S., & Senawongsa, C. (2018). Bansho: Visually sequencing mathematical ideas. *Teaching Children Mathematics, 24*(6), 362–369.

Linn, R. L., & Gronlund, N. E. (2000). *Measurement and assessment in teaching* (8th ed.). Upper Saddle River, NJ: Merrill Prentice Hall.

Lomax, K., Alfonzo, K., Dietz, S., Kleyman, E., & Kazemi, E. (2017). Trying three-act tasks with primary students. *Teaching Children Mathematics, 24*(2), 112–119.

National Association for the Education of Young Children. (2009). *Developmentally appropriate practice in early childhood programs serving children from birth through age 8.* Retrieved from http://www.naeyc.org/positionstatements

National Council of Teachers of Mathematics. (1991). Professional standards for teaching mathematics. Retrieved from http://www.nctm.org/standards/content.aspx?id=26628

National Council of Teachers of Mathematics. (2014). *Principles to actions: Ensuring mathematical success for all.* Reston, VA: Author.

National Governors Association Center for Best Practices, Council of Chief State School Officers (2010). *Common Core State Standards for Mathematics.* Washington, DC: Author.

National Reading Panel, National Institute of Child Health and Human Development. (2000). *Teaching children to read: An evidence-based assessment of the scientific research literature on reading and its implications for reading instruction.* D. N. Langenburg (Ed.). Washington, DC: U.S. Government Printing Office.

National Research Council, Committee on Early Childhood Mathematics. (2009). *Mathematics learning in early childhood: Paths toward excellence and equity.* C. T. Cross, T. A. Woods, & H. Schweingruber (Eds.). Washington, DC: National Academy Press.

Parrish, S. (2014). *Number talks: Whole number computation.* Sausalito, CA: Math Solutions.

Schlechty, P. C. (2011). *Working on the work: An action plan for teachers, principals, and superintendents.* San Francisco, CA: Jossey-Bass.

Small, M. (2012). *Good questions: Great ways to differentiate mathematics instruction* (2nd ed.). Reston, VA: National Council of Teachers of Mathematics.

Smith, M. S., & Stein, M. K. (2011). *5 practices for orchestrating productive mathematics discussions.* Reston, VA: National Council of Teachers of Mathematics.

Thunder, K. (2011). *Mathematization: Constructing and connecting mathematical knowledge in a prekindergarten classroom* (Unpublished doctoral dissertation). University of Virginia, Charlottesville, VA.

Thunder, K. (2014). *Differentiating elementary mathematics instruction.* Presentation, Harrisonburg, VA.

Thunder, K., & Berry, R. Q., III. (2016). The promise of qualitative metasynthesis for mathematics education. *Journal of Research in Mathematics Education, 47*(4), 318–337.

Thunder, K., & Demchak, A. N. (2012). *Using literacy strategies to gain deep mathematical understanding in grades 2–5.* Presentation for the Virginia School/University Partnership, Roanoke, VA.

Thunder, K., & Demchak, A. N. (2016). The math diet: An instructional framework to grow mathematicians. *Teaching Children Mathematics, 22*(7), 389–392.

Thunder, K., & Demchak, A. N. (2017). *Workshop models for literacy and math, Grades 1–4.* Presentation for Virginia School/University Partnership, Charlottesville, VA.

Trocki, A., Taylor, C., Starling, T., Sztajn, P., & Heck, D. (2014/2015). Launching a discourse-rich mathematics lesson. *Teaching Children Mathematics, 21*(5), 276–281.

Tudge, J. R. H., & Doucet, F. (2004). Early mathematical experiences: Observing young Black and White children's everyday activities. *Early Childhood Research Quarterly, 19*(1), 21–39.

Van de Walle, J. A., Karp, K. S., & Bay-Williams, J. M. (2018). *Elementary and middle school mathematics: Teaching developmentally* (10th ed.). New York, NY: Pearson Education.

Virginia Department of Education. (2016). *Mathematics 2016 standards of learning.* Richmond: Virginia Department of Education.

Wolf, N. B. (2015). *Modeling with mathematics: Authentic problem solving in middle school.* Portsmouth, NH: Heinemann Publishing.

Index

3 Ways to get started with Visible Learning^{plus}®

The power of the **Visible Learning**^{plus} **School Impact Process**—based on Professor John Hattie's research—lies in evidence-based cycles of inquiry and action that help you align your strategic priorities to the factors that accelerate student achievement.

1

Attend an Event

Discover the core concepts of the Visible Learning™ research at a local event led by one of our world-class presenters.

2

Measure Your Baseline

Determine the extent to which high-impact practices are present in your school. A certified Visible Learning™ consultant will collect your data and present an unbiased, written baseline report to help you track progress and measure growth.

3

Build a Foundation

Develop a cycle of inquiry and knowledge building into your school's professional learning planning process so that your time, energy, and resources are focused on what is having the greatest impact on your students' learning.

VLN199E1

Learn more at visiblelearningplus.com

C❂RWIN

All students should have the opportunity to be successful!

Visible Learning^plus is based on one simple belief: Every student should experience at least one year's growth over the course of one school year. Visible Learning^plus translates the groundbreaking Visible Learning research by professor John Hattie into a practical model of inquiry and evaluation. Bring Visible Learning to your daily classroom practice with these additional resources across mathematics, literacy, and science.

John Hattie, Douglas Fisher, Nancy Frey, Linda M. Gojak, Sara Delano Moore, and William Mellman

Discover the right mathematics strategy to use at each learning phase so all students demonstrate more than a year's worth of learning per school year.

John Almarode, Douglas Fisher, Joseph Assof, Sara Delano Moore, Kateri Thunder, John Hattie, and Nancy Frey

Leverage the most effective teaching practices at the most effective time to meet the surface, deep, and transfer learning needs of every mathematics student.

Douglas Fisher, Nancy Frey, and John Hattie

Ensure students demonstrate more than a year's worth of learning during a school year by implementing the right literacy practice at the right moment.

Douglas Fisher, Nancy Frey, John Hattie, and Marisol Thayre

High-impact strategies to use for all you teach—all in one place. Deliver sustained, comprehensive literacy experiences to K–12 learners each day.

Nancy Frey, John Hattie, and Douglas Fisher

Imagine students who understand their educational goals and monitor their progress. This illuminating book focuses on self-assessment as a springboard for markedly higher levels of student achievement.

John Almarode, Douglas Fisher, Nancy Frey, and John Hattie

Inquiry, laboratory, project-based learning, discovery learning? The authors reveal that it's not which strategy is used, but when, and plot a vital K–12 framework for choosing the right approach at the right time.

corwin.com

Let us know what you think!

Did the information in this book resonate with you? We're hoping you'll continue to support this book's journey to reaching teachers and having the ultimate impact in the classroom. Here are a few ways you can do that:

> > > **JOIN** the conversation! Share your comments, participate in an online book study, or post a picture of yourself with the book on social media using **#VLClassroom**.

> > > **PROVIDE** your expert review of *Teaching Mathematics in the Visible Learning Classroom, Grades K–2* on Amazon.

> > > **LEAD** or join a book study in your school or team to share ideas on how to bring the concepts presented in the book to life.

> > > **FOLLOW** our Corwin in the Classroom Facebook page and share your Visible Learning strategies in the mathematics classroom using **#VLClassroom**.

> > > **RECOMMEND** this book for your Professional Learning Community activities.

> > > **SUGGEST** this book to teacher educators.

Be sure to stay up-to-date on all things Corwin by following us on social media:
   Facebook: www.facebook.com/corwinclassroom
   Instagram: www.instagram.com/corwin_press, @corwin_press
   Twitter: twitter.com/CorwinPress, @CorwinPress
   Pinterest: www.pinterest.com/corwinpress/pins

www.corwin.com

CORWIN

A SAGE Publishing Company

Helping educators make the greatest impact

CORWIN HAS ONE MISSION: to enhance education through intentional professional learning.

We build long-term relationships with our authors, educators, clients, and associations who partner with us to develop and continuously improve the best evidence-based practices that establish and support lifelong learning.